OFFICIAL

PAST

PAPERS

WITH ANSWERS

INTERMEDIATE 2

HISTORY
2007-2011

SQA

BrightRED
PUBLISHING

Publisher's Note

We are delighted to bring you the 2011 Past Papers and you will see that we have changed the format from previous editions. As part of our environmental awareness strategy, we have attempted to make these new editions as sustainable as possible.

To do this, we have printed on white paper and bound the answer sections into the book. This not only allows us to use significantly less paper but we are also, for the first time, able to source all the materials from sustainable sources.

We hope you like the new editions and by purchasing this product, you are not only supporting an independent Scottish publishing company but you are also, in the International Year of Forests, not contributing to the destruction of the world's forests.

Thank you for your support and please see the following websites for more information to support the above statement –

www.fsc-uk.org

www.loveforests.com

© Scottish Qualifications Authority
All rights reserved. Copying prohibited. No part of this publication may be reproduced, stored in a retrieval system, or transmitted in any form or by any means, electronic, mechanical, photocopying, recording or otherwise.

First exam published in 2007.
Published by Bright Red Publishing Ltd, 6 Stafford Street, Edinburgh EH3 7AU
tel: 0131 220 5804 fax: 0131 220 6710 info@brightredpublishing.co.uk www.brightredpublishing.co.uk

ISBN 978-1-84948-200-4

A CIP Catalogue record for this book is available from the British Library.

Bright Red Publishing is grateful to the copyright holders, as credited on the final page of the Question Section, for permission to use their material. Every effort has been made to trace the copyright holders and to obtain their permission for the use of copyright material. Bright Red Publishing will be happy to receive information allowing us to rectify any error or omission in future editions.

[BLANK PAGE]

X044/201

NATIONAL
QUALIFICATIONS
2007

FRIDAY, 18 MAY
9.00 AM – 10.45 AM

HISTORY
INTERMEDIATE 2

The instructions for this paper are on *Page two*. Read them carefully before you begin your answers. Some sources in this examination have been adapted or translated.

SCOTTISH
QUALIFICATIONS
AUTHORITY

INSTRUCTIONS

Answer **one** question from Part 1, The Short Essay

Answer **one** context from Part 2, Scottish and British

Answer **one** context from Part 3, European and World

Answer **one** other context from

     either Part 2, Scottish and British

     or   Part 3, European and World

Contents

[Turn over

PART 1: THE SHORT ESSAY

Mar

Answer **one** question. For this question you should write a short essay using your own knowledge. The essay should include an introduction, development and conclusion. Each question is worth 8 marks.

SCOTTISH AND BRITISH CONTEXTS:

CONTEXT 1: MURDER IN THE CATHEDRAL: CROWN, CHURCH AND PEOPLE, 1154–1173

Question 1: Explain why Henry II quarrelled with Archbishop Becket.   **8**

CONTEXT 2: WALLACE, BRUCE AND THE WARS OF INDEPENDENCE, 1286–1328

Question 2: Explain why Robert Bruce was successful in making himself King of Scots.   **8**

CONTEXT 3: MARY, QUEEN OF SCOTS AND THE SCOTTISH REFORMATION, 1540s–1587

Question 3: Explain why Queen Elizabeth ordered the execution of Mary, Queen of Scots in 1587.   **8**

CONTEXT 4: THE COMING OF THE CIVIL WAR, 1603–1642

Question 4: Explain why James I quarrelled with the English Parliament during his reign.   **8**

CONTEXT 5: "ANE END OF ANE AULD SANG": SCOTLAND AND THE TREATY OF UNION, 1690s–1715

Question 5: Explain why the Scottish colony at Darien failed.   **8**

CONTEXT 6: IMMIGRANTS AND EXILES: SCOTLAND, 1830s–1930s

Question 6: Explain why many Scots left to go overseas between the 1830s and 1930s.   **8**

CONTEXT 7(*a*): FROM THE CRADLE TO THE GRAVE? SOCIAL WELFARE IN BRITAIN, 1890s–1951

Question 7(*a*): Explain why the social reforms of the Liberal government 1906–1914 were important in improving the welfare of the British people.   **8**

Marks

CONTEXT 7(*b*): CAMPAIGNING FOR CHANGE:
SOCIAL CHANGE IN SCOTLAND, 1900s–1979

Question 7(*b*): Explain why all women were given the vote by 1928.

8

CONTEXT 8: A TIME OF TROUBLES:
IRELAND, 1900–1923

Question 8: Explain why the Ulster Unionists opposed the Home Rule Bill.

8

EUROPEAN AND WORLD CONTEXTS:

CONTEXT 1: THE NORMAN CONQUEST, 1060–1153

Question 9: Explain why David I's reign has been called the "Normanisation" of Scotland.

8

CONTEXT 2: THE CROSS AND THE CRESCENT:
THE FIRST CRUSADE, 1096–1125

Question 10: Explain why the People's Crusade failed.

8

CONTEXT 3: WAR, DEATH AND REVOLT
IN MEDIEVAL EUROPE, 1328–1436

Question 11: Explain why Joan of Arc was executed in 1431.

8

CONTEXT 4: NEW WORLDS:
EUROPE IN THE AGE OF EXPANSION, 1480s–1530s

Question 12: Explain why Portugal was able to discover new trade routes to the East in the late fifteenth and early sixteenth centuries.

8

CONTEXT 5: "TEA AND FREEDOM":
THE AMERICAN REVOLUTION, 1763–1783

Question 13: Explain why the defeat of the French in 1763 created tensions in the American colonies.

8

CONTEXT 6: "THIS ACCURSED TRADE":
THE BRITISH SLAVE TRADE AND ITS ABOLITION, 1770–1807

Question 14: Explain why slave resistance on the plantations was mainly unsuccessful.

8

Mar

CONTEXT 7: CITIZENS!
THE FRENCH REVOLUTION, 1789–1794

Question 15: Explain why the Terror gave Robespierre complete control of France.

8

CONTEXT 8: CAVOUR, GARIBALDI
AND THE MAKING OF ITALY, 1815–1870

Question 16: Explain why Italian unification had not been achieved by 1850.

8

CONTEXT 9: IRON AND BLOOD? BISMARCK AND THE
CREATION OF THE GERMAN EMPIRE, 1815–1871

Question 17: Explain why there was a growth in German nationalism between 1815 and 1850.

8

CONTEXT 10: THE RED FLAG:
LENIN AND THE RUSSIAN REVOLUTION, 1894–1921

Question 18: Explain why there was a revolution in Russia in January 1905.

8

CONTEXT 11: FREE AT LAST?
RACE RELATIONS IN THE USA, 1918–1968

Question 19: Explain why a civil rights movement grew in the USA in the 1950s and 1960s.

8

CONTEXT 12: THE ROAD TO WAR, 1933–1939

Question 20: Explain why Germany's neighbours felt threatened by Hitler's foreign policy in the period 1933–1938.

8

CONTEXT 13: IN THE SHADOW OF THE BOMB:
THE COLD WAR, 1945–1985

Question 21: Explain why views on the Vietnam War changed in the United States.

8

[END OF PART 1: THE SHORT ESSAY]

[Turn over for PART 2: SCOTTISH AND BRITISH CONTEXTS on *Page eight*]

PART 2:

Mar

HISTORICAL STUDY: SCOTTISH AND BRITISH

> **CONTEXT 1: MURDER IN THE CATHEDRAL: CROWN, CHURCH AND PEOPLE, 1154–1173**

Answer the following questions using recalled knowledge and information from the sources where appropriate.

Source A explains why Henry II had to reform the legal system when he became king in 1154.

Source A

> When Henry became king it ended the brutal twenty-year civil war of Stephen's reign. Henry needed to gain control of his country. During the war the barons had set up their own law courts and were running the law in their own areas. Many barons had also become sheriffs and were corrupt. Although Henry had not been in charge of the country for long he needed to act quickly to remove the barons' armies from the country.

1. Why did Henry II have to reform the legal system when he became king in 1154? (Use **Source A** and recall.)   **5**

2. Describe the uses of castles in medieval times.   **5**

Source B was written by Abbot Ailred in the twelfth century. It describes life at Rievaulx Abbey in Yorkshire.

Source B

> Our food is simple, our clothes are rough, our drink is from the stream. Under our tired limbs there is only a mat when we sleep; when sleep is sweetest we must rise at a bell's bidding to services. There is no moment of idleness. Everywhere there is peace and a marvellous freedom from the cares of the world.

3. How useful is **Source B** as evidence of the life of a medieval monk?   **4**

[END OF CONTEXT 1]

Marks

HISTORICAL STUDY: SCOTTISH AND BRITISH

> **CONTEXT 2: WALLACE, BRUCE AND THE WARS OF INDEPENDENCE, 1286–1328**

Answer the following questions using recalled knowledge and information from the sources where appropriate.

Source A is a letter written by Bishop Fraser of St Andrews to King Edward in October 1290.

Source A

> A rumour has spread among the people that the Maid of Norway has died. The Bishop of Durham, Earl Warenne and I then heard that she has recovered from her sickness but that she is very weak. We have agreed to stay at Perth until we hear definite news about her. We have sent two knights to Orkney to find out exactly what has happened.

1. How useful is **Source A** as evidence about what happened while the Scots waited for the arrival of the Maid?   **4**

2. Describe what happened at the Battle of Falkirk in 1298.   **5**

Source B explains why the Scots had recognised King Edward's authority by 1305.

Source B

> In May 1303 King Edward invaded Scotland once more – but for the last time. He made an armed progress through the realm and stayed for the winter in Dunfermline. Edward then punished the Scottish nobles by making them pay fines. He exiled a few of their most troublesome leaders but there was only one execution. By 1305 King Edward felt he had secured his authority in Scotland.

3. Why did the Scots recognise King Edward's authority by 1305? (Use **Source B** and recall.)   **5**

[END OF CONTEXT 2]

Mar

HISTORICAL STUDY: SCOTTISH AND BRITISH

> **CONTEXT 3: MARY, QUEEN OF SCOTS AND THE SCOTTISH REFORMATION, 1540s–1587**

Answer the following questions using recalled knowledge and information from the sources where appropriate.

Source A explains why Scottish Protestants rebelled against Mary of Guise in 1559.

Source A

> In 1559, Mary, Queen of Scots, who claimed to be the rightful Queen of England, became Queen of France. This worried the pro-English Protestant nobles. Her mother, Mary of Guise, governed Scotland with the help of an increasing number of French officials and soldiers. At the time when Scottish worries about French control were growing, Mary of Guise began to take action against Protestants in Scotland.

1. Why did Scottish Protestants rebel against Mary of Guise in 1559? (Use **Source A** and recall.)   **5**

Source B are Queen Mary's orders to pay ministers of the Church of Scotland, issued in 1566.

Source B

> Because the ministers within Scotland have not been paid for this last year and because I determined that they should be paid in the future, I have, with the advice of my government officials, decided to allocate the sum of £10 000 for their payment. I have also ordered that this sum must be paid in full.

2. How useful is **Source B** as evidence of Mary's support for the Church of Scotland in 1566?   **4**

3. Describe the events which led to Mary, Queen of Scots being made a prisoner in Loch Leven Castle.   **5**

[END OF CONTEXT 3]

Marks

HISTORICAL STUDY: SCOTTISH AND BRITISH

**CONTEXT 4: THE COMING OF
THE CIVIL WAR, 1603–1642**

Answer the following questions using recalled knowledge and information from the sources where appropriate.

Source A is part of Parliament's Petition of Right presented to the king in 1628.

Source A

> i)   No man should be compelled to make any gift, loan, benevolence, tax or similar charge to the Crown without consent of Parliament.
>
> ii)   No free man should be detained in prison without due cause shown.
>
> iii)   Soldiers and sailors should not be billeted upon private citizens without their agreement.
>
> iv)   There should be no martial law in time of peace.

1. How useful is **Source A** as evidence of the poor relations between Crown and Parliament in the reign of King Charles I?

    4

Source B is about Charles I's problems over religion in Scotland.

Source B

> In 1633 Charles came to Scotland to be crowned, accompanied by his new Archbishop of Canterbury. The coronation service was held in St Giles with candles, crucifix and full Anglican rites. Presbyterian ministers were ordered to wear Anglican surplices at services. The General Assembly had not met since 1618 and presbyteries were threatened with dissolution. Feelings were soon running high against the king.

2. Why did Charles I encounter difficulties with the Presbyterians in Scotland? (Use **Source B** and recall.)

    5

3. Describe the main activities of the Long Parliament against the king from 1640 until the outbreak of war in 1642.

    5

[END OF CONTEXT 4]

Mar

HISTORICAL STUDY: SCOTTISH AND BRITISH

> **CONTEXT 5: "ANE END OF ANE
> AULD SANG": SCOTLAND AND
> THE TREATY OF UNION, 1690s–1715**

Answer the following questions using recalled knowledge and information from the sources where appropriate.

Source A is about Scottish opposition to the Act of Union.

Source A

> By an incorporating union, Scotland will become poorer than ever. Why so? Because Scotsmen will spend ten times more in England than they do now, and Scotland will run out of money. Scottish Members of Parliament will need money to live in London and Scottish noblemen will move there permanently as well. Some argue there would be advantages in trading with English colonies, but as I see it, English manufacturers will destroy our own industries.

1. Why did many Scots oppose the Union of 1707? (Use **Source A** and recall.)　　5

Source B is from a letter written in 1707 by the Earl of Seafield who was a member of the Scottish government.

Source B

> It is impossible to state exactly how much was given to the Duke of Atholl, the Marquis of Tweeddale and the Earls of Roxburghe, Marchmont and Cromartie without revealing exactly how much has been given to everybody else. So far, this has been kept a secret and revealing this information at present would cause embarrassment.

2. How useful is **Source B** as evidence about how some Scottish nobles were persuaded to support the Act of Union?　　4

3. Describe the events that led to the Jacobite Rising of 1715.　　5

[END OF CONTEXT 5]

Marks

HISTORICAL STUDY: SCOTTISH AND BRITISH

CONTEXT 6: IMMIGRANTS AND EXILES: SCOTLAND, 1830s–1930s

Answer the following questions using recalled knowledge and information from the sources where appropriate.

Source A explains why Irish people came to Scotland.

Source A

South-West areas of Scotland like Ayrshire were close to Ireland and so attracted Irish people to go there. A large number settled in the Glasgow area as many ships with cheap fares arrived there. During the year 1848 the number of people landing in Glasgow numbered a thousand a week. Many Irish people went to Dundee where they found work in the Dundee jute industry. Some Irish men and women came to Scotland for just part of the year and then returned home. They mainly worked on farms at times such as the harvest.

1. Why did many Irish people come to Scotland in the nineteenth century? (Use **Source A** and recall.)   5

Source B is from a statement made by a cotton manufacturer in Glasgow in 1836.

Source B

When the Irish first come over here, both the parents and the children are generally very decent and respectable. After they have been here some time their behaviour deteriorates. The change comes about by mixing with the lowest dregs of our Scottish working population.

2. How useful is **Source B** as evidence of Scottish attitudes to Irish immigrants in the 1830s?   4

3. In what ways did Scottish immigrants help develop countries where they settled?   5

[END OF CONTEXT 6]

Mar

HISTORICAL STUDY: SCOTTISH AND BRITISH

> **CONTEXT 7(a): FROM THE
> CRADLE TO THE GRAVE? SOCIAL
> WELFARE IN BRITAIN, 1890s–1951**

Answer the following questions using recalled knowledge and information from the sources where appropriate.

Source A is about conditions in London around 1890 by a campaigner against poverty.

Source A

> In one cellar a sanitary inspector reports finding a father, mother, three children and four pigs! In another room a missionary found a man ill with smallpox, his wife just recovering from the birth of her eighth child, and the children running about half naked and covered with dirt. Elsewhere was a poor widow, her three children, and a child who had been dead thirteen days.

1. How useful is **Source A** as evidence of the effects of poverty in Britain in the late nineteenth century? **4**

2. In what ways did the Second World War change people's attitude to poverty? **5**

Source B explains the effects of Labour welfare reforms.

Source B

> The National Insurance and National Assistance Acts meant everyone would be given help "from the cradle to the grave". The National Health Service Act of 1946 gave free medical care to all. All of these acts needed a lot of people to administer them. Some 200 000 homes a year were built between 1948 and 1951. The Labour government embarked on an ambitious school building programme.

3. Why were the Labour welfare reforms of 1945 to 1951 thought to be a great success? (Use **Source B** and recall.) **5**

[END OF CONTEXT 7(a)]

Marks

HISTORICAL STUDY: SCOTTISH AND BRITISH

CONTEXT 7(*b*): CAMPAIGNING FOR CHANGE: SOCIAL CHANGE IN SCOTLAND, 1900s–1979

Answer the following questions using recalled knowledge and information from the sources where appropriate.

Source A is about events on Clydeside in 1919.

Source A

> In the period just after the Great War there was a wave of working-class protest. It was feared that soldiers returning from war would find no work and many women had also lost their jobs. The government was worried that the workers of Clydeside would attempt to copy the Bolshevik revolution of 1917. There was a great deal of political unrest and some of the protesters even called for a Scottish Workers' Republic.

1. Why did some people fear that revolution was breaking out on Clydeside in 1919? (Use **Source A** and recall.)   **5**

Source B is from an interview with a radio repairman in the 1930s.

Source B

> When a radio went wrong, it was like a death in the family. Sometimes when I arrived on the street a cheer went up and people would willingly pay whatever it took to get the set working again. It made me feel terribly important as I was treated with the same respect as a doctor.

2. How useful is **Source B** as evidence about the popularity of radio in the 1930s?   **4**

3. Describe the changes that took place in industry in Scotland after 1945.   **5**

[END OF CONTEXT 7(b)]

HISTORICAL STUDY: SCOTTISH AND BRITISH

Mar

CONTEXT 8: A TIME OF TROUBLES: IRELAND, 1900–1923

Answer the following questions using recalled knowledge and information from the sources where appropriate.

Source A explains why support for Sinn Fein increased in Ireland.

Source A

> In 1917 Sinn Fein won two by-elections. One of the men elected was Eamon De Valera. He had taken part in the Easter Rising but had avoided execution because he was born in America. De Valera took charge of Sinn Fein and reorganised it. Within the year all nationalist groups in Ireland had been united and Sinn Fein became the leading Irish party. As time went on the public began to see Sinn Fein as the main opposition to British rule.

1. Why did support for Sinn Fein increase in Ireland between 1916 and 1918? (Use **Source A** and recall.)   5

2. Describe the terms of the Anglo-Irish Treaty of 1921.   5

Source B is part of a letter from a District Police Inspector to the British Minister of Home Affairs in 1923.

Source B

> Some members of these Protestant groups are little better than hooligans. Their only aim is the extermination of Catholics by any and every means. They commit the deliberate and cold-blooded murder of harmless Catholics, shooting into Catholic houses and throwing bombs into Catholic areas. They have become as bad as the rebel gunmen. No-one obeys the law.

3. How useful is **Source B** as evidence of the violence in Ireland after partition?   4

[END OF CONTEXT 8]

[END OF PART 2: SCOTTISH AND BRITISH CONTEXTS]

PART 3:

Marks

HISTORICAL STUDY: EUROPEAN AND WORLD

> ### CONTEXT 1: THE NORMAN CONQUEST, 1060–1153

Answer the following questions using recalled knowledge and information from the sources where appropriate.

Source A is about the Battle of Hastings.

Source A

> Harold greatly weakened his chances of success through his rashness in moving south to meet William before he could gather together all the men available to him. Despite this, the Normans found it difficult to break through the ranks of the English forces. They gained the upper hand only when the defenders broke their own battle-line to pursue Normans they mistakenly thought were retreating.

1. Why did King Harold lose the Battle of Hastings? (Use **Source A** and recall.)　　**5**

2. Describe William I's methods of controlling England after 1066.　　**5**

Source B is about the role of castles in the Norman Conquest. It was written by the medieval chronicler Orderic Vitalis.

Source B

> The fortifications which the Normans called castles were hardly known in England. In spite of their courage and love of fighting, this meant the English could only put up a weak show of resistance. Certainly in King William's time men suffered great oppression and much injustice because he ordered castles to be built which were a sore burden on the poor.

Source C is about castles in the Norman Conquest. It was written by the modern historian M Morris in 2003.

Source C

> Recently historians have begun to suggest the importance of castles has been exaggerated. New technical ideas such as the building of castles made little difference between the Normans and the English. Knocking out the Anglo-Saxons in battle was the key thing. Erecting huge mounds of earth with castles on them was all very well, but in fact, they were really only symbols of lordship and not weapons of conquest.

3. Compare the views of **Sources B** and **C** on the role of castles in the Norman Conquest.　　**4**

[END OF CONTEXT 1]

Mar

HISTORICAL STUDY: EUROPEAN AND WORLD

> ### CONTEXT 2: THE CROSS AND THE CRESCENT: THE FIRST CRUSADE, 1096–1125

Answer the following questions using recalled knowledge and information from the sources where appropriate.

Source A explains why people joined the First Crusade.

Source A

> After Pope Urban's speech many people set off on Crusade. Some went because they said they wanted to serve God. Others went because they believed it was their duty to help the Christians in the east. For some, their reasons for going were far more practical. Famine and plague had terrified people to the point where they were desperate to leave Europe. Recapturing Jerusalem seemed an attractive idea.

1. Why did people join the First Crusade? (Use **Source A** and recall.)   **5**

Source B describes the relationship between the Emperor Alexius and Bohemond. It was written in 1096 by a Crusader who travelled with Bohemond.

Source B

> When Alexius heard that the honourable knight Bohemond had arrived at Constantinople, he immediately began to panic. Alexius was so afraid of him that he began to think of ways to trick and to get rid of Bohemond. Only by God's will did his tricks fail. When he finally met Bohemond, Alexius insisted that he take an oath of loyalty. The emperor did this because he feared the power Bohemond had over the other knights.

Source B describes the relationship between the Emperor Alexius and Bohemond. It was written by Alexius's daughter, Anna.

Source C

> Bohemond is the most dishonest and dishonourable man I have ever met. The minute he arrived in Constantinople it was obvious that he wanted to steal Alexius's land. Alexius, knowing what kind of man Bohemond was, insisted that he take an oath of loyalty. The emperor did this because he did not trust Bohemond. This cunning tactic spoiled any of Bohemond's plans to trick Alexius and take his land.

2. Compare **Sources B** and **C** as views of the relationship between Alexius and Bohemond.   **4**

3. Describe the problems faced by the Crusaders after the capture of Jerusalem.   **5**

[END OF CONTEXT 2]

Marks

HISTORICAL STUDY: EUROPEAN AND WORLD

> **CONTEXT 3: WAR, DEATH AND
> REVOLT IN MEDIEVAL EUROPE,
> 1328–1436**

Answer the following questions using recalled knowledge and information from the sources where appropriate.

Source A is about the growing tension between England and France in 1337.

Source A

> English monarchs still had some lands in France and Edward III was looking to extend his kingdom. Also Edward's mother was a French princess which allowed him to claim that he was the rightful King of France. The French argued that no woman could have any claim to the French throne. Edward started to make preparations for war. His people were anxious to support him. They were annoyed by the way the French had stopped Flemish merchants from buying English wool.

1. Why was England preparing for war with France by 1337? (Use **Source A** and recall.)   **5**

Sources B and **C** describe the effects of the Black Death on England.

Source B

> Sheep and oxen strayed through the fields and among the crops and there was no-one to drive them off or collect them. Livestock perished in great numbers throughout all districts due to a lack of shepherds and other farm workers. In the autumn no-one could be hired for less than 4 pennies plus meals. For this reason crops perished but in the year of the plague there was so much corn it did not matter.

Source C

> There was a shortage of labour because so many people, particularly peasants, died of the disease. Many farm animals also died. Lords, who relied on their peasants to farm their land, became desperate. They were forced to pay more to each peasant worker. Wages rose so much that Edward III had to issue new coins called groats and half groats (a groat was worth 4 pennies).

2. How far do **Sources B** and **C** agree about the effects of the Black Death on England?   **4**

3. Describe Henry V's campaign in France between 1415 and 1420.   **5**

[END OF CONTEXT 3]

Mar

HISTORICAL STUDY: EUROPEAN AND WORLD

> **CONTEXT 4: NEW WORLDS:**
> **EUROPE IN THE AGE OF**
> **EXPANSION, 1480s–1530s**

Answer the following questions using recalled knowledge and information from the sources where appropriate.

1. Describe Columbus's first voyage to the New World in 1492.   **5**

Source A is from a letter written by the fifteenth-century Italian map-maker Paul Toscanelli to Christopher Columbus.

Source A

> Paul, the scholar and physician, to Christopher Columbus greetings.
> I understand your magnificent and great desire to explore and find a way to where the spices grow. I therefore send you a map made by my own hands, on which are drawn the coasts and islands from which you must begin to make your journey westwards and the places at which you should arrive.

Source B is part of a letter by the King of Spain in support of the voyage of the explorer Ferdinand Magellan in the early sixteenth century.

Source B

> According to the information and maps I have obtained from persons who have seen them, I know for certain that there are spices in the islands of the Moluccas. You are ordered to seek them with this fleet. I command that in every matter of navigation you follow the decisions of the bearer of this letter, Ferdinand Magellan, whose greatest desire is to undertake this voyage to discover new lands.

2. Compare **Sources A** and **B** as views of why voyages of exploration took place between the 1480s and 1530s.   **4**

In **Source C** a Conquistador describes a battle between the native peoples of the New World and their Spanish conquerors.

Source C

> The steady firing of our artillery and musketeers did the enemy much damage. Those who came too close to us were soon forced back by the sword-play of our men. Our horsemen were so skilful and fought so bravely that, after God who showered His blessings upon us, they were our greatest asset. However so many of the enemy charged upon us that only by a miracle of sword-play could we make them give way and maintain our battle formation.

3. Why were the native peoples of the New World unable to defeat the Spanish Conquistadors? (Use **Source C** and recall.)   **5**

[END OF CONTEXT 4]

HISTORICAL STUDY: EUROPEAN AND WORLD

Marks

> ### CONTEXT 5: "TEA AND FREEDOM": THE AMERICAN REVOLUTION, 1763–1783

Answer the following questions using recalled knowledge and information from the sources where appropriate.

1. Describe the events in Boston in 1770 which became known as the "Boston Massacre". **5**

Source A was written by George III in 1776 defending British rule in the American colonies.

Source A

> I believe the spirit of the British nation too great and the resources with which God has blessed her too numerous, to give up so many colonies which she has established with great care. We have helped these colonies grow and become successful. We have protected and defended them at the expense of much blood and at great cost to us.

Source B was written by Thomas Paine in 1776 criticising Britain's rule in the American colonies.

Source B

> America would have flourished as much and probably more, even if no European nation had taken notice of her. America is so rich because of her trade in essential goods which will always be needed by other countries. Britain has defended the American continent at not only her own expense but also at the expense of the colonists. This she has done not out of concern but for trade and power.

2. Compare the views expressed in **Sources A** and **B** about British rule in the American colonies. **4**

Source C explains the importance of French support for the colonists.

Source C

> After the American victory at Saratoga in 1778, France officially entered the war on the American side. The French wanted to avenge their defeat in 1763. From the beginning the French secretly lent the American government money to keep the war going. At the battle of Yorktown the majority of Washington's army was equipped and supplied by the French. Indeed the majority of the 15 000 soldiers were French. The French navy also trapped Cornwallis's soldiers in Yorktown.

3. Why was French support important to the colonists throughout the Revolutionary War? (Use **Source C** and recall.) **5**

[END OF CONTEXT 5]

Ma

HISTORICAL STUDY: EUROPEAN AND WORLD

> ### CONTEXT 6: "THIS ACCURSED TRADE": THE BRITISH SLAVE TRADE AND ITS ABOLITION, 1770–1807

Answer the following questions using recalled knowledge and information from the sources where appropriate.

1. Describe the ways Britain profited from the slave trade.　**5**

Sources A and **B** describe the effects of the Atlantic slave trade on Africa and its peoples.

Source A

> Nowhere in history have a people experienced such a terrible ordeal as Africans during the Atlantic slave trade. Over nearly four centuries of the trade, millions of healthy men, women and children were savagely torn from their homeland, herded into ships, and dispersed all over the so called New World. Although there is no way to work out exactly how many people perished, it has been estimated that about 10 million Africans survived the Middle Passage.

Source B

> The Atlantic slave trade spelled disaster for Africa and its peoples. For four hundred years, millions of the healthiest young people of the region were stolen from their homeland. No-one is sure exactly how many were sold into slavery but probably about 11 million African people arrived in the New World between 1450 and 1850. Add to that the number who died in war or on the journey and you can begin to see the devastating effect on families at that time.

2. How far do **Sources A** and **B** agree about the effects of the slave trade on Africa and its peoples?　**4**

Source C explains why it took so long to abolish the slave trade.

Source C

> The supporters of the slave trade were well organised and influential. Although Wilberforce introduced his first bill to abolish it in 1789, it took a full eighteen years to end the evil. Plantation owners were often Members of Parliament who also had the support of George III. As a result, they created many difficulties for the abolitionists.

3. Why did it take so long to persuade parliament to abolish the slave trade? (Use **Source C** and recall.)　**5**

[END OF CONTEXT 6]

Marks

HISTORICAL STUDY: EUROPEAN AND WORLD

> **CONTEXT 7: CITIZENS! THE
> FRENCH REVOLUTION, 1789–1794**

Answer the following questions using recalled knowledge and information from the sources where appropriate.

1. Describe the difficulties faced by Louis XVI's government by 1789.   **5**

Source A is from a list of complaints sent to the Estates General from a village in the south of France, 1789.

Source A

> We are heavily burdened by feudal dues even though our soil is barren. When our rents and taxes have been paid, we have hardly a penny left. The landlords grow fat from our labours yet pay no taxes. We pay, indeed, without understanding what we are paying for. There is only one thing that we ask of the Estates General – to find a way to relieve our poverty.

Source B is from a list of complaints from a village in the west of France, 1789.

Source B

> We most humbly ask that all citizens, no matter who they are, contribute to all the taxes according to their income. We should be told who takes a share of the taxes – for example, how much goes to the army. Bear in mind that the land grows every day more unproductive and that our burdens should be lightened.

2. How far do **Sources A** and **B** agree about the complaints of French peasants before the Revolution?   **4**

Source C explains the feelings of many French people in 1791.

Source C

> The Third Estate had fought together against the privileges of the Church, nobility and monarchy yet it had become increasingly clear that the revolution was fast becoming a victory for the middle class. The aristocracy were to be given compensation for the loss of their feudal rights. Lands taken away from the Church were sold in such a way that poorer peasants could not afford to buy them. Workshops for the unemployed were closed down.

3. Why were many French people disappointed in the revolution by 1791? (Use **Source C** and recall.)   **5**

[END OF CONTEXT 7]

HISTORICAL STUDY: EUROPEAN AND WORLD

> ### CONTEXT 8: CAVOUR, GARIBALDI AND THE MAKING OF ITALY, 1815–1870

Answer the following questions using recalled knowledge and information from the sources where appropriate.

In **Sources A** and **B** two historians discuss the effects of the Crimean War.

Source A

> Piedmont's participation in the Crimean War had been unpopular and unproductive. However, the war did change the international situation in Piedmont's favour. Austria's hesitant approach to the war meant that she lost the friendship of Russia. This left her isolated. Her failure to support Britain and France meant she could not expect help from these two great powers when it came to controlling the Italian states. Austria's isolation would prove crucial in helping to bring about Italian unification.

Source B

> The Crimean War was a critical turning point for the cause of Italian unification. Austria was now isolated diplomatically. She had lost her great ally, Russia, and was forced to ally with unreliable Prussia. Neither France nor Britain would be sympathetic to maintaining Austrian power in northern Italy and its dominant position over the whole peninsula. Piedmont's participation in the Crimean War also confirmed her position as the leading state in Italy.

1. To what extent do **Sources A** and **B** agree about the effects of the Crimean War on Austria's diplomatic position?   4

In **Source C** a journalist from the time describes Mazzini's role in Italian unification.

> Guiseppe Mazzini did more than anyone to publicise the great aim of Italian unity. He was an active member of the Carbonari but when it became clear to him that its badly organised conspiracies were making no progress he founded a national movement called Young Italy. He was sentenced to death for his activities and spent most of his life in exile hatching plots against the rulers of the Italian states.

2. Why was Guiseppe Mazzini important to Italian unification? (Use **Source C** and recall.)   5

3. Describe the contribution of Guiseppe Garibaldi to Italian unification.   5

[END OF CONTEXT 8]

Marks

HISTORICAL STUDY: EUROPEAN AND WORLD

> **CONTEXT 9: IRON AND BLOOD?**
> **BISMARCK AND THE CREATION OF**
> **THE GERMAN EMPIRE, 1815–1871**

Answer the following questions using recalled knowledge and information from the sources where appropriate.

1. Describe the events of the 1848 Revolution in Germany.   5

In **Source A** the Prussian Field Marshal, von Moltke, describes Prussia's preparations for the war against Austria in 1866.

Source A

> Our leaders prepared carefully for the war with Austria. We ensured the support of other countries. They did not wish to increase the size of Prussia but wanted to increase our influence. Austria had to give up her control over the German states but not a bit of territory was to be taken from her. Austria had exhausted her strength. Prussia felt it was her duty to assume the leadership of the German races and now felt strong enough to do so.

In **Source B** a modern historian describes the preparations of Prussia for the war against Austria in 1866.

Source B

> In preparation for the war against Austria, Bismarck's leadership was crucial. He secured the neutrality of Napoleon III and made an alliance with Italy to attack Austria in the rear if war should come. Bismarck insisted that not a bit of Austrian territory should be annexed by Prussia. The object was to ensure the supremacy of Prussia over the north German states.

2. How far do **Sources A** and **B** agree about Prussia's preparations for the war against Austria in 1866?   4

Source C explains the growing hostility between Prussia and France from 1868 to 1870.

Source C

> In 1868 the new government of Spain began to look for a new monarch. They approached Prince Leopold of Hohenzollern. This was opposed by France since having a German as king in Spain would alter the balance of power against France. The news of the Hohenzollern candidature caused a hostile reaction in Paris. The French government demanded the King of Prussia's guarantee that the Hohenzollerns would never claim the Spanish throne. At Ems, the king politely refused to give any such guarantee.

3. Why was there growing hostility between Prussia and France between 1868 and 1870? (Use **Source C** and recall.)   5

[END OF CONTEXT 9]

Mar

HISTORICAL STUDY: EUROPEAN AND WORLD

> ### CONTEXT 10: THE RED FLAG: LENIN AND THE RUSSIAN REVOLUTION, 1894–1921

Answer the following questions using recalled knowledge and information from the sources where appropriate.

1. What methods did the Tsar use to maintain his control over Russia before 1914?   **5**

Source A is part of a letter from the Tsarina to the Tsar describing the situation in Petrograd in February 1917.

Source A

> The trouble comes from a few idlers, well-dressed people, wounded soldiers and school girls. We hear of students coming into town and telling people to stay off the streets in the morning or they could be shot. What lies! Of course the cab-drivers and motormen are now on strike. But it is all different from 1905. The people all worship you and only want bread.

Source B is part of a letter from the President of the Duma to the Tsar. It also describes the situation in Petrograd in February 1917.

Source B

> The situation is serious. Petrograd is in a state of chaos. The government is paralysed; the transport system has broken down so supplies of fuel are completely disorganised. Discontent is general and on the increase. There is wild shooting in the streets. It is urgent that someone whom the people trust should form a new government.

2. How far do **Sources A** and **B** disagree about the unrest in Petrograd in February 1917?   **4**

In **Source C** Trotsky explains why the Red Army was victorious in the Civil War.

Source C

> A flabby, panicky mob could be transformed in two or three weeks into an efficient fighting force. What was needed for this? It needed a few dozen good commanders who were experienced fighters. Communists ready to make any sacrifice for the revolution were essential. Supplies such as boots for the barefooted, underwear, food, tobacco and matches attracted new recruits who were also encouraged by an energetic propaganda campaign.

3. Why was the Red Army victorious in the Civil War? (Use **Source C** and recall.)   **5**

[END OF CONTEXT 10]

Marks

HISTORICAL STUDY: EUROPEAN AND WORLD

> CONTEXT 11: FREE AT LAST? RACE
> RELATIONS IN THE USA, 1918–1968

Answer the following questions using recalled knowledge and information from the sources where appropriate.

Source A is by a Senator from Alabama in 1921. He is explaining why he wanted immigration controls.

Source A

> As soon as the immigrants step off the decks of their ships our problem has begun – Bolshevism, red anarchy, crooks and kidnappers. Thousands come here who never take the oath to support our Constitution and to become citizens of the United States. They do not respect what our flag represents. They pay allegiance to some other country and flag while they live upon the benefits of our own. They are of no service whatever to our people. They constitute a menace and a danger to us every day.

Source B is a description by Robert Coughlan of the growth of support for the Ku Klux Klan in the 1920s.

Source B

> It may be asked why, then, did the town take so enthusiastically to the Klan? Many old stock Americans believed they were in danger of being overrun. The "foreigners were ruining our country"; and so anything "foreign" was "un-American" and a menace. Cars were draped with the American flag and some carried homemade signs with Klan slogans such as "America for the Americans".

1. How far do **Sources A** and **B** agree about American attitudes to immigrants in the 1920s? 4

2. Describe the events of the Montgomery bus boycott. 5

Source C explains why the Black Panthers gained support.

Source C

> The leaders of the Black Panthers argued that black Americans were victims of white aggression and it was now time to defend black Americans. When Huey Newton said things like "The police have never been our protectors", the big newspapers gave the Panthers a negative image. Journalists did not publicise the self-help programmes organised by the Black Panthers, who also had a ten-point programme. This included demands for freedom and the release of all black people held in prisons.

3. Why did the Black Panthers gain support from many black Americans? (Use **Source C** and recall.) 5

[END OF CONTEXT 11]

Mar

HISTORICAL STUDY: EUROPEAN AND WORLD

CONTEXT 12: THE ROAD TO WAR, 1933–1939

Answer the following questions using recalled knowledge and information from the sources where appropriate.

Source A is about the reoccupation of the Rhineland, 1936.

Source A

> Germany was able to score an important victory without having to fire a shot. Hitler knew that his strategy had required taking a great risk because France was much stronger. After he had shown strong leadership Hitler was treated with greater respect abroad. France's allies in Eastern Europe began to see Germany as the stronger nation while in the west the Belgians moved towards a position of neutrality instead of supporting France.

1. Why was the reoccupation of the Rhineland in 1936 important for Hitler? (Use **Source A** and recall.)   5

2. Describe the events of the Czechoslovakian crisis of 1938 that led to the Munich Settlement.   5

In **Sources B** and **C** two modern historians give their views on appeasement.

Source B

> Appeasement was a practical solution to make peace and settle disputes with Germany. This approach was adopted because it was believed that Germany had been treated unfairly at Versailles. For the British and French leaders it was not a policy of cowardice or weakness in the face of threats. Instead, it was a policy of preventing war in the belief that Europe could not survive a bloodbath such as the Great War.

Source C

> Appeasement often meant a surrender of principles. Chamberlain's approach to appeasement was based on the belief that Nazism, horrible as it was, was here to stay and Britain ought to deal with it. Under his direction it became a policy of cowardice and dishonour – a way of gaining short-term peace at someone else's expense.

3. How far do **Sources B** and **C** disagree about the policy of appeasement?   4

[END OF CONTEXT 12]

Marks

HISTORICAL STUDY: EUROPEAN AND WORLD

**CONTEXT 13: IN THE SHADOW OF
THE BOMB: THE COLD WAR,
1945–1985**

Answer the following questions using recalled knowledge and information from the sources where appropriate.

1. What was meant by "the Cold War"?　　5

Source A is from the speech by President Kennedy on television to the American people, 22 October 1962.

Source A

> To halt this build up, a strict quarantine of all offensive military equipment being shipped to Cuba is being introduced. All ships of any kind bound for Cuba from whatever nation or port will, if found to contain cargoes of offensive weapons, be turned back. We are not at this time, however, denying the necessities of life as the Soviets attempted to do in their Berlin blockade of 1948.

Source B is from the letter sent by Nikita Khrushchev to President Kennedy, 24 October 1962.

Source B

> You, Mr President, are not declaring quarantine, but rather an ultimatum, and you are threatening that if we do not obey your orders, you will use force to turn back the ships. Think about what you are saying! And you want to persuade me to agree to this! What does it mean to agree to these demands? It would mean for us to conduct our relations with other countries not by reason, but by yielding to tyranny. You are not appealing to reason; you want to intimidate us.

2. Compare the views in **Sources A** and **B** on the Cuban Missile Crisis.　　4

Source C explains why there was a thaw in the Cold War in the late 1960s.

Source C

> The tensions of the 1960s, which had brought them to the brink of nuclear war, caused the superpowers to rethink their plans. This led to a thaw in the Cold War. Both sides had important reasons to seek a relaxation in tensions. Leonid Brezhnev and the rest of the Soviet leadership felt the economic burden of the nuclear arms race was too great. The American economy was also in financial trouble as a result of the Vietnam War. Johnson, and to a lesser extent Nixon, were having difficulty funding the government welfare programme.

3. Why did both sides want détente by the late 1960s? (Use **Source C** and recall.)　　5

[END OF CONTEXT 13]

[END OF PART 3: EUROPEAN AND WORLD CONTEXTS]

[END OF QUESTION PAPER]

[BLANK PAGE]

[BLANK PAGE]

X044/201

| NATIONAL QUALIFICATIONS 2008 | MONDAY, 26 MAY 9.00 AM – 10.45 AM | HISTORY INTERMEDIATE 2 |

The instructions for this paper are on *Page two*. Read them carefully before you begin your answers. Some sources in this examination have been adapted or translated.

INSTRUCTIONS

Answer **one** question from Part 1, The Short Essay

Answer **one** context from Part 2, Scottish and British

Answer **one** context from Part 3, European and World

Answer **one** other context from

>   **either**   Part 2, Scottish and British
>
>   **or**   Part 3, European and World

Contents

[Turn over

PART 1: THE SHORT ESSAY

Ma

Answer **one** question. For this question you should write a short essay using your own knowledge. The essay should include an introduction, development and conclusion. Each question is worth 8 marks.

SCOTTISH AND BRITISH CONTEXTS:

CONTEXT 1: MURDER IN THE CATHEDRAL: CROWN, CHURCH AND PEOPLE, 1154–1173

Question 1: Explain why the Church was important in the Middle Ages.

8

CONTEXT 2: WALLACE, BRUCE AND THE WARS OF INDEPENDENCE, 1286–1328

Question 2: Explain why there was a succession problem in Scotland between 1286 and 1292.

8

CONTEXT 3: MARY, QUEEN OF SCOTS AND THE SCOTTISH REFORMATION, 1540s–1587

Question 3: Explain why her marriage to Darnley caused problems for Mary, Queen of Scots.

8

CONTEXT 4: THE COMING OF THE CIVIL WAR, 1603–1642

Question 4: Explain why Charles I declared war on Parliament in 1642.

8

CONTEXT 5: "ANE END OF ANE AULD SANG": SCOTLAND AND THE TREATY OF UNION, 1690s–1715

Question 5: Explain why some Scots thought a Union with England would make Scotland richer.

8

CONTEXT 6: IMMIGRANTS AND EXILES: SCOTLAND, 1830s–1930s

Question 6: Explain why many Scots resented immigrants from Ireland in the nineteenth century.

8

CONTEXT 7(*a*): FROM THE CRADLE TO THE GRAVE? SOCIAL WELFARE IN BRITAIN, 1890s–1951

Question 7(*a*): Explain why the Labour welfare reforms after 1945 were successful in meeting the needs of the people.

8

Marks

CONTEXT 7(b): CAMPAIGNING FOR CHANGE: SOCIAL CHANGE IN SCOTLAND, 1900s–1979

Question 7(b): Explain why many Scottish women were able to lead better lives in the period 1918–1939.

8

CONTEXT 8: A TIME OF TROUBLES: IRELAND, 1900–1923

Question 8: Explain why the Easter Rising of 1916 failed.

8

EUROPEAN AND WORLD CONTEXTS:

CONTEXT 1: THE NORMAN CONQUEST, 1060–1153

Question 9: Explain why Anglo-Saxon opposition to William was ineffective after 1066.

8

CONTEXT 2: THE CROSS AND THE CRESCENT: THE FIRST CRUSADE, 1096–1125

Question 10: Explain why the First Crusade was able to achieve its aims.

8

CONTEXT 3: WAR, DEATH AND REVOLT IN MEDIEVAL EUROPE, 1328–1436

Question 11: Explain why the French were eventually successful in the Hundred Years' War.

8

CONTEXT 4: NEW WORLDS: EUROPE IN THE AGE OF EXPANSION, 1480s–1530s

Question 12: Explain why developments in technology were important in encouraging voyages of exploration.

8

CONTEXT 5: "TEA AND FREEDOM": THE AMERICAN REVOLUTION, 1763–1783

Question 13: Explain why some American colonists remained loyal to Britain.

8

CONTEXT 6: "THIS ACCURSED TRADE": THE BRITISH SLAVE TRADE AND ITS ABOLITION, 1770–1807

Question 14: Explain why many people were in favour of the Slave Trade in the eighteenth century.

8

Ma

CONTEXT 7: CITIZENS!
THE FRENCH REVOLUTION, 1789–1794

Question 15:   Explain why France became a republic in 1792.

8

CONTEXT 8: CAVOUR, GARIBALDI
AND THE MAKING OF ITALY, 1815–1870

Question 16:   Explain why Italy became a unified country by 1870.

8

CONTEXT 9: IRON AND BLOOD? BISMARCK AND THE
CREATION OF THE GERMAN EMPIRE, 1815–1871

Question 17:   Explain why Prussia succeeded in uniting Germany by 1871.

8

CONTEXT 10: THE RED FLAG:
LENIN AND THE RUSSIAN REVOLUTION, 1894–1921

Question 18:   Explain why there was discontent among Russian industrial workers in the years leading up to 1914.

8

CONTEXT 11: FREE AT LAST?
RACE RELATIONS IN THE USA, 1918–1968

Question 19:   Explain why the Ku Klux Klan was feared in the 1920s and 1930s.

8

CONTEXT 12: THE ROAD TO WAR, 1933–1939

Question 20:   Explain why Britain allowed Germany to ignore the Treaty of Versailles during the 1930s.

8

CONTEXT 13: IN THE SHADOW OF THE BOMB:
THE COLD WAR, 1945–1985

Question 21:   Explain why a Cold War developed after the Second World War.

8

[END OF PART 1: THE SHORT ESSAY]

[Turn over for PART 2: SCOTTISH AND BRITISH CONTEXTS on *Page eight*

PART 2:

HISTORICAL STUDY: SCOTTISH AND BRITISH

Ma

> ### CONTEXT 1: MURDER IN THE CATHEDRAL: CROWN, CHURCH AND PEOPLE, 1154–1173

Answer the following questions using recalled knowledge and information from the sources where appropriate.

Source A explains why Henry II was forced to increase his power when he became king in 1154.

Source A

> Henry's first task was to destroy all the castles that had been built without the king's permission. Nineteen years of civil war had increased the power of the barons and reduced the authority of the king. Within three weeks of becoming king, Henry marched on Scarborough castle and defeated the Earl of York. Soon after, Henry dealt with the sheriffs who were deciding the law in their own areas. They were also corrupt and could no longer be trusted.

1. Why was Henry II forced to increase his power when he became king in 1154? (Use **Source A** and recall.)   5

2. Describe the role of a knight in medieval society.   5

Sources B and **C** describe the quarrel between Henry II and Archbishop Becket.

Source B

> It was the king's wish that members of the clergy who committed crimes be tried in the king's court and not in the Church court. Becket completely refused to agree to this. He argued that only God and not the king had the right to judge the clergy. Henry felt betrayed by Becket's defence of the Church. He immediately threatened Becket with exile and death.

Source C

> Becket's actions angered the king. Henry expected Becket to support him and not the Church. To his amazement Becket would not agree to the clergy being tried in the king's court. Henry threatened and bullied Becket but this did not work. Becket argued that the king received his power from God and therefore had no authority to judge clergymen.

3. How far do **Sources B** and **C** agree about the quarrel between Henry II and Archbishop Becket?   4

[END OF CONTEXT 1]

Marks

HISTORICAL STUDY: SCOTTISH AND BRITISH

CONTEXT 2: WALLACE, BRUCE
AND THE WARS OF
INDEPENDENCE, 1286–1328

Answer the following questions using recalled knowledge and information from the sources where appropriate.

1. Describe what happened when Edward I attacked Berwick in 1296.

5

Sources A and **B** describe the meeting of Bruce and the Red Comyn in 1306.

Source A

> While they were speaking, Bruce suddenly accused Comyn of betraying him. Comyn denied this. Just as he had planned, Bruce hit Comyn with a sword and left. When some evil folk told Bruce that Comyn would live, he ordered them to kill him beside the high altar.

Source B

> When Bruce accused Comyn of telling King Edward about him, Comyn said this was a lie. This evil speaker was then stabbed and wounded. Later, the monks laid Comyn beside the altar but, when he said that he thought he would live, his enemies hit him again. Thus he was taken away from this world.

2. How far do **Sources A** and **B** agree about what happened when Bruce and the Red Comyn met at Greyfriars Kirk in 1306?

4

Source C is about the Battle of Bannockburn.

Source C

> Bruce's careful preparations for battle were ruined when Edward II moved his army to attack from the east and not from the south. However, this gave the much larger English army no room to move because they were surrounded by marshes and streams. Bruce decided to take advantage of this mistake and to attack them. The English were so jammed together and so tangled up that their leaders struggled to organise any defence and they lost all confidence in Edward II for leading them into this trap.

3. Why did the Scots win the Battle of Bannockburn? (Use **Source C** and recall.)

5

[END OF CONTEXT 2]

Mar

HISTORICAL STUDY: SCOTTISH AND BRITISH

> **CONTEXT 3: MARY, QUEEN OF SCOTS AND THE SCOTTISH REFORMATION, 1540s–1587**

Answer the following questions using recalled knowledge and information from the sources where appropriate.

1. Describe the events which forced Mary, Queen of Scots to leave Scotland in 1548.   **5**

Source A is about the unpopularity of Riccio, Mary's secretary.

Source A

> Riccio had arrived in Scotland as a musician but he won the attention and friendship of Mary who made him a secretary. Darnley blamed Riccio for Mary's refusal to make him king. He also grew jealous of Mary's friendship with Riccio whose lively and witty company she enjoyed. Many of the Scottish nobles detested this low born Italian and believed him to be a secret agent of the Pope.

2. Why did many Scots dislike Riccio? (Use **Source A** and recall.)   **5**

Sources B and **C** describe Mary's return to Edinburgh after her capture at Carberry, 1567.

Source B

> To her horror, Mary was placed under the guard of two very wicked young men. Dirty and so exhausted and faint, Mary was escorted back to Edinburgh. As she rode through the streets of Edinburgh, people shouted abuse at her, calling her a murderess and screaming "Burn her! Drown her!". By now, Mary was weeping.

Source C

> As she rode through the streets of Edinburgh the people shouted "Burn her! Kill her! Drown her! She is not fit to live." Two evil young thugs were guarding her and they joined in insulting her. Amazed, almost stunned, the Queen allowed tears of shock and humiliation to pour down her cheeks.

3. How far do **Sources B** and **C** agree about what happened to Mary after her capture at Carberry in 1567?   **4**

[END OF CONTEXT 3]

Marks

HISTORICAL STUDY: SCOTTISH AND BRITISH

> **CONTEXT 4: THE COMING OF
> THE CIVIL WAR, 1603–1642**

Answer the following questions using recalled knowledge and information from the sources where appropriate.

Sources A and **B** describe the attitude of the Stuarts to Scotland after the Union of the Crowns.

Source A

> After 1603 the Stuarts lost interest in Scotland and were really only concerned with England, which was the richer and more powerful kingdom. Scotland was governed like a distant province. The Stuarts only cared about Scotland when they needed men and money for their armies. From James VI onwards, they were glad to escape from a country with its troublesome Presbyterians.

Source B

> Scotland and England were much closer in size and wealth in the 1600s, so it's not true to say that Scotland was neglected because England was richer. The Stuarts remained vitally interested in Scottish affairs as Scotland was their original power base. The Stuarts were especially keen to impose their views on the Church as they saw the Presbyterians as a threat to their authority.

1. How far do **Sources A** and **B** agree about the attitude of the Stuarts to Scotland?   **4**

Source C explains why James VI and I was unpopular with the English Parliament.

> The new king lost respect by giving money and power to his favourites at court. His coronation cost £20,000 and he spent lavishly on hunting and banquets. By 1610 he was seriously short of money. He increased his income by raising the customs duties on imported goods. The Members of Parliament argued that the king could not raise taxes without their permission. The sale of monopolies also brought in a great deal of money but made Parliament angry.

2. Why was James VI and I unpopular with the English Parliament between 1603 and 1625? (Use **Source C** and recall.)   **5**

3. Describe the ways the Scots opposed Charles I over religion between 1637 and 1640.   **5**

[END OF CONTEXT 4]

Mar

HISTORICAL STUDY: SCOTTISH AND BRITISH

> **CONTEXT 5: "ANE END OF ANE AULD SANG": SCOTLAND AND THE TREATY OF UNION, 1690s–1715**

Answer the following questions using recalled knowledge and information from the sources where appropriate.

1. Describe the events leading up to the execution of Captain Green of the Worcester in 1705.   **5**

Source A is about why Queen Anne wanted a Union between Scotland and England.

Source A

> Union was the solution favoured by Queen Anne and by Lord Godolphin. She found it difficult to govern Scotland from Westminster. Union would avoid any arguments about the succession because Anne was determined to secure the Protestant Succession. She also thought that the Union of the two countries would create a more powerful state. Besides, Union would protect England from any French threat in the future if the discontented Scots ever wanted to revive the Auld Alliance.

2. Why did Queen Anne want a Union between England and Scotland? (Use **Source A** and recall.)   **5**

Sources B and **C** describe Scottish reaction to the Union between 1707 and 1714.

Source B

> The Scots soon became disillusioned with the Union because it did not bring immediate prosperity. The Church of Scotland was outraged when patronage was reintroduced to the Church of Scotland and Episcopalians were to be tolerated. The Malt Tax was introduced and many were angry as this broke the Treaty. It appeared to many Scots that politicians in London had the power to re-write the Treaty.

Source C

> For most people, life in most matters was unchanged but some were soon disappointed. Within a few years significant changes were made which they thought broke the terms of the Treaty of Union. Church Patronage obviously broke the Church of Scotland's Act of Security and angered its ministers. Many Scots were unhappy with the introduction of the Malt Tax as this could have had serious consequences.

3. How far do **Sources B** and **C** agree about the reasons for Scottish anger after the Union?   **4**

[END OF CONTEXT 5]

Marks

HISTORICAL STUDY: SCOTTISH AND BRITISH

CONTEXT 6: IMMIGRANTS AND EXILES: SCOTLAND, 1830s–1930s

Answer the following questions using recalled knowledge and information from the sources where appropriate.

Sources A and **B** explain why many Irish immigrated to Scotland in the 1840s.

Source A

> Irish immigration continued steadily until the 1840s. The Irish potato famine of the mid 1840s however led to a sharp increase in this immigration. It led to great poverty and some landlords evicted those who could not pay their rent. Transport costs were cheap, and wages in the west of Scotland continued to be higher than those in Ireland.

Source B

> In the mid and late 1840s the potato crops in Ireland were destroyed by blight, which caused the death of many people and led many others to leave. Many landlords used the crisis to take away people's homes. The very low wages paid in Ireland meant that the higher wages on offer in Scotland were attractive. Irish people found it was not far to travel to Scotland and that plenty of ships travelled the route, so the cost was cheap. Travelling conditions were miserable.

1. How far do **Sources A** and **B** agree about the reasons for Irish immigration to Scotland?   **4**

2. In what ways were Scots encouraged to emigrate between the 1830s and 1930s?   **5**

Source C explains why Andrew Carnegie became successful.

> Andrew Carnegie's family left Dunfermline for the USA when Andrew was twelve. He managed to get a job with the Pennsylvania Railroad Company. Here he prospered because of his energy and ability. He began the Company's sleeping car service. He also had great financial skills, borrowing a lot of money to invest. These investments proved to be enormously successful and made it possible for him to buy up iron and steel businesses, coalfields and steamships. In 1901 he sold his businesses to the US Steel Corporation. This made him the richest man in the world.

3. Why did many Scots emigrants, like Andrew Carnegie, became successful abroad? (Use **Source C** and recall.)   **5**

[END OF CONTEXT 6]

Mar

HISTORICAL STUDY: SCOTTISH AND BRITISH

CONTEXT 7(*a*): FROM THE CRADLE TO THE GRAVE? SOCIAL WELFARE IN BRITAIN, 1890s–1951

Answer the following questions using recalled knowledge and information from the sources where appropriate.

Sources A and **B** are about the causes of poverty in the early twentieth century.

Source A

> The investigations of Booth and Rowntree both revealed the problems facing the poorer classes in Britain. They identified some of the direct causes of poverty. The main reasons were that a man's earnings were not enough to support himself and his family. They were not able to obtain employment when trade was bad. Some men could not work due to sickness. Bad habits, such as drinking and gambling, also caused problems.

Source B

> Although many people thought Britain was experiencing a golden age, there was increasing unemployment and thirty per cent of the population were living in poverty. Of those living in poverty, about two-thirds were in that position because of low pay or irregular earnings. About one quarter were poor because of illness. Only about one-tenth were poor because of personal failings such as drunkenness or gambling.

1. How far do **Sources A** and **B** agree about the causes of poverty in the early twentieth century?   4

2. Describe the social reforms of the Liberal government between 1906 and 1914.   5

Source C is about the Home Front during the Second World War.

> During the Second World War the Home Front was treated and run like a battlefield. The priority was to ensure "fair shares for all" and to avoid waste. The war caused the government to get more involved in all areas of life. The Ministry of Food established the responsibility of the government to ensure the nation's health and safe food supply. War wounded, including bomb victims, were given free treatment. It soon became clear people expected the government to continue to do more for them after the war.

3. Why did the Second World War lead people to expect improvements in social welfare? (Use **Source C** and recall.)   5

[END OF CONTEXT 7(a)]

Marks

HISTORICAL STUDY: SCOTTISH AND BRITISH

> **CONTEXT 7(*b*): CAMPAIGNING FOR CHANGE: SOCIAL CHANGE IN SCOTLAND, 1900s–1979**

Answer the following questions using recalled knowledge and information from the sources where appropriate.

1. Describe the methods used by women to campaign for the vote in the period 1900 to 1914.

    5

Sources A and **B** are people's memories of going to the cinema in the 1930s.

Source A

> I used to go to the cinema almost every Saturday. We handed over two jam jars which covered the entrance charge of one penny. The action films were quite violent but nobody took them seriously with kids shouting things such as, "Look, the man's got a knife! Mind yer back, Jimmy!" We all enjoyed ourselves enormously and hammered our hands on the plain wooden seats. We must have made an outrageous amount of noise. Looking back, it was basic and in poor condition.

Source B

> For a penny we not only saw the show but sometimes received a free comic or small bag of sweeties as well. The programme comprised of a "funny" and a more dramatic film such as "The Hooded Terror" or "Tarzan", which had plenty of fighting in them. We compared the various cinemas and all agreed that our local was a "flea pit". Some theatres had individual seats instead of benches.

2. How far do **Sources A** and **B** agree about cinema entertainment in the 1930s?

    4

Source C is from a report about Scottish industry after 1945.

Source C

> We have the disadvantage of an outdated railway network and road building is much too slow. Many of the country's factory buildings are greatly in need of modernisation. Many shortages of skilled workers are appearing in industry. We must be ready to accept government and local authority help to solve the problem. To keep up with our competitors abroad, industry must encourage far greater levels of scientific and technical training.

3. Why did Scotland's industries find it difficult to compete with other countries after 1945? (Use **Source C** and recall.)

    5

[END OF CONTEXT 7(b)]

Ma

HISTORICAL STUDY: SCOTTISH AND BRITISH

CONTEXT 8: A TIME OF
TROUBLES: IRELAND, 1900–1923

Answer the following questions using recalled knowledge and information from the sources where appropriate.

Sources A and **B** are two Irish reactions to the outbreak of the First World War.

Source A

The interests of Ireland are at stake in this war. Your duty is to fight against Germany and everything it stands for. If we refuse to fight and stay at home then we will be disgracing our nation. Now is not the time for rebellion. By helping Britain, we help ourselves. I call on the men of Ireland to prove their bravery and courage by volunteering for this war.

Source B

If you are itching to fight, then your duty is to fight for Ireland and not for an empire we do not want to belong to. We have waited long enough. Now is the moment to start the rebellion. We gain nothing by helping the British fight this war. Our interests lie in an independent Ireland and nothing else. Only the foolish and misguided will go to fight in France.

1. How far do **Sources A** and **B** agree about whether or not the Irish should fight in the First World War?   4

2. Describe the actions taken by both sides in the Anglo-Irish War, 1919–1921.   5

Source C explains why the 1921 Treaty caused divisions amongst the nationalists.

Source C

By 1921 most members of the IRA accepted that a war against the British could not be won. Despite this, De Valera encouraged people to reject the Treaty. Moreover, the British were still in Ireland and had not been driven out. His supporters also believed that Ulster should not be partitioned. In particular De Valera objected to the oath of allegiance to the king. Even though the Irish public wanted peace, the anti-treaty forces were prepared to use violence to get what they wanted.

3. Why did some Irish nationalists refuse to accept the 1921 Treaty? (Use **Source C** and recall.)   5

[END OF CONTEXT 8]

[END OF PART 2: SCOTTISH AND BRITISH CONTEXTS]

Marks

PART 3:

HISTORICAL STUDY: EUROPEAN AND WORLD

CONTEXT 1: THE NORMAN CONQUEST, 1060–1153

Answer the following questions using recalled knowledge and information from the sources where appropriate.

1. What advantages did William have over his enemies at the Battle of Hastings?   **5**

Source A explains the influence of Norman England on David I.

Source A

> In 1072 William brought a great army to Scotland in response to Scottish raids on his kingdom. The Scottish king, Malcolm III, agreed to accept William as his overlord. When Malcolm's son David I became king in 1124 he too had to accept this and was determined to copy Norman ways. Furthermore, he had married the Anglo-Norman, Ada de Varene. This brought him estates in Huntingdonshire and Northamptonshire. David saw how the Anglo-Norman king kept a tight grip over England using the nobles to help him govern the country.

2. Why was David I influenced by Norman England? (Use **Source A** and recall.)   **5**

Source B is from a charter granting lands to Robert Bruce in 1124.

Source B

> David, by the grace of God, king of the Scots, does hereby give to his faithful servant, Robert Bruce, all the lands of Annandale and the castle of Lochmaben which is to be the centre of the Lordship. In return Robert will provide ten knights fully armed and each with a good horse to fight in the army of the king when called upon to do so.

3. How useful is **Source B** as evidence of the importance of the Bruce lords of Annandale?   **4**

[END OF CONTEXT 1]

Ma

HISTORICAL STUDY: EUROPEAN AND WORLD

> CONTEXT 2: THE CROSS AND THE
> CRESCENT: THE FIRST CRUSADE,
> 1096–1125

Answer the following questions using recalled knowledge and information from the sources where appropriate.

Source A was written by Abbot Guibert, who interviewed followers of Peter the Hermit.

Source A

> I do not remember any other man being held in such honour. Peter was generous to the poor and brought peace to every village he visited. He had great authority and a wonderful ability as a speaker. He seemed so holy that even the hairs from his donkey's tail were plucked as relics.

1. How useful is **Source A** as evidence of the popularity of Peter the Hermit?   **4**

2. What problems did the Crusaders face on their journey from Europe to Jerusalem?   **5**

Source B explains why Jerusalem was difficult to capture.

Source B

> Massive walls and flanking towers surrounded the city of Jerusalem. Starving the garrison into surrender was not easy because those inside had prepared well for an attack. They used drainage systems to reduce the possibility of disease. They had large water cisterns to provide them with a good supply of water. Although the Crusaders were overjoyed at seeing the Holy City, they knew they had an enormous task to complete.

3. Why did the First Crusade find Jerusalem difficult to capture? (Use **Source B** and recall.)   **5**

[END OF CONTEXT 2]

Marks

HISTORICAL STUDY: EUROPEAN AND WORLD

CONTEXT 3: WAR, DEATH AND
REVOLT IN MEDIEVAL EUROPE,
1328–1436

Answer the following questions using recalled knowledge and information from the sources where appropriate.

1. Describe the campaigns of the Black Prince in France.   5

Source A is about the reasons for discontent among the French peasants in 1358.

Source A

> France suffered a humiliating defeat in 1358. The English leaders withdrew to Bordeaux and agreed to a truce. During this time the great companies of mercenaries from the English forces pillaged the French countryside. The French peasants were further enraged by the nobles' demands for heavier payments of feudal dues and by the order of the Dauphin Charles that the peasants rebuild the castles of their aristocratic oppressors.

2. Why did the French peasants revolt in 1358? (Use **Source A** and recall.)   5

Source B is from an account of the Peasants' Revolt in England in the Anonimalle Chronicle written in the late fourteenth century.

Source B

> At this time the common people had as their advisor an evil churchman named John Ball. He advised them to get rid of all the lords, archbishops, abbots and priors. He said that the wealth of these men should be distributed among the people. He was respected by the commoners as a prophet and he worked to increase their hatred.

3. How useful is **Source B** as evidence of the aims of the Peasants' Revolt of 1381?   4

[END OF CONTEXT 3]

Ma

HISTORICAL STUDY: EUROPEAN AND WORLD

> ### CONTEXT 4: NEW WORLDS: EUROPE IN THE AGE OF EXPANSION, 1480s–1530s

Answer the following questions using recalled knowledge and information from the sources where appropriate.

Source A explains why the Europeans wanted to expand overseas.

Source A

> Each of the European states began exploration at different times. To increase their wealth they began to explore in search of a variety of products to trade. In the North Atlantic Ocean, an enormously valuable trade in fish encouraged boats of all European nations to search for fishing grounds farther from Europe. Spices drew explorers around the tip of Africa to Southeast Asia because they needed spices to preserve the meat they ate. By trading directly with the East, Europeans could avoid costly customs duties, or taxes, charged by rulers of every country.

1. Why did European countries want to explore overseas between 1480 and 1540? (Use **Source A** and recall.) **5**

Source B is from a letter from the African ruler, King Affonso of Angola, to the king of Portugal in the sixteenth century.

Source B

> We cannot say how great the damage is since Portuguese merchants seize our people, sons of farmers, sons of nobles, servants and relatives daily. They also wish to take the goods and produce of this kingdom. They grab them and sell them. Their wickedness and evil is so great that our country is losing its entire people.

2. How useful is **Source B** as evidence of the effects of Portugal's exploration of Africa? **4**

3. Describe the methods used by the Spanish Conquistadors to defeat either the **Aztecs** or the **Incas**. **5**

[END OF CONTEXT 4]

Marks

HISTORICAL STUDY: EUROPEAN AND WORLD

> **CONTEXT 5: "TEA AND FREEDOM":**
> **THE AMERICAN REVOLUTION,**
> **1763–1783**

Answer the following questions using recalled knowledge and information from the sources where appropriate.

1. Describe the complaints of the American colonists against British rule.   **5**

Source A is an extract from the diary of one of George Washington's army surgeons, in 1777.

Source A

> The army now begins to grow sickly from the continued tiredness they have suffered during this campaign. Poor food, hard living conditions, cold weather, nasty clothes, nasty food and vomiting out of my senses, I tell you the devil's in it. I can't endure it. Why are we sent here to starve and freeze?

2. How useful is **Source A** as evidence of the poor condition of Washington's Continental Army at the start of the War of Independence?   **4**

Source B explains why Britain lost the American war.

Source B

> When the revolution began, Britain was a great power with an experienced army and a strong navy. It had economic resources and a king determined to keep the colonies intact. However things went wrong. Britain never had a clear strategy for winning the war. Supply and communication were also problems. In addition to this, Washington was able to hold his army together and maintained morale. At home the British Parliament was not united behind the war.

3. Why did the British lose the war with the American colonists? (Use **Source B** and recall.)   **5**

[END OF CONTEXT 5]

Mar

HISTORICAL STUDY: EUROPEAN AND WORLD

> ### CONTEXT 6: "THIS ACCURSED TRADE": THE BRITISH SLAVE TRADE AND ITS ABOLITION, 1770–1807

Answer the following questions using recalled knowledge and information from the sources where appropriate.

Source A is from a book by Mungo Park, an eighteenth century explorer in Africa.

Source A

> The African captives are usually secured by putting the right leg of one and the left leg of another into the same pair of fetters. By supporting the fetters with a string, they can just walk, though very slowly. Every four slaves are likewise fastened together by their necks with a strong rope or twisted thongs and at night extra fetters are put on their hands.

1. How useful is **Source A** as evidence of the treatment of Africans when they were first captured?

   4

2. Describe what happened to slaves at the end of the Middle Passage.

   5

Source B is about the campaign to abolish the slave trade.

Source B

> In 1787 a small group of Quakers launched a public campaign against the British slave trade. Baptists and Methodists found a new social and political voice by supporting the campaign. Slavery seemed offensive in the world after the French Revolution, when more and more people talked of liberty. British manufacturers now supported the idea of free labour. At last many people saw the approach of the end of such an abominable practice.

3. Why was the slave trade abolished in 1807? (Use **Source B** and recall.)

   5

[END OF CONTEXT 6]

Marks

HISTORICAL STUDY: EUROPEAN AND WORLD

CONTEXT 7: CITIZENS! THE FRENCH REVOLUTION, 1789–1794

Answer the following questions using recalled knowledge and information from the sources where appropriate.

Source A is about the ideas of the "Philosophers" who questioned the way France was ruled in 1789.

Source A

> Diderot declared that governments should be influenced by scientific ideas and not just the will of the king. Montesquieu stated that power should be shared between the monarchy and parliament. He argued that the making of laws and raising taxes should be the role of parliament. Many Frenchmen learned of Montesquieu's ideas when they were sent to help in the American War of Independence. Rousseau attacked the idea that the king and the nobles were born to rule over the people.

1. Why did new ideas encourage people to question the way France was ruled in 1789? (Use **Source A** and recall.)   **5**

2. Describe the events leading up to the storming of the Bastille in July 1789.   **5**

Source B is a description of the execution of Louis XVI by one of the men who sentenced him to death, written in 1792.

Source B

> His blood flows and there is a cry of joy as 80,000 armed men cheer. His blood flows and there are people who dip a fingertip or scrap of paper in it. An executioner sells small bundles of his hair and people buy ribbons to tie it with. Everyone carries off a small bloodstained fragment of his clothing.

3. How useful is **Source B** as evidence of how people felt about Louis XVI's death?   **4**

[END OF CONTEXT 7]

Ma

HISTORICAL STUDY: EUROPEAN AND WORLD

CONTEXT 8: CAVOUR, GARIBALDI AND THE MAKING OF ITALY, 1815–1870

Answer the following questions using recalled knowledge and information from the sources where appropriate.

Source A is from a poem by the Italian nationalist Leopardi. It was written in 1818.

Source A

> O my fatherland, I see the greatness that was Rome
> And the arches and the columns and
> The marble towers of our Roman ancestors
> Where is that glory now?

1. How useful is **Source A** as evidence of the growth of nationalist feeling in Italy after 1815?   4

2. Describe the difficulties faced by the Italian nationalists during the revolutions of 1848–1849.   5

Source B explains the development of Piedmont in the 1850s.

Source B

> In 1851 Piedmont signed trade agreements with France, Britain and Belgium. This resulted in a growth in trade. Between 1850 and 1859 imports and exports grew by 300%. By this time 850 kilometres of railway track were in operation in Piedmont. In 1853 an electric telegraph link was set up between Turin and Paris. A canal building programme began in 1857 which helped the growth of industry. By 1859 Piedmont was considered to be the most modern state in Italy.

3. Why had Piedmont become a wealthy and powerful state by 1859? (Use **Source B** and recall.)   5

[END OF CONTEXT 8]

Marks

HISTORICAL STUDY: EUROPEAN AND WORLD

CONTEXT 9: IRON AND BLOOD? BISMARCK AND THE CREATION OF THE GERMAN EMPIRE, 1815–1871

Answer the following questions using recalled knowledge and information from the sources where appropriate.

1. Describe the growth of nationalism in the German states between 1815 and 1850.　　**5**

Source A is about the failure of the 1848 revolutions.

Source A

> In 1848 revolutions broke out all over Europe. In Germany there were wide differences in the aims of the revolutionaries. The liberals wanted a united German Empire with a national parliament. Other groups didn't want to abolish the monarchy but wanted to give more power to the ordinary people. They could not agree about the borders of the new Germany. It is therefore no surprise that the 1848 revolutions collapsed.

2. Why did the 1848 revolutions in Germany fail? (Use **Source A** and recall.)　　**5**

Source B is from a letter written by Bismarck to the King of Prussia in 1866.

Source B

> We have to avoid punishing Austria too severely because we do not want her to be bitter and wanting revenge. We ought to keep the possibility of becoming friends again. If Austria is punished she will become the ally of France and every other country who is opposed to us.

3. How useful is **Source B** as evidence of why Prussia wanted a lenient treaty after the Austro-Prussian War in 1866?　　**4**

[END OF CONTEXT 9]

Mar

HISTORICAL STUDY: EUROPEAN AND WORLD

> ### CONTEXT 10: THE RED FLAG: LENIN AND THE RUSSIAN REVOLUTION, 1894–1921

Answer the following questions using recalled knowledge and information from the sources where appropriate.

Source A is about Stolypin's agricultural reforms.

Source A

> Peasants were allowed to buy up strips of land from their neighbours to make a single land holding. Stolypin set up a peasants' bank to provide loans for them to do this. This would also allow them to use more modern methods of agriculture. Stolypin believed that this would create a new class of prosperous "kulaks" who would be loyal to the government. About 15 % of peasants took up the offer and made greater profits when grain production increased.

1. Why did the lives of some peasants improve as a result of Stolypin's reforms? (Use **Source A** and recall.)   **5**

2. Describe the problems facing the Provisional Government in 1917.   **5**

Source B is from the diary of a French diplomat living in Russia in February 1918.

Source B

> We are now living in a madhouse. In the last few days there has been an avalanche of decrees. First comes a decree cancelling all banking transactions, then comes one confiscating housing. A law is made to take the children of middle class parents into care. In this way differences in education will be avoided.

3. How useful is **Source B** as evidence of life in Russia after the Bolshevik revolution?   **4**

[END OF CONTEXT 10]

Marks

HISTORICAL STUDY: EUROPEAN AND WORLD

> ### CONTEXT 11: FREE AT LAST? RACE RELATIONS IN THE USA, 1918–1968

Answer the following questions using recalled knowledge and information from the sources where appropriate.

1. Describe the effects of the Jim Crow laws on Black Americans.   **5**

Source A is about the events in Birmingham, Alabama, in 1963.

Source A

> In January 1963, Martin Luther King announced that the SCLC was going to Birmingham, Alabama, the most racist city in America. King knew that civil rights protesters would be risking their lives when they arrived in Birmingham. Racists had the support of the Birmingham police department. King knew if they could lead a successful demonstration in Birmingham they might spark off big changes across the South. On May 2 the march began and the police were waiting for them. Over nine hundred children were jailed that day.

2. Why was the protest in Birmingham in 1963 an important event in the civil rights campaign in the USA? (Use **Source A** and recall.)   **5**

Source B is from a speech by Stokely Carmichael in Greenwood on 17 June 1966.

Source B

> This is the twenty-seventh time I have been arrested – and I ain't going to jail no more. The only way we gonna stop them white men from whuppin' us is to take over. We been saying freedom for six years and we ain't got nothin'. What we gonna start saying now is Black Power.

3. How useful is **Source B** as evidence of the beliefs of the Black Power movement?   **4**

[END OF CONTEXT 11]

Ma

HISTORICAL STUDY: EUROPEAN AND WORLD

**CONTEXT 12: THE ROAD TO WAR,
1933–1939**

Answer the following questions using recalled knowledge and information from the sources where appropriate.

1. In what ways did Hitler increase German military power in the years after 1933?   **5**

Source A is the opinion of Lord Tweedsmuir, a British politician, about the Anschluss, March 1938.

Source A

> I don't see what the problem is. Austria will be much happier as part of Germany. The Treaty of Versailles said that Germany and Austria must never unite but that was foolish. Some people say that Czechoslovakia will be Hitler's next target but that is not our problem.

2. How useful is **Source A** as evidence of British attitudes to the Anschluss?   **4**

Source B explains German complaints against Poland.

Source B

> Germany had signed a non-aggression treaty with Poland in 1934 which made Poland feel safe. Yet this was the country that the Nazis hated most of all and not just for racial reasons. The creation of Poland meant that large areas of land had been taken from Germany and because of this millions of Germans were forced to live under Polish rule. The German city of Danzig had been taken away from Germany and was run by the League of Nations to suit the Poles.

3. Why did Germany declare war on Poland in 1939? (Use **Source B** and recall.)   **5**

[END OF CONTEXT 12]

Marks

HISTORICAL STUDY: EUROPEAN AND WORLD

> ### CONTEXT 13: IN THE SHADOW OF THE BOMB: THE COLD WAR, 1945–1985

Answer the following questions using recalled knowledge and information from the sources where appropriate.

Source A is from a document by President Kennedy on the situation in Berlin in 1961.

Source A

> It seems particularly stupid to risk killing a million Americans over an argument about access rights on a motorway or because the Germans want Germany reunited. If I'm going to threaten Russia with nuclear war, it will have to be for much bigger and more important reasons than that.

1. How useful is **Source A** as evidence of American policy towards the Berlin Crisis in 1961?

4

2. Describe the part played by the USA in the Cuban Missile Crisis of 1962.

5

Source B explains why the USA lost the war in Vietnam.

Source B

> North Vietnam suffered widespread destruction but it still triumphed. America realised too late that the real war in Vietnam was not just a military one but one for "the hearts and minds" of the peasants. American troops failed to cope with the guerrilla tactics of the Viet Cong. The communists were backed militarily by China and Russia. By the late 1960s all that the American troops wanted was to go home.

3. Why did the USA lose the war in Vietnam? (Use **Source B** and recall.)

5

[END OF CONTEXT 13]

[END OF PART 3: EUROPEAN AND WORLD CONTEXTS]

[END OF QUESTION PAPER]

[BLANK PAGE]

2009

[BLANK PAGE]

X044/201

NATIONAL QUALIFICATIONS 2009	TUESDAY, 2 JUNE 9.00 AM – 10.45 AM	HISTORY INTERMEDIATE 2

The instructions for this paper are on *Page two*. Read them carefully before you begin your answers.
Some sources in this examination have been adapted or translated.

INSTRUCTIONS

Answer **one** question from Part 1, The Short Essay

Answer **one** context* from Part 2, Scottish and British

Answer **one** context* from Part 3, European and World

Answer **one** other context* from

     either   Part 2, Scottish and British

     or   Part 3, European and World

*Answer all the questions in each of your chosen contexts.

Contents

[Turn over

PART 1: THE SHORT ESSAY

Mar

Answer **one** question. For this question you should write a short essay using your own knowledge. The essay should include an introduction, development and conclusion. Each question is worth 8 marks.

SCOTTISH AND BRITISH CONTEXTS:

CONTEXT 1: MURDER IN THE CATHEDRAL: CROWN, CHURCH AND PEOPLE, 1154–1173

Question 1:   Explain why knights were important in the twelfth century.   **8**

CONTEXT 2: WALLACE, BRUCE AND THE WARS OF INDEPENDENCE, 1286–1328

Question 2:   Explain why John Balliol lost his position as King of Scots in 1296.   **8**

CONTEXT 3: MARY, QUEEN OF SCOTS AND THE SCOTTISH REFORMATION, 1540s–1587

Question 3:   Explain why Mary, Queen of Scots, faced difficulties ruling Scotland when she returned in 1561.   **8**

CONTEXT 4: THE COMING OF THE CIVIL WAR, 1603–1642

Question 4:   Explain why there were problems between Crown and Parliament during the reign of James VI and I.   **8**

CONTEXT 5: "ANE END OF ANE AULD SANG": SCOTLAND AND THE TREATY OF UNION, 1690s–1715

Question 5:   Explain why there was so much opposition to a Union in Scotland before 1707.   **8**

CONTEXT 6: IMMIGRANTS AND EXILES: SCOTLAND, 1830s–1930s

Question 6:   Explain why Scots emigrants made a valuable contribution in Canada and the United States.   **8**

CONTEXT 7(*a*): FROM THE CRADLE TO THE GRAVE? SOCIAL WELFARE IN BRITAIN, 1890s–1951

Question 7(*a*):   Explain why the Liberal reforms, 1906–1914, failed to solve the problems of the poor.   **8**

Marks

CONTEXT 7(b): CAMPAIGNING FOR CHANGE: SOCIAL CHANGE IN SCOTLAND, 1900s–1979

Question 7(b): Explain why many industries in Scotland experienced problems in the years between the two world wars.

8

CONTEXT 8: A TIME OF TROUBLES: IRELAND, 1900–1923

Question 8: Explain why support for Sinn Fein increased after 1916.

8

EUROPEAN AND WORLD CONTEXTS:

CONTEXT 1: THE NORMAN CONQUEST, 1060–1153

Question 9: Explain why David I introduced feudalism to Scotland.

8

CONTEXT 2: THE CROSS AND THE CRESCENT: THE FIRST CRUSADE, 1096–1125

Question 10: Explain why Pope Urban II called the First Crusade.

8

CONTEXT 3: WAR, DEATH AND REVOLT IN MEDIEVAL EUROPE, 1328–1436

Question 11: Explain why the Hundred Years' War broke out between England and France in 1337.

8

CONTEXT 4: NEW WORLDS: EUROPE IN THE AGE OF EXPANSION, 1480s–1530s

Question 12: Explain why European countries wanted to search for new lands between the 1480s and 1530s.

8

CONTEXT 5: "TEA AND FREEDOM": THE AMERICAN REVOLUTION, 1763–1783

Question 13: Explain why the colonists won the American War of Independence.

8

CONTEXT 6: "THIS ACCURSED TRADE": THE BRITISH SLAVE TRADE AND ITS ABOLITION, 1770–1807

Question 14: Explain why there was increasing support for the campaign against the slave trade by the 1780s.

8

Ma

CONTEXT 7: CITIZENS!
THE FRENCH REVOLUTION, 1789–1794

Question 15: Explain why few French people supported Louis XVI in 1789.

8

CONTEXT 8: CAVOUR, GARIBALDI
AND THE MAKING OF ITALY, 1815–1870

Question 16: Explain why Cavour was important to Italian unification.

8

CONTEXT 9: IRON AND BLOOD? BISMARCK AND THE
CREATION OF THE GERMAN EMPIRE, 1815–1871

Question 17: Explain why Bismarck's leadership was important to the unification of the German states.

8

CONTEXT 10: THE RED FLAG:
LENIN AND THE RUSSIAN REVOLUTION, 1894–1921

Question 18: Explain why the Reds won the Civil War.

8

CONTEXT 11: FREE AT LAST?
RACE RELATIONS IN THE USA, 1918–1968

Question 19: Explain why black people rioted in many American cities in the 1960s.

8

CONTEXT 12: THE ROAD TO WAR, 1933–1939

Question 20: Explain why events after Munich, September 1938, led to the outbreak of war in 1939.

8

CONTEXT 13: IN THE SHADOW OF THE BOMB:
THE COLD WAR, 1945–1985

Question 21: Explain why the USA became involved in a crisis over Cuba in 1962.

8

[END OF PART 1: THE SHORT ESSAY]

[Turn over for PART 2: SCOTTISH AND BRITISH CONTEXTS on *Page eight*

PART 2:

HISTORICAL STUDY: SCOTTISH AND BRITISH

Ma*

> **CONTEXT 1: MURDER IN THE CATHEDRAL: CROWN, CHURCH AND PEOPLE, 1154–1173**

Answer the following questions using recalled knowledge and information from the sources where appropriate.

Source A was written in 1177 by Peter of Blois, Henry II's secretary.

Source A

> Every day the king travels around his kingdom. He never rests and works tirelessly to make sure that his people are at peace. On occasion, he attacks the barons but this is only so that the law of the country can be upheld. No one is more honest, more polite and more generous to the poor than the king. He is truly loved by his people.

1. How useful is **Source A** as evidence of the character of Henry II?   4

2. Describe the life of a monk in medieval times.   5

Source B explains why Henry II and Archbishop Becket quarrelled.

Source B

> Henry II appointed Thomas Becket as Archbishop of Canterbury in 1162. Almost immediately their friendship was tested when Becket resigned as Chancellor. Until then Becket had been a loyal servant, so this action stunned the king. Becket then refused to sign the Constitutions of Clarendon and would not agree to reduce the power of the Church. When summoned to appear at the Northampton trial, Becket fled to France without the king's permission. He remained there for six years protected by the king of France.

3. Why did Henry II and Archbishop Becket quarrel? (Use **Source B** and recall.)   5

[END OF CONTEXT 1]

Marks

HISTORICAL STUDY: SCOTTISH AND BRITISH

> **CONTEXT 2: WALLACE, BRUCE AND THE WARS OF INDEPENDENCE, 1286–1328**

Answer the following questions using recalled knowledge and information from the sources where appropriate.

Source A was written by a Scottish chronicler some time after the death of Alexander III in 1286.

Source A

> On 19th March, the king was delayed by the ferry at South Queensferry until dusk on a dark, stormy night. When advised by his companions not to go beyond Inverkeithing that night, he rejected their advice and with an escort of knights he hurried along a very steep track towards Kinghorn. To the west of that place, his horse stumbled and he was killed.

1. How useful is **Source A** as evidence about the death of King Alexander III?   4

2. Describe what happened at the Battle of Stirling Bridge.   5

Source B explains why the Scots sent the Declaration of Arbroath to the Pope in 1320.

Source B

> In the years after Bannockburn, although Bruce controlled Scotland, he was not accepted internationally as its king. Earlier efforts to gain recognition by invading the north of England had failed. They had only annoyed Edward. The Scots then tried to increase the pressure on Edward by invading Ireland, but this ended in disaster when Edward Bruce was killed in 1318. When they sent the declaration to the Pope in 1320, they hoped he would recognise Bruce as king.

3. Why did the Scots send the Declaration of Arbroath to the Pope in 1320? (Use **Source B** and recall.)   5

[END OF CONTEXT 2]

Ma

HISTORICAL STUDY: SCOTTISH AND BRITISH

> ### CONTEXT 3: MARY, QUEEN OF SCOTS AND THE SCOTTISH REFORMATION, 1540s–1587

Answer the following questions using recalled knowledge and information from the sources where appropriate.

Source A explains why Protestantism spread in Scotland in the 1540s and 1550s.

Source A

> In Germany, the ideas of Martin Luther had started the Reformation movement. Some Scots began questioning the teachings of the Catholic Church. During the Rough Wooing, English invaders had encouraged this by distributing English translations of the Bible so people could study the Bible for themselves. The Catholic Church continued to use the Latin Bible. Religious pamphlets, smuggled into Scotland from Europe, also spread Protestant ideas. The "Good and Godly Ballads" made these ideas popular. Protestantism began to spread more quickly in Scotland.

1. Why did Protestantism spread in Scotland in the 1540s and 1550s? (Use **Source A** and recall.)   5

2. Describe the events surrounding the murder of Darnley in 1567.   5

Source B is part of a letter written by Mary, Queen of Scots, to Queen Elizabeth in 1582.

Source B

> While I was in Scotland, my subjects were encouraged to speak, act and finally to rebel against me by the agents, spies and secret messengers sent there in your name. I do not have any specific proof of that except for the confession of one person whom you rewarded very generously for his hard work at that time.

3. How useful is **Source B** as evidence of Mary's opinion of Queen Elizabeth?   4

[END OF CONTEXT 3]

Marks

HISTORICAL STUDY: SCOTTISH AND BRITISH

> ### CONTEXT 4: THE COMING OF THE CIVIL WAR, 1603–1642

Answer the following questions using recalled knowledge and information from the sources where appropriate.

Source A is from "A Concise History of Scotland" by Fitzroy McLean, published in 1974.

Source A

> The new service book was read for the first time in St Giles on 23 July 1637 amid scenes of violence which soon developed into a riot. Tradition says the females of the congregation played a leading part, egged on by a certain Jenny Geddes. Before long, the Privy Council were forced to shut themselves in Holyroodhouse to escape the mob.

1. How useful is **Source A** as evidence of how the Scots reacted to Charles I's introduction of the Common Prayer Book in 1637?   **4**

Source B explains why Charles I became unpopular in England between 1629 and 1640.

Source B

> Since the Middle Ages, only people who lived near the coast had to pay Ship Money. In 1635 Charles I made people from inland areas pay Ship Money tax as well. There were strong objections because the king had imposed this new tax without the consent of Parliament. He also fined people who had built on common land, or in royal forests. Anyone who refused to pay was tried in special courts. The king was seen as a tyrant. People turned against him.

2. Explain why Charles I became unpopular in England between 1629 and 1640. (Use **Source B** and recall.)   **5**

3. Describe the events between 1640 and 1642 which led to the outbreak of the Civil War.   **5**

[END OF CONTEXT 4]

Ma

HISTORICAL STUDY: SCOTTISH AND BRITISH

> ### CONTEXT 5: "ANE END OF ANE AULD SANG": SCOTLAND AND THE TREATY OF UNION, 1690s–1715

Answer the following questions using recalled knowledge and information from the sources where appropriate.

Source A is a public notice published by the Directors of the Company of Scotland in 1698.

Source A

> The Court of Directors now have ships ready and loaded with provisions and all manner of things needed for their intended expedition to settle a colony in the Indies. They give notice that to encourage people to go on this expedition, they promise to give them fifty acres of good ground to grow their crops.

1. How useful is **Source A** as evidence about Scottish preparations for the Darien Expedition? **4**

Source B explains why many Scottish nobles agreed to the Act of Union.

Source B

> The Scottish nobility has been criticised for "betraying" Scotland at the time of the Union. There was, however, a considerable effort put into convincing them of the wealth which a Union would bring to Scotland. They would prosper by having access to England's colonies and after the Union many did invest in the sugar trade of the West Indies. Besides, a Union would guarantee the Protestant Succession and its supporters would gain both royal approval and the benefits it brought.

2. Why did many Scottish nobles agree to the Act of Union? (Use **Source B** and recall.) **5**

3. In what ways did Scotland change as a result of the Act of Union? **5**

[END OF CONTEXT 5]

Marks

HISTORICAL STUDY: SCOTTISH AND BRITISH

> ## CONTEXT 6: IMMIGRANTS AND EXILES: SCOTLAND, 1830s–1930s

Answer the following questions using recalled knowledge and information from the sources where appropriate.

Source A is evidence given to a government enquiry in 1836 by a Catholic priest in Aberdeen.

Source A

> The number of cotton and linen factories in Aberdeen has continued to grow since the Irish people were encouraged to come to us. Finding work is easy and fairly good wages are offered to them in these factories. A considerable number of Irish people have come to the city and have brought their families with them.

1. How useful is **Source A** as evidence of the reasons Irish people came to Scotland after 1830?

    4

2. Describe the experience of Irish immigrants in the west of Scotland.

    5

Source B explains why many Scots emigrated overseas in the twentieth century.

Source B

> Mr Macdonald, the headmaster, said that he had faith in Canada. Many of his best pupils who were now living in Canada were succeeding. This was obvious from the money and letters they sent home to their parents. He then introduced the Canadian immigration agent, who spoke first in Gaelic and then in English. He said Canada was a huge country which offered great opportunities for farming. He enthusiastically praised the country as he showed view after view of scenes of Canada on the screen.

3. Why did many Scots emigrate overseas in the twentieth century? (Use **Source B** and recall.)

    5

[END OF CONTEXT 6]

Ma

HISTORICAL STUDY: SCOTTISH AND BRITISH

**CONTEXT 7(*a*): FROM THE
CRADLE TO THE GRAVE? SOCIAL
WELFARE IN BRITAIN, 1890s–1951**

Answer the following questions using recalled knowledge and information from the sources where appropriate.

Source A comments on changing attitudes towards poverty.

Source A

> By the start of the twentieth century, attitudes towards the poor in Britain were changing. Trade unions felt the Liberals and Conservatives did not do enough for the poor. There was also a growth in Socialist thinking which felt very strongly that a high level of poverty was wrong. The Labour Party was formed in 1900. It stood for practical reforms to tackle poverty. The Labour Party threatened to take support away from the Liberals. Frightened by this, the Liberals began to think of ways to help the poor.

1. Why did attitudes towards poverty change in the early twentieth century? (Use **Source A** and recall.)   5

Source B is a cartoon from the Daily Herald newspaper in 1942.

Source B

2. How useful is **Source B** as evidence of the ideas in the Beveridge Report?   4

3. Describe the reforms introduced by Labour after 1945 to improve the lives of the British people.   5

[END OF CONTEXT 7(a)]

HISTORICAL STUDY: SCOTTISH AND BRITISH

Marks

> **CONTEXT 7(b): CAMPAIGNING FOR CHANGE: SOCIAL CHANGE IN SCOTLAND, 1900s–1979**

Answer the following questions using recalled knowledge and information from the sources where appropriate.

1. Describe the ways sport became more popular in Scotland between 1900 and 1939.   **5**

Source A explains why women had not gained the right to vote by 1914.

Source A

> In the years before the Great War, the government had a number of problems to deal with and did not regard votes for women as very important. In addition, the Prime Minister, Mr Asquith, was personally opposed to giving women the franchise. Emmeline Pankhurst founded the Women's Social and Political Union even though most men believed that women should not get involved in politics. When women began militant actions such as breaking shop windows, they were accused of being irresponsible.

2. Why had women not gained the right to vote by 1914? (Use **Source A** and recall.)   **5**

Source B is a photograph of a class being taught to wash clothes in a Dundee school in 1938.

Source B

3. How useful is **Source B** as evidence of the way Scottish children were educated in the 1930s?   **4**

[END OF CONTEXT 7(b)]

HISTORICAL STUDY: SCOTTISH AND BRITISH

CONTEXT 8: A TIME OF TROUBLES: IRELAND, 1900–1923

Answer the following questions using recalled knowledge and information from the sources where appropriate.

Source A explains why the Ulster Unionists were against Home Rule for Ireland.

Source A

> Unionists knew that the Home Rule Bill could not be defeated in parliament. The Unionists argued that Home Rule would destroy their way of life. Ulster was far richer than the rest of Ireland and many believed that they would be forced into poverty if the law was accepted. Led by MPs such as Edward Carson, as many as 50,000 Unionists attended meetings in Belfast. They were afraid that Ulster would be isolated from the Empire and that the Protestant Church could be weakened.

1. Why were the Ulster Unionists against Home Rule for Ireland? (Use **Source A** and recall.)

Source B is a poster produced by the Irish National Party in 1915.

Source B

2. How useful is **Source B** as evidence of Irish Nationalists' attitudes towards the First World War?

3. Describe the Civil War which broke out in Ireland in 1922.

[END OF CONTEXT 8]

[END OF PART 2: SCOTTISH AND BRITISH CONTEXTS]

Marks

PART 3:

HISTORICAL STUDY: EUROPEAN AND WORLD

CONTEXT 1: THE NORMAN CONQUEST, 1060–1153

Answer the following questions using recalled knowledge and information from the sources where appropriate.

Sources A and **B** are about Earl Harold's right to become King of England in 1066.

Source A

> King Edward died in London having reigned for twenty three years. The next day he was buried amid the bitter grieving of all present. After the burial, Harold, whom Edward had nominated as his rightful successor, was chosen as King by all the powerful lords of England and on the same day was crowned legitimately and with great ceremony by Aldred, Archbishop of York.

Source B

> Harold did not wait for public support but broke the oath he had taken to support William's rightful claim to the throne. With the help of a few of his supporters, he seized the throne on the day of Edward's funeral at the very time when all the people were mourning their loss. He was illegally crowned by Stigund of Canterbury, who had been excommunicated by the Pope.

1. How far do **Sources A** and **B** disagree about Harold's right to be King of England?   **4**

2. Describe the methods used by William to increase his royal authority.   **5**

Source C explains why there was an increase in the number of abbeys and monasteries in Scotland.

Source C

> David was the youngest son of the saintly Queen Margaret and was very religious. He began a building of abbeys and monasteries such as would never be known again in Scotland. Much of the wealth that David gained from his burghs was poured into these great new projects. David encouraged his nobles to leave land to the church. Master craftsmen were brought from England and France. The kingdom was alive with a new spirit and his work was carried on by the kings that followed.

3. Why did the number of abbeys and monasteries in Scotland increase during the reign of David I? (Use **Source C** and recall.)   **5**

[END OF CONTEXT 1]

M

HISTORICAL STUDY: EUROPEAN AND WORLD

> **CONTEXT 2: THE CROSS AND THE CRESCENT: THE FIRST CRUSADE, 1096–1125**

Answer the following questions using recalled knowledge and information from the sources where appropriate.

Source A explains why the Peoples' Crusade failed.

Source A

> After months of travelling, Peter the Hermit arrived at Constantinople. The journey had been difficult and many in his army had already been killed. Emperor Alexius warned the Crusaders not to attack the Muslims but to wait for the knights. The Crusaders were eager to get to Jerusalem and so ignored this advice. Soon afterwards, the Crusaders began arguing amongst themselves. They elected their own leaders and no longer listened to Peter the Hermit. In despair he left the Crusade and returned to Constantinople.

1. Why did the Peoples' Crusade fail? (Use **Source A** and recall.)   5

2. Describe the capture of Nicaea by the First Crusade.   5

Sources B and **C** describe the Crusaders' victory at Antioch.

Source B

> Kerbogha and the Muslim forces attacked the Crusaders the minute they left the city. Bohemond led the Crusaders and organised the knights. Without his leadership they would have been defeated. Although they were tired and hungry, they continued to fight. The Muslims were brave and did not give up. Eventually the Crusaders forced them to flee the battlefield and won a great victory.

Source C

> Although the Muslim forces surrounded Antioch, they did not attack the Crusaders when they left the city. Bohemond commanded the army but could not organise his knights and was nearly defeated. The Crusaders were only victorious because the Muslims did not respect Kerbogha. They refused to fight and fled the battlefield. Their cowardly behaviour meant the Muslims lost the battle.

3. How far do **Sources B** and **C** disagree about the Crusaders' victory at Antioch?   4

[END OF CONTEXT 2]

Marks

HISTORICAL STUDY: EUROPEAN AND WORLD

> **CONTEXT 3: WAR, DEATH AND REVOLT IN MEDIEVAL EUROPE, 1328–1436**

Answer the following questions using recalled knowledge and information from the sources where appropriate.

Source A explains why the Black Death spread across Europe in the fourteenth century.

Source A

> When a rat died of plague its fleas would leave and carry the disease to humans. This happened because humans and rats lived close together. Trading ships were often infested with rats. If these rats died of plague their fleas could give it to sailors and the people in the ports. A ship would therefore carry the plague until the sailors died of it. Diseased rats could also get into merchants' wagons and be carried across the country. This explanation of the spread of the plague is called the trade route theory.

1. Why did the Black Death spread across Europe in the fourteenth century? (Use **Source A** and recall.)   5

Sources B and **C** describe the role of Henry V in the Hundred Years' War.

Source B

> Henry V was the last great Plantagenet king. He believed strongly in his right to the French throne and convinced many Frenchmen that his cause was just. His great speech to his archers before Agincourt inspired victory. He was a leader who expected discipline from others and showed great self-discipline himself. However, under the stress of war he could become cruel towards his defeated enemies.

Source C

> Henry had no right to the crown of France. He had no right to that of England either. According to the legend, the war with France showed Henry's military genius. Really, it was a story of gambler's luck. The superior French army got stuck in the mud at Agincourt. At Agincourt, he was a war criminal, massacring prisoners in defiance of the conventions of war.

2. How far do **Sources B** and **C** disagree about the role of Henry V in the Hundred Years' War?   4

3. What part did Joan of Arc play in reawakening French national pride?   5

[END OF CONTEXT 3]

Ma

HISTORICAL STUDY: EUROPEAN AND WORLD

> ### CONTEXT 4: NEW WORLDS: EUROPE IN THE AGE OF EXPANSION, 1480s–1530s

Answer the following questions using recalled knowledge and information from the sources where appropriate.

Source A is about shipbuilding and navigation.

Source A

> The Age of Exploration was possible because of new inventions. The most important of these inventions was the carrack. This ship had a lateen sail which made ships faster and far more manouverable. Longer journeys were possible which encouraged European rulers to search for new lands. Astrolabes helped sailors identify their location at sea. The development of log lines helped sailors calculate their speed and longitude. A great deal of expansion was then achieved in just fifty years.

1. Why did developments in shipbuilding and navigation make voyages of exploration easier between the 1480s and 1530s? (Use **Source A** and recall.)   5

Sources B and **C** describe Columbus's arrival in the New World.

Source B

> They arrived at a small island. Soon the local people came to watch them. The Admiral went on shore with Vicente Yanez, the captain of the Nina. The Admiral called to the two captains and to the others who leaped on shore, and said that they should bear faithful testimony that he had taken possession of the said island for the King and Queen. He presented the natives with red caps and strings of beads to wear upon the neck.

Source C

> After a voyage of more than two months the fleet sighted land. On 12th October Columbus set foot in the New World. Watched by naked, silent natives, he took control of the island in the name of the King and Queen of Spain and gave thanks to God. Gifts were exchanged with the natives. Columbus believed they were somewhere in the Indies, near Cipangu.

2. How far do **Sources B** and **C** agree about what happened when Christopher Columbus first arrived in the New World?   4

3. Describe the exploration of North America up to 1540.   5

[END OF CONTEXT 4]

Marks

HISTORICAL STUDY: EUROPEAN AND WORLD

> **CONTEXT 5: "TEA AND FREEDOM":**
> **THE AMERICAN REVOLUTION,**
> **1763–1783**

Answer the following questions using recalled knowledge and information from the sources where appropriate.

Source A is about the colonists' relationship with Britain.

Source A

> Many colonists were suffering as trade was poor and they believed the British government was responsible. Despite this, the Americans hoped that the economy would soon improve. However, Granville, a British government minister, introduced tough trade policies which made things worse. Consequently, the colonists saw British naval officers and customs men as greedy and unwanted. They represented a distant and unsympathetic government. This helped push many well-to-do colonists towards opposition to Britain and increased the likelihood of armed rebellion.

1. Why were many colonists unhappy with British rule by 1776? (Use **Source A** and recall.)

5

Sources B and **C** are about the American forces which fought against the British army.

Source B

> The Revolutionary War was waged by small armies. The American forces were often led by inefficient, even incompetent, commanders who fought muddled campaigns. The men gathering in Boston were enthusiastic but badly armed and lacking supplies. The American commander, George Washington, could rely on no more than 5000 regular soldiers. Most men were part-time and served for only a few months. Britain's professional army was larger but not large enough to subdue the Americans.

Source C

> Many officers who led the American forces were not trained in the different types of warfare. The whole army was short of artillery, cavalry and almost all sorts of supplies. Within each state there were part-time soldiers. Many were militiamen who met and trained in their spare time and, although they did not have a uniform, they still came to fight for their country's freedom.

2. To what extent do **Sources B** and **C** agree about the condition of the American army? **4**

3. Describe the events leading up to the British surrender at Saratoga in 1777. **5**

[END OF CONTEXT 5]

Ma

HISTORICAL STUDY: EUROPEAN AND WORLD

> **CONTEXT 6: "THIS ACCURSED TRADE": THE BRITISH SLAVE TRADE AND ITS ABOLITION, 1770–1807**

Answer the following questions using recalled knowledge and information from the sources where appropriate.

1. Describe conditions for slaves during the Middle Passage. **5**

Sources A and **B** describe slave auctions in the West Indies.

Source A

> Slaves were treated in most cases like cattle. A man went about the country buying up slaves and he was called a "speculator". Then he would sell them to the highest bidder. Oh! It was pitiful to see children taken from their mothers' breasts, mothers sold, husbands sold to a different owner than their wives. One woman had a baby and he wouldn't buy the baby.

Source B

> The slave master made us hold up our heads while customers felt our hands and arms and looked at our teeth, precisely as someone examines a horse which he is about to purchase. All the time the auction was going on one mother was crying aloud. She begged the man not to buy her son unless he also bought her; but the boy was sold on his own to the man who offered the most money.

2. How far do **Sources A** and **B** agree about what happened during slave auctions? **4**

Source C explains why people were in favour of the slave trade.

Source C

> The slave trade continued to be defended by businessmen who made large profits from it. Evidence from Bristol and Liverpool indicated that profits of 30 per cent from slave voyages were common. The Triangular Trade linked Britain, West Africa and the Caribbean. The Triangular Trade also helped Britain's industrial development. In Manchester, for example, it was said to have helped the growth in manufacturing. Work was provided for many at the port of Liverpool.

3. Why were some people in favour of the slave trade? (Use **Source C** and recall.) **5**

[END OF CONTEXT 6]

Marks

HISTORICAL STUDY: EUROPEAN AND WORLD

> ### CONTEXT 7: CITIZENS! THE
> ### FRENCH REVOLUTION, 1789–1794

Answer the following questions using recalled knowledge and information from the sources where appropriate.

1. Describe the changes introduced by the Legislative Assembly in 1791.   **5**

Source A describes the growth of feeling against the monarchy in France in 1792.

Source A

> Although Louis had been allowed to live comfortably in his palace he made no secret that he disliked having to share power with the Legislative Assembly. He supported war with Austria hoping that French defeat would restore his royal authority. The radicals imprisoned the king and his family after the storming of the Tuileries. Louis rejected the advice of moderate advisors to fully implement the Constitution of 1791. By then many people suspected that Louis was privately encouraging counter-revolution.

2. Why was there growing dislike of the monarchy in France in 1792? (Use **Source A** and recall.)   **5**

Sources B and **C** describe the events of September 1792 which came to be known as the September Massacres.

Source B

> On August 10th 1792, Danton's supporters seized control and set up the Commune which became the real power in Paris. Danton gave a violent speech encouraging the Paris mobs to rise up. The sans-culottes attacked the prisons which they believed were secretly sheltering enemies of the revolution. They killed about one and a half thousand people. Street fights continued and barricades were set up all over the city.

Source C

> The news of the invasion of France by the Prussian army led to panic in Paris. Working class people began rioting, believing they were defending the revolution. From the night of September 2nd, in three prisons in Paris at least fifteen hundred women, priests and soldiers were brutally murdered. Although Danton condemned the massacres, he must take the blame for having stirred up the sans-culottes.

3. How far do **Sources B** and **C** agree about the events of the September Massacres in Paris in 1792?   **4**

[END OF CONTEXT 7]

Ma

HISTORICAL STUDY: EUROPEAN AND WORLD

> ### CONTEXT 8: CAVOUR, GARIBALDI AND THE MAKING OF ITALY, 1815–1870

Answer the following questions using recalled knowledge and information from the sources where appropriate.

1. Describe the growth of nationalism in Italy between 1815 and 1847.   5

Sources A and **B** describe the events of the 1848 revolutions in Milan and Naples.

Source A

> Early in the year trouble broke out in Milan. The sight of Austrian soldiers smoking in the streets was an excuse for the people to show their dislike of the troops. Small-scale fights broke out, quickly followed by larger riots and eventually by a full scale revolution. The Austrian commander decided to withdraw his troops from the area. The revolutionaries set up a provisional government and prepared to continue the fight against Austria.

Source B

> There were clashes between the people and the troops in Naples. Arms were handed out to the townspeople and the next day protest grew as peasants from outside the city arrived to join the rising. The army replied by shelling the city and two days later reinforcements of 5000 troops arrived. Despite this, by April the revolutionaries had taken over. The middle and upper-class nationalists set up a provisional government.

2. How far do **Sources A** and **B** agree about the events of the 1848 revolutions in the Italian cities?   4

Source C describes the importance of Garibaldi.

Source C

> As a military leader Garibaldi was a good, sometimes brilliant, commander, excellent at sizing up the situation. He inspired great enthusiasm and devotion in his men. His conquest of the south was a remarkable achievement. His chance meeting with Mazzini in 1833 gave him a cause to fight for. All Garibaldi's actions can be explained by his total devotion to the idea of Italian unity. It became the driving obsession of his life.

3. Why was Garibaldi important to the unification of Italy in 1861? (Use **Source C** and recall.)   5

[END OF CONTEXT 8]

Marks

HISTORICAL STUDY: EUROPEAN AND WORLD

> ### CONTEXT 9: IRON AND BLOOD?
> ### BISMARCK AND THE CREATION OF
> ### THE GERMAN EMPIRE, 1815–1871

Answer the following questions using recalled knowledge and information from the sources where appropriate.

Sources A and **B** describe actions against the student movement in Germany in the early nineteenth century.

Source A

> At a student demonstration an Austrian spy was murdered. The Austrian government was determined to prevent further incidents. At a meeting of the Confederation of Carlsbad in 1819, it was agreed to set up inspectors to oversee the universities. In addition to this, student organisations were outlawed. In most German states a strict press censorship was enforced. The effect of the decrees was the dismissal of a number of professors.

Source B

> The first sign of nationalist feeling occurred in the Students' Unions in the universities. Metternich and the Austrian government were determined to stop this. At a meeting of the Confederation at Carlsbad in 1819, decrees were passed which suppressed the student societies, causing many university teachers to be dismissed. Student societies re-emerged in the 1830s. Flags of black, red and gold came to symbolise liberal ideas.

1. How far do **Sources A** and **B** agree about the actions taken against the student movement?   4

Source C is about the growth of nationalism in the German states.

Source C

> The folk tales of the Brothers Grimm celebrated Germany's past and looked forward to the day when it would at last be one nation. United by language, it was felt by many that the German states should also be united by the same government. By 1836, twenty five of the thirty nine German states had joined the Zollverein. The development of the railways in the 1830s and 1840s had made the German states co-operate, ending their isolation from one another. By 1850 over 3000 miles of railways had been laid.

2. Why did nationalism grow within the German states between 1815 and 1850? (Use **Source C** and recall.)   5

3. Describe the events leading to Austria's defeat by Prussia in 1866.   5

[END OF CONTEXT 9]

HISTORICAL STUDY: EUROPEAN AND WORLD

Ma

CONTEXT 10: THE RED FLAG: LENIN AND THE RUSSIAN REVOLUTION, 1894–1921

Answer the following questions using recalled knowledge and information from the sources where appropriate.

Source A is about the outbreak of the 1905 Revolution.

Source A

> By 1905 there was a growing desire to overthrow the repressive government of Nicholas II. There was a great deal of poverty in the cities and the countryside. The revolutionary movement gained strength following Russia's humiliating defeat by Japan. In January an uprising to remove the Tsar began. The non-Russian areas of the empire witnessed violent disturbances. Revolutionary groups became much more organised. They formed a soviet in St Petersburg. A soviet was a type of worker's parliament.

1. Why was there a revolution in Russia in 1905? (Use **Source A** and recall.)   5

2. Describe the effects of the First World War on the Russian people.   5

In **Sources B** and **C**, Bolshevik leaders argue about the decision to call a revolution in October 1917.

Source B is from a letter by Lenin.

Source B

> The Bolsheviks can and must take state power immediately into their own hands. They can do so because revolutionary elements in Petrograd and Moscow are now very strong. We can and must overcome our opponents' resistance and gain power. By promising peace and land we will be able to form a government that no-one will be able to overthrow. The majority of the people are on our side. By seizing power in Moscow and Petrograd we shall win absolutely and unquestionably.

Source C is from a letter by two Bolsheviks, Kamenev and Zinoviev.

Source C

> We are convinced that to call an uprising now would put the party and the revolution at risk. Our party is strong but the workers and soldiers are not ready to take to the streets now. The right mood does not exist. The party must be given time to grow. An uprising now will destroy what we have already achieved. We raise a voice against this ruinous policy.

3. How far do **Sources B** and **C** disagree about the decision to call a revolution in October 1917?   4

[END OF CONTEXT 10]

Marks

HISTORICAL STUDY: EUROPEAN AND WORLD

CONTEXT 11: FREE AT LAST? RACE RELATIONS IN THE USA, 1918–1968

Answer the following questions using recalled knowledge and information from the sources where appropriate.

1. What problems faced black Americans who moved north in the 1920s and 1930s?

5

Source A explains black Americans' reaction to the Civil Rights Movement.

Source A

> Between 1945 and 1959, the Civil Rights Movement made much progress. Black activists, especially the NAACP, were the moving force behind Supreme Court decisions. The Supreme Court had declared segregated schools unconstitutional in 1954. Progress in carrying out this declaration was very slow over the next ten years. Unending black pressure forced President Eisenhower to propose a Civil Rights Act in 1957. The Civil Rights Movement was gaining heroes such as Rosa Parks during this period, though there were also victims such as Emmett Till.

2. Why did black Americans feel that progress towards civil rights had been made between 1945 and 1959? (Use **Source A** and recall.)

5

Sources B and **C** describe the sit-ins.

Source B

> Some Civil Rights workers believed that the sit-ins showed students that they could take action themselves. Young black people realised that they could make a difference to Civil Rights by winning the support of both black and white Americans. However, sit-ins only achieved limited success in some of the towns and cities where the protests were used. Much more needed to be done to improve Civil Rights.

Source C

> The very act of protesting meant the students believed they could make a difference. When they "sat in" these young people practiced non-violence, they dressed in their best clothes and they studied books. This helped to encourage black community support and won the respect and even admiration of some white Americans. However, the sit-ins only enjoyed success in a few Southern states. In the Deep South, white Americans refused to desegregate and the protestors faced resistance from the white authorities.

3. How far do **Sources B** and **C** agree about the success of the sit-ins?

4

[*END OF CONTEXT 11*]

M

HISTORICAL STUDY: EUROPEAN AND WORLD

> ### CONTEXT 12: THE ROAD TO WAR, 1933–1939

Answer the following questions using recalled knowledge and information from the sources where appropriate.

Source A is about Britain's policy of Appeasement in the 1930s.

Source A

> The Great Depression meant that money could not be found for rearmament and the government knew that the British people were totally opposed to war. Chamberlain, who had been Chancellor before becoming Prime Minister in 1937, had a reputation as a social reformer. Chamberlain was in favour of personal, face to face talks among Europe's leaders and believed he could negotiate directly with Hitler. The British Government took the view that communist Russia was the real threat to peace in the world.

1. Why did Britain follow a policy of Appeasement in the 1930s? (Use **Source A** and recall.)

    5

2. Describe the aims of Hitler's foreign policy.

    5

Sources B and **C** are opinions about the Anschluss between Germany and Austria in 1938.

Source B

> It is clear that Anschluss is popular among the Austrian people who are, after all, German in language and culture. Keeping Germany and Austria apart had been one of the more spiteful terms of Versailles and this wrong is now made right. Therefore Europe is likely to benefit from a period of peace and prosperity as Germany moves into a brighter future.

Source C

> Germany has taken over Austria. Any intelligent person can see that an even more powerful Germany is a threat to the peace and stability of Europe. The decision in 1919 to forbid Anschluss had been a very sensible one for limiting the war-like ambitions of Germany. We have permitted Hitler to brutally invade an independent country whose population has no love for Nazism.

3. How far do **Sources B** and **C** disagree about the Anschluss?

    4

[END OF CONTEXT 12]

HISTORICAL STUDY: EUROPEAN AND WORLD

CONTEXT 13: IN THE SHADOW OF THE BOMB: THE COLD WAR, 1945–1985

Answer the following questions using recalled knowledge and information from the sources where appropriate.

Source A is about the Berlin Wall.

Source A

> On 12 August 1961 a record 4000 East Germans fled to West Berlin to start a new life in the West. Those who left were often young and well educated. In the small hours of 13 August, Soviet and East German "shock workers" closed the border and put barbed wire across the streets. The East Germans claimed that enemy agents had been stationed in West Berlin. The agents were using Berlin as a centre of operations against East Germany and the Soviet Union. Berlin had become a divided city.

1. Why did the Soviet Union build the Berlin Wall in 1961? (Use **Source A** and recall.) **5**

Sources B and **C** are about the tactics of the Vietcong.

Source B

> The Vietcong, or "Charlie" as the Americans called them, were the locally born guerrilla fighters of South Vietnam. The Vietcong consisted of three groups: units of regular soldiers, provincial forces, and part-time guerrillas. The Vietcong generally avoided large scale attacks on the enemy but continually harassed their troops and installations causing heavy American casualties. They travelled light, carrying basic weapons and few supplies.

Source C

> Our first real battle was in the Michelin Rubber Plantation. Thousands of Vietcong launched wave after wave of attacks on our camp. But they had all kinds of Chinese and Russian weapons, such as flamethrowers and rocket launchers. Eventually we counter-attacked and pushed them back. Fortunately, we only lost around seven guys. The Vietcong body count was reported to have been 800, but I thought it was more.

2. How far do **Sources B** and **C** disagree about the tactics used by the Vietcong? **4**

3. Describe the steps taken to reduce tension between the USA and the USSR during the 1960s and 1970s. **5**

[END OF CONTEXT 13]

[END OF PART 3: EUROPEAN AND WORLD CONTEXTS]

[END OF QUESTION PAPER]

[BLANK PAGE]

[BLANK PAGE]

X044/201

NATIONAL
QUALIFICATIONS
2010

WEDNESDAY, 26 MAY
9.00 AM – 10.45 AM

HISTORY
INTERMEDIATE 2

The instructions for this paper are on *Page two*. Read them carefully before you begin your answers.
Your Invigilator will tell you which contexts to answer in Parts 2 and 3 of the examination.

INSTRUCTIONS

Answer **one** question from Part 1, The Short Essay

Answer **one** context* from Part 2, Scottish and British

Answer **one** context* from Part 3, European and World

Answer **one** other context* from

> **either** Part 2, Scottish and British
>
> **or**   Part 3, European and World

*Answer all the questions in each of your chosen contexts.

Contents

[Turn over

PART 1: THE SHORT ESSAY

Ma

Answer **one** question. For this question you should write a short essay using your own knowledge. The essay should include an introduction, development and conclusion. Each question is worth 8 marks.

SCOTTISH AND BRITISH CONTEXTS:

**CONTEXT 1: MURDER IN THE CATHEDRAL:
CROWN, CHURCH AND PEOPLE, 1154–1173**

Question 1:   Explain why Henry II faced difficulties on becoming king in 1154.   **8**

**CONTEXT 2: WALLACE, BRUCE AND THE
WARS OF INDEPENDENCE, 1286–1328**

Question 2:   Explain why the Scots won the battle at Bannockburn.   **8**

**CONTEXT 3: MARY, QUEEN OF SCOTS AND THE
SCOTTISH REFORMATION, 1540s–1587**

Question 3:   Explain why Riccio became unpopular with Darnley and the Scottish nobles.   **8**

CONTEXT 4: THE COMING OF THE CIVIL WAR, 1603–1642

Question 4:   Explain why Charles I was an unpopular monarch in England by 1640.   **8**

**CONTEXT 5: "ANE END OF ANE AULD SANG":
SCOTLAND AND THE TREATY OF UNION, 1690s–1715**

Question 5:   Explain why many Scots were disappointed by the Act of Union by 1715.   **8**

**CONTEXT 6: IMMIGRANTS AND EXILES:
SCOTLAND, 1830s–1930s**

Question 6:   Explain why Irish immigrants were attracted to Scotland between 1830 and 1930.   **8**

**CONTEXT 7: FROM THE CRADLE TO THE GRAVE?
SOCIAL WELFARE IN BRITAIN, 1890s–1951**

Question 7:   Explain why the Liberal government passed social welfare reforms between 1906 and 1914.   **8**

Marks

CONTEXT 8: CAMPAIGNING FOR CHANGE: SOCIAL CHANGE IN SCOTLAND, 1900s–1979

Question 8: Explain why there was still a need to improve many women's lives after 1918.

8

CONTEXT 9: A TIME OF TROUBLES: IRELAND, 1900–1923

Question 9: Explain why the Anglo-Irish War broke out in 1919.

8

EUROPEAN AND WORLD CONTEXTS:

CONTEXT 1: THE NORMAN CONQUEST, 1060–1153

Question 10: Explain why knights were important in medieval society.

8

CONTEXT 2: THE CROSS AND THE CRESCENT: THE FIRST CRUSADE, 1096–1125

Question 11: Explain why the Crusaders were able to keep control of the Holy Land after 1097.

8

CONTEXT 3: WAR, DEATH AND REVOLT IN MEDIEVAL EUROPE, 1328–1436

Question 12: Explain why France was unsuccessful in the war against England between 1415 and 1422.

8

CONTEXT 4: NEW WORLDS: EUROPE IN THE AGE OF EXPANSION, 1480s–1530s

Question 13: Explain why the Spaniards were able to defeat **either** the Aztecs **or** the Incas.

8

CONTEXT 5: "TEA AND FREEDOM": THE AMERICAN REVOLUTION, 1763–1783

Question 14: Explain why the American War of Independence broke out in 1775.

8

CONTEXT 6: "THIS ACCURSED TRADE": THE BRITISH SLAVE TRADE AND ITS ABOLITION, 1770–1807

Question 15: Explain why it took so long for Britain to abolish the slave trade.

8

Ma

CONTEXT 7: CITIZENS!
THE FRENCH REVOLUTION, 1789–1794

Question 16: Explain why the French people were unhappy with their government by 1789.

8

CONTEXT 8: CAVOUR, GARIBALDI
AND THE MAKING OF ITALY, 1815–1870

Question 17: Explain why Garibaldi's leadership was important to the unification of Italy.

8

CONTEXT 9: IRON AND BLOOD? BISMARCK AND THE
CREATION OF THE GERMAN EMPIRE, 1815–1871

Question 18: Explain why the nationalist movement had failed to unite the German states by 1850.

8

CONTEXT 10: THE RED FLAG:
LENIN AND THE RUSSIAN REVOLUTION, 1894–1921

Question 19: Explain why the Tsar was able to remain in power following the 1905 revolution.

8

CONTEXT 11: FREE AT LAST?
RACE RELATIONS IN THE USA, 1918–1968

Question 20: Explain why the demand for civil rights continued to grow after 1945.

8

CONTEXT 12: THE ROAD TO WAR, 1933–1939

Question 21: Explain why Hitler's actions created problems in Europe between 1933 and 1939.

8

CONTEXT 13: IN THE SHADOW OF THE BOMB:
THE COLD WAR, 1945–1985

Question 22: Explain why America lost the war in Vietnam.

8

[END OF PART 1: THE SHORT ESSAY]

[Turn over for PART 2: SCOTTISH AND BRITISH CONTEXTS on *Page eight*

PART 2:

Ma

HISTORICAL STUDY: SCOTTISH AND BRITISH

> ### CONTEXT 1: MURDER IN THE CATHEDRAL: CROWN, CHURCH AND PEOPLE, 1154–1173

Answer the following questions using recalled knowledge and information from the sources where appropriate.

Source A explains why castles were important in the twelfth century.

Source A

> During Henry II's reign, castles were built of stone and with extra walls and towers. These castles became a key symbol of power. They were also the administrative centres of each town. The numerous rooms inside a castle meant that it was an ideal base for the local garrison carrying out guard duty. Although many castles had been built illegally during the civil war there was no doubt that they were useful during times of attack when food, drink and other supplies could be stored there.

1. Why were castles important in the twelfth century? (Use **Source A** and recall.)   5

Sources B and **C** describe the life of a monk in medieval times.

Source B

> At 2 o'clock in the morning, monks were woken for a service in the chapel. Although they were given time to sleep, monks were expected to pray at least 8 times a day. Breakfast included bread and fruit and was eaten in silence. After breakfast, monks were allowed a little free time but were expected to spend most of the day working in the fields or carrying out other duties.

Source C

> Many monks lived their lives by St Benedict's rule. During meal times talking was strictly forbidden so monks listened to prayers or to readings from holy books. Services began in the middle of the night and every monk was expected to pray in church several times a day. Isolated from the local community, monks were not allowed to leave the monastery and had to forget their previous life.

2. How far do **Sources B** and **C** agree about the lives of monks in medieval times?   4

3. Describe the murder of Archbishop Becket.   5

[END OF CONTEXT 1]

Marks

HISTORICAL STUDY: SCOTTISH AND BRITISH

> CONTEXT 2: WALLACE, BRUCE
> AND THE WARS OF
> INDEPENDENCE, 1286–1328

Answer the following questions using recalled knowledge and information from the sources where appropriate.

1. Describe the events between 1286 and 1292 that led to Edward I becoming overlord of Scotland.

   5

Source A explains why the leadership of William Wallace was important.

Source A

> Wallace has become a folk hero in Scotland. Although he was only the second son of an unimportant knight, for a short while he became Guardian of Scotland uniting people under his leadership. He reorganised the army of Scotland and prepared for an English invasion. He also looked for foreign help. Bishop Lamberton was sent to Rome and Paris to plead Scotland's cause there. Wallace also renewed trade with Germany to obtain iron for weapons which he needed for his army.

2. Why was the leadership of William Wallace important during the Wars of Independence? (Use **Source A** and recall.)

   5

Sources B and **C** are about the amount of support Robert Bruce had in 1320.

Source B

> In the Declaration of Arbroath of 1320, the Scottish nobles explained to the Pope why all the Scots thought Robert Bruce was their king. They argued that he had royal blood and that his actions had won him the support of the Scottish people. On top of that, they argued that they wanted him as king because he had saved Scotland from being taken over by the King of England.

Source C

> Even while the Declaration of Arbroath was being written, some Scottish nobles were plotting against Robert Bruce. They felt he was a ruthless thug who had murdered his main rival in a church. Other Scottish nobles claimed to be more closely related to the Scottish royal family than Bruce. They, however, had not been successful in war. These disagreements caused problems in Scotland.

3. How far do **Sources B** and **C** disagree about the amount of support Robert Bruce had in 1320?

   4

[END OF CONTEXT 2]

Mar

HISTORICAL STUDY: SCOTTISH AND BRITISH

> ### CONTEXT 3: MARY, QUEEN OF SCOTS AND THE SCOTTISH REFORMATION, 1540s–1587

Answer the following questions using recalled knowledge and information from the sources where appropriate.

Source A explains why Henry VIII ordered the invasions of Scotland after 1544.

Source A

> The death of King James V after the Scottish defeat at Solway Moss gave King Henry VIII the opportunity to break the Auld Alliance between France and Scotland. He freed Scottish prisoners of war on condition they supported the marriage of Mary to his son, Edward. Within a year the Scots had agreed to this in the Treaty of Greenwich. However, when Henry then made more and more demands on them, the French encouraged the Scots to resist. Finally the Scots announced that the Treaty was broken.

1. Why did Henry VIII of England order the invasions of Scotland after 1544? (Use **Source A** and recall.)   5

2. Describe the events leading up to the signing of the Treaty of Edinburgh in 1560.   5

Sources B and **C** are about how well Mary, Queen of Scots ruled Scotland.

Source B

> Mary returned to Scotland as Queen in 1561. Mary was a Roman Catholic who believed that she should rule England instead of her Protestant cousin, Elizabeth. She neglected the government of Scotland by leaving the running of the country to a group of Protestant nobles. She did not really care about the issue of religion in Scotland.

Source C

> Until Mary allowed her heart to rule her head by marrying Darnley, she had been a successful ruler in Scotland. She had defeated the nobles who challenged her authority and had established a successful government under her half-brother Moray. As a Roman Catholic, her tolerant treatment of Scotland's new Protestant church was ahead of its time.

3. How far do **Sources B** and **C** disagree about how well Mary, Queen of Scots ruled Scotland?   4

[END OF CONTEXT 3]

Marks

HISTORICAL STUDY: SCOTTISH AND BRITISH

> ## CONTEXT 4: THE COMING OF
> ## THE CIVIL WAR, 1603–1642

Answer the following questions using recalled knowledge and information from the sources where appropriate.

Sources A and **B** describe James VI and I.

Source A

> James VI and I was well educated and clever. The Union of the Crowns united the monarchs of Scotland and England and James became king of both countries. He claimed that kings were appointed by God, and could do as they wished. He lost people's respect by giving money and power to favourites at court. His son, Charles I was to prove a less popular king.

Source B

> The reign of the Stuarts began in 1603. James VI and I was a highly intelligent man. From the start of his reign he spent a lot of money, not only on himself but on gifts and pensions to courtiers. Although he believed in the Divine Right of Kings he did not try to be an absolute monarch in his relations with Parliament. Charles I would use his royal prerogative to a greater extent.

1. How far do **Sources A** and **B** agree about James VI and I?   4

2. Describe the methods used by James VI and I to raise money during his reign.   5

Source C explains why Charles I faced opposition to his rule in Scotland.

Source C

> When Charles decided to enforce his religious views on the Scottish people, he met fierce resistance. Many Scots were Presbyterians who carried out their own religious services and they disliked these changes. They showed this when they signed the National Covenant in 1638, sometimes in blood. The Scots also resented Charles because he was an absentee King and he visited Scotland only once during his reign. Scotland was a poor country and many Scots thought Charles did not care. Deep resentment and suspicion grew across Scotland.

3. Why did Charles I face opposition to his rule in Scotland? (Use **Source C** and recall.)   5

[END OF CONTEXT 4]

M

HISTORICAL STUDY: SCOTTISH AND BRITISH

> ### CONTEXT 5: "ANE END OF ANE AULD SANG": SCOTLAND AND THE TREATY OF UNION, 1690s–1715

Answer the following questions using recalled knowledge and information from the sources where appropriate.

1. Describe what happened during the Worcester affair.

Source A explains why Queen Anne wanted a Treaty of Union.

Source A

> Queen Anne came to the throne of Scotland and England in 1702. She wanted a complete Union of the two countries because she found it difficult to control the Scottish Parliament. She also faced complaints that her policies were harming Scotland. The Scottish Parliament was even threatening to end the Union of the Crowns. However, at first, these problems with Scotland made it more difficult for England to fight the war against France.

2. Why did Queen Anne want a Treaty of Union between England and Scotland? (Use **Source A** and recall.)

Sources B and **C** are about Scottish attitudes to the Treaty of Union.

Source B

> The Treaty of Union was passed in 1707. Scots thought the Equivalent was money to help the country recover from the Darien Scheme. Scots felt they would have influence in a new and more powerful kingdom. They thought their traders would benefit from access to English colonies.

Source C

> Scots feared that, once they lost their independence, they would have little influence over government decisions. Others worried that businesses in Scotland would suffer from competition from English imports. They also thought the money paid to Scotland was a bribe to rich and powerful men—the only way that a Union could be passed.

3. How far do **Sources B** and **C** disagree about Scottish attitudes to the Treaty of Union?

[END OF CONTEXT 5]

Marks

HISTORICAL STUDY: SCOTTISH AND BRITISH

CONTEXT 6: IMMIGRANTS AND EXILES: SCOTLAND, 1830s–1930s

Answer the following questions using recalled knowledge and information from the sources where appropriate.

Sources A and **B** are about Scottish attitudes to Irish immigration.

Source A

> Irish immigrants tended to concentrate in particular areas because they were disliked by the native Scots. It was natural that the immigrants should live together but the determination to stick to their own culture was looked upon with suspicion. There were accusations that they did not wish to become "new Scots". In addition, the Irish did not receive much credit for their contribution to the Scottish economy.

Source B

> There was a reluctance to admit that Irish workers were essential to the development of industry in Scotland even though they were to be found wherever work needed doing. Many Scots criticised immigrants for keeping to their native language and religion. It became clear that there was a great deal of resentment against the immigrants in Scotland.

1. How far do **Sources A** and **B** agree about Scottish attitudes to Irish immigration?   **4**

Source C explains why poor Scots were able to emigrate in the nineteenth century.

Source C

> Some landlords saw it as in their own interests to encourage poor tenants to seek their fortunes elsewhere. The landlords were willing to pay the full travelling costs, especially to Canada. Landlords often wrote off rent arrears so that the tenants would have some money for their new life and some even bought their cattle which provided the emigrant with some extra help. Glasgow and Edinburgh feared a massive influx of Highlanders and the city authorities made a contribution towards their expenses in emigrating.

2. Why were many poor Scots able to emigrate during the nineteenth century? (Use **Source C** and recall.)   **5**

3. In what ways did Scots help to improve the lands to which they emigrated?   **5**

[END OF CONTEXT 6]

HISTORICAL STUDY: SCOTTISH AND BRITISH

> **CONTEXT 7: FROM THE CRADLE TO THE GRAVE? SOCIAL WELFARE IN BRITAIN, 1890s–1951**

Answer the following questions using recalled knowledge and information from the sources where appropriate.

Sources A and **B** describe the Old Age Pensions Act of 1908.

Source A

> The Liberal government passed a series of welfare reforms to help the old, the young and the sick. A pensioner with a yearly income of up to £21 received the full 25p a week. Pensions were not made available to those who had been in prison during the previous ten years. The pension was not a generous amount. The Liberals were criticised for not doing enough to tackle the real causes of poverty.

Source B

> The Pensions Act entitled people over seventy with an annual income of up to £21 to 25p a week of a pension. The government stated that these payments were not meant to be a complete solution to the problem of poverty in old age. However, the foundation stones of the welfare state had been laid. Any seventy year old was entitled to a pension provided they had avoided imprisonment in the previous ten years and they had not continually avoided work.

1. How far do **Sources A** and **B** agree about the Old Age Pensions Act of 1908?

2. Describe the ways the Beveridge Report of 1942 suggested tackling the social problems facing Britain.

Source C is about the welfare reforms passed by the Labour government between 1945 and 1951.

Source C

> Poor housing and homelessness were still serious problems by 1951. The Labour government also did little to enhance the educational opportunities for working class children, most of whom left school at fifteen with no paper qualifications. People thought the National Health Service was a great success but there was still a shortage of hospitals and health centres. There was still a long way to go before the problems of poverty and deprivation were adequately solved. The Labour Party lost the General Election of 1951.

3. Why were some people disappointed with the Labour welfare reforms by 1951? (Use **Source C** and recall.)

[END OF CONTEXT 7]

HISTORICAL STUDY: SCOTTISH AND BRITISH

Marks

> ### CONTEXT 8: CAMPAIGNING FOR CHANGE: SOCIAL CHANGE IN SCOTLAND, 1900s–1979

Answer the following questions using recalled knowledge and information from the sources where appropriate.

Sources A and **B** describe changes to Scots drinking habits in the early twentieth century.

Source A

> By 1900, people were drinking less alcohol. The number of public houses decreased and convictions for drunkenness fell. This was due more to the increased tax on alcohol than to the temperance movement. People also preferred to spend their money on the new consumer and household goods which were increasingly available, as well as on leisure activities.

Source B

> As the twentieth century progressed Scottish men were drinking much less than they had in the nineteenth century. The reasons for this are many. One was the development of many different things to do. The number of pubs in some areas fell where people voted for this. Alcohol became much more expensive when the government raised the tax on spirits by 34% in 1909 and then cut pub opening times to five and a half hours a day in 1914.

1. How far do **Sources A** and **B** agree about reasons why people were drinking less in Scotland in the early 20th century?   **4**

2. Describe the unrest on Red Clydeside between 1915 and 1919.   **5**

Source C describes the effects of North Sea Oil on the north of Scotland.

Source C

> Oil had a huge impact upon the north of Scotland. Aberdeen became the oil capital of Europe and the boom spread to smaller east coast towns such as Fraserburgh, Peterhead and Montrose. Giant rigs became a common sight in the Moray and Cromarty Firths because of the construction yards at Ardersier and Nigg. There were almost 3,000 new jobs created in the Shetland Islands. Dozens of companies moved to the north east to provide support and other services to the industry.

3. Why was the development of North Sea Oil so important for the economy of the north of Scotland? (Use **Source C** and recall.)   **5**

[END OF CONTEXT 8]

M.

HISTORICAL STUDY: SCOTTISH AND BRITISH

> ### CONTEXT 9: A TIME OF
> ### TROUBLES: IRELAND, 1900–1923

Answer the following questions using recalled knowledge and information from the sources where appropriate.

Sources A and **B** are two Irish opinions on the Union with Britain.

Source A

> The Irish people have benefited greatly from the Union. We are better housed, fed and receive better wages for our work. Our freedom and rights have been protected and this has led to great success. In the past Ireland was a poor country with little or no future. Today Ireland works in partnership with Britain. It would be a disaster to listen to those who want to destroy all that Ireland has achieved.

Source B

> Until Ireland has the right to make its own laws we will have no freedom. For years we have been the losers in the Union with Britain. Although the Union is against the wishes of the people, the British are unwilling to listen. Unemployment and poor wages have made many Irish men and women desperate yet the British government does nothing to help. Conditions are so bad, Irish families are being forced to emigrate abroad in an attempt to try and improve their lives.

1. How far do **Sources A** and **B** disagree about the Union?

2. Describe the actions taken by the Unionists against the Home Rule Bill.

Source C explains why De Valera opposed the 1921 Treaty.

Source C

> After months of negotiations the Irish delegation in London reluctantly signed the 1921 Treaty. De Valera had remained in Dublin and was furious that terms had been agreed without consulting him. He refused to accept that six counties in the north of Ireland would be separated from the rest of the country. He also refused to swear an oath of allegiance to the British King. Although most people in Ireland wanted an end to the war, De Valera argued that only full independence would lead to peace.

3. Why did De Valera oppose the 1921 Treaty? (Use **Source C** and recall.)

[END OF CONTEXT 9]

[END OF PART 2: SCOTTISH AND BRITISH CONTEXTS]

Marks

PART 3:

HISTORICAL STUDY: EUROPEAN AND WORLD

> ### CONTEXT 1: THE NORMAN CONQUEST, 1060–1153

Answer the following questions using recalled knowledge and information from the sources where appropriate.

Source A is about the events leading up to the Battle of Hastings.

Source A

> William arrived at Pevensey with a huge army. He had countless horsemen and archers. When it was reported that William had landed, Harold at once forced his exhausted army to march south. Although he knew that some of the bravest of the Saxons had fallen in the two previous battles he advanced with full speed into the south of England. On 14 October Harold fought with the Normans nine miles from Hastings. However some of his soldiers refused to remain loyal to him and deserted from his army.

1. Why did Harold lose the battle of Hastings? (Use **Source A** and recall.)   **5**

Source B describes how William gained control of England after the Battle of Hastings. It was written by his priest in 1077.

Source B

> William went to various parts of his kingdom. He tried to organise everything to suit his people as well as himself. Wherever he went the people surrendered to him. There was no resistance, but everywhere men submitted to him and asked for his peace. He gave rich fiefs to the men he had brought over from France but no Frenchman was given anything that had been unjustly taken from an Englishman.

2. How useful is **Source B** as evidence about William's attempts to control England after 1066?   **4**

3. In what ways did Scotland change during the reign of David I?   **5**

[END OF CONTEXT 1]

M(

HISTORICAL STUDY: EUROPEAN AND WORLD

> ### CONTEXT 2: THE CROSS AND THE CRESCENT: THE FIRST CRUSADE, 1096–1125

Answer the following questions using recalled knowledge and information from the sources where appropriate.

Source A explains why Pope Urban II called the First Crusade.

Source A

> In 1095 Emperor Alexius sent messages to the Pope begging him for help against the Turks. Although Urban II had not been Pope for very long, he could see that the Turks were a threat to Christianity. Eight months later the Pope delivered a successful speech at Clermont. Almost immediately peasants and knights left their homes and took the cross. The Pope hoped the Crusade would stop western knights fighting amongst themselves and encourage them to recapture Jerusalem from the Turks.

1.   Why did Pope Urban II call the First Crusade? (Use **Source A** and recall.)   5

2.   Describe the siege and capture of Antioch by the First Crusade.   5

Source B describes the behaviour of the Crusaders at Marrat au Numan. It was written by a priest who went on the First Crusade.

Source B

> Although many knights stayed in Antioch or returned home, the main Crusading army continued the journey to Jerusalem. On the way we stayed at Marrat au Numan. Our men were starving and desperate for food. Some Crusaders began to rip up the bodies of their dead enemies. They cut their flesh into slices, cooked and ate them. Many of us were shocked by what we saw and could not wait to leave.

3.   How useful is **Source B** as evidence of the Crusaders' behaviour in the Holy Land?   4

[END OF CONTEXT 2]

Marks

HISTORICAL STUDY: EUROPEAN AND WORLD

CONTEXT 3: WAR, DEATH AND
REVOLT IN MEDIEVAL EUROPE,
1328–1436

Answer the following questions using recalled knowledge and information from the sources where appropriate.

1. Describe the problem of succession to the French throne after 1328.   **5**

Source A is about the effects of the Battle of Poitiers on France. It was written by Froissart the chronicler in 1388.

Source A

> The battle was fought on the 19th day of September 1356. The finest knights of France died on that day. This severely weakened the realm of France. The country fell into great misery. In all, 17 lords were taken prisoner. Between 500 and 700 men-at-arms were killed. In all, 6,000 Frenchmen died.

2. How useful is **Source A** as evidence of the effects of the Battle of Poitiers on France?   **4**

Source B is about the end of the Peasants' Revolt.

Source B

> The King was determined that the revolt would not succeed. He sent out his messengers to capture those who had led the revolt. Many were hanged. Gallows were set up all around the city of London and in other cities and boroughs to put people off joining in the revolt. At last the King, seeing that too many of his subjects would die, took pity. He granted pardons to some of the troublemakers on condition that they should never rebel again on pain of losing their lives. So this wicked revolt ended.

3. Why was the King able to crush the Peasants' Revolt? (Use **Source B** and recall.)   **5**

[END OF CONTEXT 3]

Ma

HISTORICAL STUDY: EUROPEAN AND WORLD

> ### CONTEXT 4: NEW WORLDS: EUROPE IN THE AGE OF EXPANSION, 1480s–1530s

Answer the following questions using recalled knowledge and information from the sources where appropriate.

Source A is from a letter by Columbus to a friend of Queen Isabella, written in 1500.

Source A

> I was sent as a captain from Spain to the Indies to conquer a large and warlike people, who had customs and beliefs very different from ours. These people live in mountains and forest without any settled townships. Here by God's will I have brought this new world under the dominion of Spain. By doing this, Spain, which was thought of by some people as poor, has now become rich.

1. How useful is **Source A** as evidence of reasons for European exploration between 1480 and 1530?   4

2. In what ways did Vasco da Gama's voyage benefit Europe?   5

Source B explains some of the problems faced by Magellan on his voyage round the world.

Source B

> Magellan left Seville with five ships full of goods to trade in the east. As a Portuguese captain commanding a Spanish fleet he was unpopular. He kept the destination secret so that the crew would not be afraid but this made him seem untrustworthy. In Patagonia the other captains plotted a mutiny against him. He crushed this and brutally executed the ringleaders. Further south, his ships had to pass through a stormy narrow straight which now bears his name. Two of his ships were lost there.

3. Why did Magellan face difficulties during his voyage round the world? (Use **Source B** and recall.)   5

[END OF CONTEXT 4]

Marks

HISTORICAL STUDY: EUROPEAN AND WORLD

> ### CONTEXT 5: "TEA AND FREEDOM": THE AMERICAN REVOLUTION, 1763–1783

Answer the following questions using recalled knowledge and information from the sources where appropriate.

1. Describe the Boston Tea Party and the British government's response to it.

5

Source A is from a letter written by the leaders of the 13 colonies when they met in May 1775.

Source A

> On the 19th day of April, General Gage sent out a large detachment of his army who made an unprovoked attack on the inhabitants of the town of Lexington. They murdered eight of the inhabitants and wounded many others. The troops then proceeded to the town of Concord, where they cruelly slaughtered several people and wounded many more, until they were forced to retreat by a group of brave colonists suddenly assembled to repel this cruel aggression.

2. How useful is **Source A** as evidence about what happened at Lexington and Concord in April 1775?

4

Source B explains the effects of the involvement of foreign countries in the American War of Independence.

Source B

> Representatives of America and France signed an alliance on 6 February 1778. The entry of France into the war added enormously to Britain's difficulties. The French attacked Britain's colonies in the Caribbean and elsewhere undermining Britain's control. They harassed British shipping in the Atlantic interfering with Britain's trade. Spain and the Netherlands had joined the anti-British alliance by 1780. As a result, Britain lost control of the seas for the first time that century. It became ever more difficult for Britain to reinforce and supply its forces in America.

3. Why did the involvement of foreign countries cause difficulties for Britain in the War of Independence? (Use **Source B** and recall.)

5

[END OF CONTEXT 5]

M

HISTORICAL STUDY: EUROPEAN AND WORLD

> ### CONTEXT 6: "THIS ACCURSED TRADE": THE BRITISH SLAVE TRADE AND ITS ABOLITION, 1770–1807

Answer the following questions using recalled knowledge and information from the sources where appropriate.

1. Describe the different stages of the triangular trade.

In **Source A**, a modern historian describes slave revolts in the West Indies.

Source A

> The British needed all the military help they could get in the 1790s when they faced slave unrest in Dominica, St Lucia, St Vincent and Grenada. Their greatest concern was for Jamaica, which was the biggest, the richest and most troublesome of their slave colonies. By the early nineteenth century, the island was undergoing what seemed like an endless series of revolts. In one of the worst rebellions, 226 properties were damaged at a cost estimated to be £1 million.

2. How useful is **Source A** as evidence of slave resistance in the West Indies?

Source B explains why the slave trade was abolished in Britain.

Source B

> During the late nineteenth century, attitudes towards the slave trade were changing. More people began to think of Africans as fellow human beings and felt that they should be treated as such. Britain's trading interests were also changing. Trade with India and East Asia was growing while trade with the West Indies had become less important to Britain. Many merchants supported free trade. They argued that slavery was an inefficient way to produce sugar. In 1807, a new law made it illegal for British people to buy slaves in Africa.

3. Why was the slave trade abolished by Britain in 1807? (Use **Source B** and recall.)

[END OF CONTEXT 6]

Marks

HISTORICAL STUDY: EUROPEAN AND WORLD

CONTEXT 7: CITIZENS! THE FRENCH REVOLUTION, 1789–1794

Answer the following questions using recalled knowledge and information from the sources where appropriate.

Source A is from the Tennis Court Oath agreed by the Third Estate in June 1789.

Source A

> Wherever the members of the Third Estate choose to meet, that is legally the National Assembly. No one has the right to prevent the members of the Assembly from gathering together when they want to. The National Assembly has the task of writing the constitution of France and to restore public order.

1. How useful is **Source A** as evidence of the relationship between the Third Estate and the King in June 1789?

4

Source B explains why France was at war with other European countries after 1791.

Source B

> Austria and Prussia went to war because they objected to the way that Marie Antoinette, an Austrian Princess, was being treated. Louis XVI also wanted war but only because he secretly hoped that a French defeat would mean an end to the Revolution. On the other hand the revolutionaries wanted to spread their ideas throughout Europe. Only some of the radical Jacobins opposed war, preferring to consolidate and expand the Revolution at home. Britain joined the war against France to prevent the French interfering in other countries.

2. Why did war break out between France and her neighbours after 1791? (Use **Source B** and recall.)

5

3. Describe the Reign of Terror.

5

[END OF CONTEXT 7]

M

HISTORICAL STUDY: EUROPEAN AND WORLD

> ### CONTEXT 8: CAVOUR, GARIBALDI AND THE MAKING OF ITALY, 1815–1870

Answer the following questions using recalled knowledge and information from the sources where appropriate.

Source A is about the failure of the Italian nationalist movement up to 1850.

Source A

> Before 1848 there was little sign of Italian nationalism, except as a wild idea. Mazzini's dream of a democratic republic lost support. The nationalists failed to work together. The revolutionaries of Sicily wanted nothing to do with those of Naples. The revolutionary leaders did not encourage mass participation. The middle classes feared that democratic government would give power to the lower classes. The revolutions were not supported by autocratic leaders, such as King Ferdinand of Sicily.

1. Why did the revolutions of 1848–1849 fail to unite Italy? (Use **Source A** and recall.)

2. Describe the steps taken by Piedmont to bring about Italian unification up to 1860.

Source B was written by a politician in Piedmont in 1861.

Source B

> Count Cavour has the talent to assess a situation and the possibilities of exploiting it. It is this wonderful ability that has helped to bring about a united Italy. Cavour had to seek out opportunities wherever he could. He manipulated events to suit his purpose. He was Prime Minister of an unimportant country so he did not have the resources of a great power like Britain or France.

3. How useful is **Source B** as evidence of the skills of Cavour as a leader?

[END OF CONTEXT 8]

Marks

HISTORICAL STUDY: EUROPEAN AND WORLD

> ### CONTEXT 9: IRON AND BLOOD?
> ### BISMARCK AND THE CREATION OF
> ### THE GERMAN EMPIRE, 1815–1871

Answer the following questions using recalled knowledge and information from the sources where appropriate.

Source A is about the growth of Prussia before 1862.

Source A

> Prussia came to be regarded as the natural leader of a united Germany and therefore emerged as the champion of German nationalism. Prussia controlled the rivers Rhine and Elbe, which were vital communication and trade routes. Other states hoped to benefit from Prussia's industrial development. Prussia took the lead in improving roads and railways. After the revolutions of 1848 Frederick William IV of Prussia promised to work for a united Germany.

1. Why was Prussia able to take the lead in German unification by 1862? (Use **Source A** and recall.)

   5

Source B is from the memoirs of Otto von Bismarck in 1898.

Source B

> I assumed that a united Germany was only a question of time, that the North German Confederation was only the first step in its solution. I did not doubt that a Franco-Prussian War must take place before the construction of a united Germany could be realised. At that time my mind was taken up with the idea of delaying the outbreak of war until our military strength had increased.

2. How useful is **Source B** as evidence of the methods used by Bismarck to bring about the unification of the German states in 1871?

   4

3. Describe the events that led to war between France and Prussia in 1870.

   5

[END OF CONTEXT 9]

HISTORICAL STUDY: EUROPEAN AND WORLD

Ma

> **CONTEXT 10: THE RED FLAG:**
> **LENIN AND THE RUSSIAN**
> **REVOLUTION, 1894–1921**

Answer the following questions using recalled knowledge and information from the sources where appropriate.

Source A explains the treatment of national minorities in the Russian Empire.

Source A

> The diversity of the Empire made it difficult to govern. Many minorities resented the policy of Russification. It made non-Russians use the Russian language instead of their own. Russian style clothes were to be worn and Russian customs were to be adopted. Russian officials were put in to run regional government in non-Russian parts of the Empire like Poland, Latvia and Finland. When Poles complained they were treated as second class citizens, they were told to change and become Russian citizens.

1. Why did national minorities dislike the policy of Russification? (Use **Source A** and recall.)   5

Source B is from a letter by the leader of the Provisional Government to his parents on 3 July 1917.

Source B

> Without doubt the country is heading for chaos. We are facing famine, defeat at the front and the collapse of law and order in the cities. There will be wars in the countryside as desperate refugees from the cities fight each other for food and land.

2. How useful is **Source B** as evidence of the problems facing the Provisional Government?   4

3. In what ways did the Civil War affect the Russian people?   5

[END OF CONTEXT 10]

Marks

HISTORICAL STUDY: EUROPEAN AND WORLD

> CONTEXT 11: FREE AT LAST? RACE
> RELATIONS IN THE USA, 1918–1968

Answer the following questions using recalled knowledge and information from the sources where appropriate.

1. Describe the problems facing European immigrants to the USA in the 1920s. **5**

Source A is from a speech made in 1954 by the Grand Dragon of the Federated Klans of Alabama.

Source A

> The Klan don't hate nobody! In fact, the Klan is the black man's best friend. He should behave himself and not allow himself to be fooled by the lies of Northerners. Then he will reap the rewards of hard work, instead of the disappointments of chasing unrealistic dreams!

2. How useful is **Source A** as evidence of attitudes towards Black Americans in the southern states at the time of the Civil Rights movement? **4**

Source B is about the Civil Rights march in Selma, Alabama in 1965.

Source B

> Late in 1964 President Johnson told King that there was little immediate hope that Congress would pass any more Civil Rights legislation. King decided that Johnson, like Kennedy before him, needed a "push". King decided to mount a new protest in Selma, Alabama. The local police chief, Sheriff Clark, was a crude, violent racist. Like Bull Connor he would make a wonderfully obvious enemy. King decided to lead a march from Selma to the state capital Montgomery to protest to Governor George Wallace about police brutality and racism.

3. Why did Martin Luther King plan a Civil Rights protest in Selma, Alabama in 1965? (Use **Source B** and recall.) **5**

[END OF CONTEXT 11]

M

HISTORICAL STUDY: EUROPEAN AND WORLD

> ### CONTEXT 12: THE ROAD TO WAR, 1933–1939

Answer the following questions using recalled knowledge and information from the sources where appropriate.

1. In what ways did Britain appease Germany between 1933 and 1936?

5

Source A explains why Germany wanted Anschluss with Austria.

Source A

> The Treaty of Versailles had forbidden unification with Austria. It was obvious that Austria was the key to south eastern Europe, where Germany wanted to spread her influence. Also, Austria had a close relationship with Hungary whom Germany wanted as an ally. Strategically, joining up with Austria would surround western Czechoslovakia and prevent it from being a base for Germany's enemies. Ever since 1918, German governments wanted to unite with Austria. Germany and Austria were joined economically in 1936 so political union was the next logical step.

2. Why did Germany want Anschluss in 1938? (Use **Source A** and recall.)

5

Source B is from a report by the British ambassador to Germany, August 1938.

Source B

> No matter how badly the Germans behave, we must also condemn Czechoslovakia. No one has much faith in the Czech government's honesty or even their ability to do the right thing over the Sudetenland. We must not blame the Germans for preparing their army because they are convinced that the Czechs want to start a war as soon as possible so they can drag Britain and France into it.

3. How useful is **Source B** as evidence of Britain's attitude to Czechoslovakia in 1938?

4

[END OF CONTEXT 12]

HISTORICAL STUDY: EUROPEAN AND WORLD

Marks

> ### CONTEXT 13: IN THE SHADOW OF THE BOMB: THE COLD WAR, 1945–1985

Answer the following questions using recalled knowledge and information from the sources where appropriate.

Source A explains why the Cold War broke out after 1945.

Source A

> The Allies met at Potsdam in July, 1945. The new American leader, Truman, distrusted the Russians and Stalin did not trust him. Stalin had good reason for being uneasy. While the Allies met at Potsdam a message had reached Truman informing him that America had successfully tested its first atomic bomb. On the 6th of August, the USA dropped an atomic bomb on Hiroshima; three days later, it dropped a second on Nagasaki. Truman had not told Stalin that this was about to happen. Wartime friends, who had fought together to defeat a common enemy, were about to become peacetime enemies.

1. Why did the Cold War break out after 1945? (Use **Source A** and recall.)   **5**

2. Describe the part played by the USSR in the Cuban Missile Crisis.   **5**

Source B is from a speech to the American people by President Reagan in March 1983.

Source B

> Our efforts to rebuild America's forces began two years ago. For twenty years the Soviet Union has been accumulating enormous military might. They didn't stop building their forces, even when they had more than enough to defend themselves. They haven't stopped now. I know that all of you want peace, and so do I. However, the freeze on building nuclear weapons would make us less, not more, secure and would increase the risk of war.

3. How useful is **Source B** as evidence of why the process of détente had come to a halt by the early 1980s?   **4**

[END OF CONTEXT 13]

[END OF PART 3: EUROPEAN AND WORLD CONTEXTS]

[END OF QUESTION PAPER]

[BLANK PAGE]

[BLANK PAGE]

X044/201

NATIONAL
QUALIFICATIONS
2011

FRIDAY, 20 MAY
9.00 AM – 10.45 AM

HISTORY
INTERMEDIATE 2

The instructions for this paper are on *Page two*. Read them carefully before you begin your answers.

Your Invigilator will tell you which contexts to answer in Parts 2 and 3 of the examination.

INSTRUCTIONS

Answer **one** question from Part 1, The Short Essay

Answer **one** context* from Part 2, Scottish and British

Answer **one** context* from Part 3, European and World

Answer **one** other context* from

       either   Part 2, Scottish and British

       or   Part 3, European and World

*Answer all the questions in each of your chosen contexts.

Contents

[Turn over

PART 1: THE SHORT ESSAY

M

Answer **one** question. For this question you should write a short essay using your own knowledge. The essay should include an introduction, development and conclusion. Each question is worth 8 marks.

SCOTTISH AND BRITISH CONTEXTS:

CONTEXT 1: MURDER IN THE CATHEDRAL: CROWN, CHURCH AND PEOPLE, 1154–1173

Question 1: Explain why Henry II and Archbishop Becket quarrelled so violently.

8

CONTEXT 2: WALLACE, BRUCE AND THE WARS OF INDEPENDENCE, 1286–1328

Question 2: Explain why some Scots were reluctant to accept the Maid of Norway as their ruler.

8

CONTEXT 3: MARY, QUEEN OF SCOTS AND THE SCOTTISH REFORMATION, 1540s–1587

Question 3: Explain why Mary, Queen of Scots, was forced to abdicate in 1567.

8

CONTEXT 4: THE COMING OF THE CIVIL WAR, 1603–1642

Question 4: Explain why the reign of Charles I was opposed in Scotland.

8

CONTEXT 5: "ANE END OF ANE AULD SANG": SCOTLAND AND THE TREATY OF UNION, 1690s–1715

Question 5: Explain why some people thought that Scotland would benefit from a Union with England in 1707.

8

CONTEXT 6: IMMIGRANTS AND EXILES: SCOTLAND, 1830s–1930s

Question 6: Explain why life was difficult for many Irish immigrants to Scotland between 1830 and 1930.

8

CONTEXT 7: FROM THE CRADLE TO THE GRAVE? SOCIAL WELFARE IN BRITAIN, 1890s–1951

Question 7: Explain why the Liberal Government reforms of 1906–1914 were important in improving the lives of children and the elderly.

8

Marks

CONTEXT 8: CAMPAIGNING FOR CHANGE: SOCIAL CHANGE IN SCOTLAND, 1900s–1979

Question 8: Explain why Scottish education in the 1930s was in need of reform. **8**

CONTEXT 9: A TIME OF TROUBLES: IRELAND, 1900–1923

Question 9: Explain why the Unionists were against the Home Rule Bill. **8**

EUROPEAN AND WORLD CONTEXTS:

CONTEXT 1: THE NORMAN CONQUEST, 1060–1153

Question 10: Explain why there was so little opposition to William I after 1066. **8**

CONTEXT 2: THE CROSS AND THE CRESCENT: THE FIRST CRUSADE, 1096–1125

Question 11: Explain why people joined the First Crusade. **8**

CONTEXT 3: WAR, DEATH AND REVOLT IN MEDIEVAL EUROPE, 1328–1436

Question 12: Explain why the Black Death had serious consequences for England. **8**

CONTEXT 4: NEW WORLDS: EUROPE IN THE AGE OF EXPANSION, 1480s–1530s

Question 13: Explain why Christopher Columbus was an important figure in European exploration. **8**

CONTEXT 5: "TEA AND FREEDOM": THE AMERICAN REVOLUTION, 1763–1783

Question 14: Explain why the colonists were able to achieve victory in their war against the British by 1783. **8**

CONTEXT 6: "THIS ACCURSED TRADE": THE BRITISH SLAVE TRADE AND ITS ABOLITION, 1770–1807

Question 15: Explain why the Middle Passage was such a dreadful experience for slaves. **8**

CONTEXT 7: CITIZENS!
THE FRENCH REVOLUTION, 1789–1794

Question 16: Explain why so many people were frightened of the Committee of Public Safety in 1793.

CONTEXT 8: CAVOUR, GARIBALDI
AND THE MAKING OF ITALY, 1815–1870

Question 17: Explain why the 1848–49 revolutions failed to bring about Italian unification.

CONTEXT 9: IRON AND BLOOD? BISMARCK AND THE
CREATION OF THE GERMAN EMPIRE, 1815–1871

Question 18: Explain why the 1848–49 revolutions failed to bring about German unification.

CONTEXT 10: THE RED FLAG:
LENIN AND THE RUSSIAN REVOLUTION, 1894–1921

Question 19: Explain why the Provisional Government had lost popular support by October 1917.

CONTEXT 11: FREE AT LAST?
RACE RELATIONS IN THE USA, 1918–1968

Question 20: Explain why the attitudes of Americans towards immigration changed after 1918.

CONTEXT 12: THE ROAD TO WAR, 1933–1939

Question 21: Explain why Britain did not want to go to war with Germany in the 1930s.

CONTEXT 13: IN THE SHADOW OF THE BOMB:
THE COLD WAR, 1945–1985

Question 22: Explain why the USA and USSR had begun the process of détente by the 1970s.

[END OF PART 1: THE SHORT ESSAY]

[Turn over for PART 2: SCOTTISH AND BRITISH CONTEXTS on *Page eight*

M

PART 2:

HISTORICAL STUDY: SCOTTISH AND BRITISH

> **CONTEXT 1: MURDER IN THE CATHEDRAL: CROWN, CHURCH AND PEOPLE, 1154–1173**

Answer the following questions using recalled knowledge and information from the sources where appropriate.

1. Describe the actions taken by Henry II to increase his power when he became king in 1154.

Source A was written in the twelfth century, by a French poet, about chivalry.

Source A

> Many knights are failing to live by the Code of Chivalry. They steal money from churches and rob pilgrims of their possessions. They attack whoever they please and show disrespect to children and the elderly. They speak of honour and bravery when they practise neither. Even though knights have spent years training to be the perfect soldier and role model they often forget their vows.

2. How useful is **Source A** as evidence of the behaviour of knights in the twelfth century?

Source B explains why priests were important in the twelfth century.

Source B

> Famine and disease meant that life in medieval times was uncertain and extremely difficult. The village priest offered support and hope that life after death would be better. At mass, the priest taught people how to behave and fulfil their Christian duties. In return the priest received some of the village's harvest to feed and keep him. Key ceremonies such as baptism, marriage and funerals were all carried out by the priest. They also taught boys to read and write and prepared them for a career in the Church.

3. Why were priests important in the twelfth century? (Use **Source B** and recall.)

[END OF CONTEXT 1]

Marks

HISTORICAL STUDY: SCOTTISH AND BRITISH

> **CONTEXT 2: WALLACE, BRUCE
> AND THE WARS OF
> INDEPENDENCE, 1286–1328**

Answer the following questions using recalled knowledge and information from the sources where appropriate.

Source A was written by the English chronicler, Walter of Guisborough in 1298.

Source A

> On one side of a little hill close to Falkirk, the Scots placed their soldiers in four round circles with their pikes held outwards at an angle. Between these circles, which are called schiltrons, were the archers and behind them was the cavalry. When our men attacked, the Scots horsemen fled without striking a sword's blow.

1. How useful is **Source A** as evidence about what happened at Falkirk?   **4**

2. Describe the events that led to the death of John Comyn at Dumfries in 1306.   **5**

Source B explains why Bruce was not fully accepted as King of Scots until 1328.

Source B

> It took almost twenty-two years of fighting before Bruce was accepted as King of Scots. He had to force many Scots to abandon King John Balliol, and others to reject the claims of Edward II as overlord. Bruce emphasised his own royal blood to justify his claim and his victory at Bannockburn as a sign of God's approval. However, he was unable to change the mind of Edward II. Bruce was also unsuccessful in his attempts to increase pressure on Edward II by spreading the war to other parts of Britain.

3. Why did it take so long for Robert Bruce to be accepted as King of Scots? (Use **Source B** and recall.)   **5**

[END OF CONTEXT 2]

M

HISTORICAL STUDY: SCOTTISH AND BRITISH

> **CONTEXT 3: MARY, QUEEN OF SCOTS AND THE SCOTTISH REFORMATION, 1540s–1587**

Answer the following questions using recalled knowledge and information from the sources where appropriate.

Source A is John Knox's description of the way in which the Earl of Arran broke the Treaty of Greenwich in 1543.

Source A

> That dishonest man, Arran, sneaked away from the Palace of Holyrood and went to Stirling. There, he apologised to Cardinal Beaton and the people who were with him for making a treaty with England. He then made a deal with the Devil by giving up his Protestant faith and also by breaking the oath that he had made to keep the Treaty of Greenwich with England.

1. How useful is **Source A** as evidence about the way in which the Earl of Arran broke the Treaty of Greenwich?

Source B explains why the Scots rebelled against Mary of Guise in 1559.

Source B

> The marriage of Mary, Queen of Scots and the Dauphin of France took place in 1558. Her mother, Mary of Guise, continued to rule Scotland on behalf of her daughter who stayed in France. Guise took strong action against Protestants in Scotland, especially after Elizabeth became Queen of England in November of the same year. She made more use of French officials and used more French soldiers to control key strongholds in Scotland. She demanded a new tax, but the Scottish nobles were determined not to allow that.

2. Why did the Scots rebel against Mary of Guise in 1559? (Use **Source B** and recall.)

3. Describe the events that led to the execution of Mary, Queen of Scots, in 1587.

[END OF CONTEXT 3]

Marks

HISTORICAL STUDY: SCOTTISH AND BRITISH

> ### CONTEXT 4: THE COMING OF THE CIVIL WAR, 1603–1642

Answer the following questions using recalled knowledge and information from the sources where appropriate.

1. Describe the changes in the way Scotland was governed after 1603.   **5**

Source A explains how Charles I raised money during his reign.

Source A

> From 1629 until 1640 Charles I raised money without calling Parliament even though monarchs were supposed to ask Parliament for permission to raise taxes. In return MPs could express their concerns about issues. In the years 1626 and 1627 a forced loan was introduced and five knights who refused to pay it were put in prison without a fair trial. Ship money was also collected. This tax was normally paid by counties with coastlines to pay for the navy to protect them but Charles forced all counties to pay ship money. He increased his income from £600,000 a year to £900,000 a year.

2. Why was there opposition to the methods used by Charles I to raise money? (Use **Source A** and recall.)   **5**

Source B is from a letter written by Thomas Wiseman of London, on 6 January 1642.

Source B

> Twelve bishops were wrongly accused of high treason by the Parliament. This week five of the leading members of the House of Commons and the Lord Mandeville in the House of Lords were accused by the King. This has bred so much anger, and rightly so, both in the city and Houses of Parliament, that we are afraid of rebellion.

3. How useful is **Source B** as evidence of the causes of the Civil War?   **4**

[END OF CONTEXT 4]

M

HISTORICAL STUDY: SCOTTISH AND BRITISH

> **CONTEXT 5: "ANE END OF ANE AULD SANG": SCOTLAND AND THE TREATY OF UNION, 1690s–1715**

Answer the following questions using recalled knowledge and information from the sources where appropriate.

1. Describe Scotland's economic problems in the years before the Union.

Source A explains why opponents of the Union were unable to stop it being passed in Scotland.

Source A

> There was very clear opposition to the Union in Scotland and some towns sent petitions against it to Edinburgh. Opponents of the Union in the Scottish Parliament were not well enough organised to take advantage of this popular opinion. Some were actually frightened by the riots and violence in the city. Their figurehead, Hamilton, was found to be unreliable. On the other hand, the government had sent secret agents to promote the advantages of a Union to Scotland and, if that did not work, the government had money to offer.

2. Why were opponents of the Union unable to stop it being passed in Scotland? (Use **Source A** and recall.)

Source B was written by Daniel Defoe in 1727.

Source B

> Now that their Parliament is gone, the Scottish nobles and gentlemen spend their time and consequently their money in England. The Union has opened the door to English manufacturers and ruined Scottish ones. Their cattle are sent to England, but money is spent there too. The troops raised in Scotland are in English service and Scotland receives no money from them either.

3. How useful is **Source B** as evidence about the effects of the Union on Scotland?

[END OF CONTEXT 5]

Marks

HISTORICAL STUDY: SCOTTISH AND BRITISH

**CONTEXT 6: IMMIGRANTS AND
EXILES: SCOTLAND, 1830s–1930s**

Answer the following questions using recalled knowledge and information from the sources where appropriate.

Source A is a picture showing an Irish family produced for a British magazine in the 1840s.

Source A

1. How useful is **Source A** as evidence of why so many people left Ireland for Scotland in the 1840s?

    4

Source B explains why Scots moved away from the Highlands.

Source B

> The lairds had discovered that their land would yield far greater profits from sheep and therefore encouraged their tenant farmers to leave. Poor soil and harsh weather made farming difficult and life in the Highlands became even worse with the repeated failure of the potato crop after 1846. In fact the Highland Scot was affected by conditions over which he had no control. However, many Highlanders preferred the countries of the Empire to Scotland's dismal industrial cities. Many Lowland craftsmen were also leaving at this time.

2. Why did so many Highland Scots emigrate? (Use **Source B** and recall.)   **5**

3. Describe the ways emigrants created Scottish communities in their new homelands.   **5**

[END OF CONTEXT 6]

HISTORICAL STUDY: SCOTTISH AND BRITISH

> **CONTEXT 7: FROM THE CRADLE
> TO THE GRAVE? SOCIAL WELFARE
> IN BRITAIN, 1890s–1951**

Answer the following questions using recalled knowledge and information from the sources where appropriate.

Source A is by the Aberdeen Association for Improving the Conditions of the Poor, in the late 19th century.

Source A

> Our aims are to encourage, in every available way, the efforts of the poor to live sober lives and to discourage idleness. In general, we want to help those who are sober and hardworking but who through illness or accident are in danger of being plunged into poverty. These are the only people who deserve our help.

1. How useful is **Source A** as evidence of attitudes to the poor at the end of the 19th century?

Source B explains the effects of the Second World War on welfare reform.

Source B

> During the war the government had to take more responsibility for the welfare of its citizens. The Ministry of Food was established and raised standards of health among the poorer classes. Rationing helped establish the idea of a universal and equal share of the country's food supply. Damage to homes affected rich and poor, with the government assisting all who were affected. Classes were mixing in society who previously had little in common. War brought many problems for civilians that could only be overcome by government action.

2. Why did the Second World War change people's attitudes towards welfare reform? (Use **Source B** and recall.)

3. Describe the limitations of the Labour Government reforms of 1945–1951.

[END OF CONTEXT 7]

Marks

HISTORICAL STUDY: SCOTTISH AND BRITISH

> **CONTEXT 8: CAMPAIGNING FOR CHANGE: SOCIAL CHANGE IN SCOTLAND, 1900s–1979**

Answer the following questions using recalled knowledge and information from the sources where appropriate.

Source A is an extract from rules introduced by the British Museum in 1914 after a painting was slashed by a Suffragette.

Source A

> The British Museum is open to men and also to women if accompanied by men who are willing to guarantee their good behaviour and take full responsibility. Unaccompanied women are only allowed in if they present a letter of introduction from a responsible person guaranteeing the woman's good behaviour and accepting responsibility for her actions.

1. How useful is **Source A** as evidence of attitudes to Suffragettes by 1914?   **4**

2. Describe the effects of the economic slump in Scotland in the 1920s and 1930s.   **5**

Source B is about increasing use of the countryside for recreation in Scotland.

Source B

> The 1920s and 1930s was the time when the "Outdoor Movement" had popular appeal. New organisations such as youth hostels, cycling clubs and rambling associations were set up. Cheap motor bikes helped get people to the countryside. While mountaineering remained an upper class sport in most of Britain, by the 1930s the unemployed in the West of Scotland were joining climbing clubs. Many people were pleased to be away from the overcrowded cities. The Scottish Rights of Way and Recreation Society campaigned for walkers' rights to roam in private estates.

3. Why did more Scots use the countryside for recreation between the wars? (Use **Source B** and recall.)   **5**

[END OF CONTEXT 8]

M

HISTORICAL STUDY: SCOTTISH AND BRITISH

> ### CONTEXT 9: A TIME OF
> ### TROUBLES: IRELAND, 1900–1923

Answer the following questions using recalled knowledge and information from the sources where appropriate.

Source A is part of a letter written by an Irish MP to the British Government in 1916.

Source A

> I admit the rebels were wrong to start an uprising but they fought a clean fight and no cruel acts against the British army were committed. The rebels should have been tried in court, sentenced and sent to jail. Executing the leaders has only increased support and sympathy for them. Already people in Dublin, who ten days ago refused to help the rebels, have changed their minds. Their anger against the British is spreading dangerously across the country.

1. How useful is **Source A** as evidence of Irish attitudes to the executions following the Easter Rising?

2. Describe the terms of the Anglo-Irish Treaty of 1922.

Source B explains why the Free State Army won the Irish Civil War.

Source B

> In June 1922, the Free State Army were supplied with artillery by the British government which they used to attack the Republicans. Within days they had won back the Four Courts and other important buildings which gave them control of Dublin. Despite this success, the Free State Army suffered a blow when their leader, Michael Collins, was killed. In response, Republican leaders were captured and executed. These executions shocked Ireland but the Catholic Church and most of the public supported the Free State Army and their attempts to end the war. Although the fighting continued for another year, the Free State Army eventually won.

3. Why did the Free State Army win the Irish Civil War in 1923? (Use **Source B** and recall.)

[END OF CONTEXT 9]

[END OF PART 2: SCOTTISH AND BRITISH CONTEXTS]

Marks

PART 3:

HISTORICAL STUDY: EUROPEAN AND WORLD

> ### CONTEXT 1: THE NORMAN CONQUEST, 1060–1153

Answer the following questions using recalled knowledge and information from the sources where appropriate.

Source A explains William's success as Duke of Normandy.

Source A

> At the age of nineteen William was already capable of leading the Normans into battle. He soon showed he was willing to use ruthless methods. When the town of Alençon refused to surrender he ordered that 34 prisoners should have their eyes gouged out as a warning. However, he also realised that he needed allies. He married Matilda, the daughter of the powerful Count Baldwin of Flanders in order to gain his support. The couple looked strange together as William was over 6 feet tall while his wife was 4 feet 2 inches.

1. Why did William become a successful leader of Normandy? (Use **Source A** and recall.)   **5**

Sources B and **C** describe the way in which David I ruled Scotland.

Source B

> David I supported the development of monasticism in Scotland by founding many abbeys including Holyrood and Dryburgh. The monks significantly improved the economy of Scotland through their expertise in sheep farming, coal working and salt production. David also established a series of royal burghs, such as Stirling, Perth and Dunfermline. He brought many Anglo-Normans into the southern half of the country to help strengthen his rule. He also took direct control of Moray after a revolt against him there.

Source C

> David established many of Scotland's most important towns. These became the King's burghs where traders were given special rights and privileges. They also benefited from the minting of Scotland's first coins. He extended the amount of land under direct royal control and used his Norman knights to put down rebellions against his rule. He helped to end the quarrel between Roman and Celtic churches and encouraged the work of Cistercian monks at Melrose and Kinloss.

2. How far do **Sources B** and **C** agree about the way in which David I ruled Scotland?   **4**

3. Describe the features of Norman government which were introduced to Scotland after 1124.   **5**

[END OF CONTEXT 1]

M

HISTORICAL STUDY: EUROPEAN AND WORLD

> **CONTEXT 2: THE CROSS AND THE CRESCENT: THE FIRST CRUSADE, 1096–1125**

Answer the following questions using recalled knowledge and information from the sources where appropriate.

Sources A and **B** describe what happened to Jewish communities during the First Crusade.

Source A

> After only a few weeks of travelling, Peter the Hermit and his followers came upon a Jewish community in Germany. Many of the Crusaders were poor and hungry so they began stealing food and possessions from the Jews. As the Crusaders thought the Jews were the enemy of Christ, most believed they could treat them as they wished. Some forced the Jews to change religion and become Christian. Others, against the orders of Peter the Hermit, slaughtered the Jews.

Source B

> A rumour spread amongst the Crusaders that whoever killed a Jew would have all their sins forgiven. Immediately Peter the Hermit's army began attacking and killing Jewish men, women and children. Although some Jews tried to fight back they had few weapons and were easily defeated. In the riot that followed, houses were robbed and valuables stolen. Those Jews who survived the massacre were forced to give up their faith and become Christians.

1. How far do **Sources A** and **B** agree about what happened to Jews during the First Crusade?

Source C explains why Emperor Alexius and the Crusaders had a poor relationship.

Source C

> When Emperor Alexius freed the Muslims inside Nicaea the Crusaders were outraged. They had taken a vow to kill all Muslims and did not expect them to be shown mercy. Worse still, Alexius insulted the Crusaders by denying them the chance to plunder the city to take their share of the treasure. Although the Crusaders needed the Emperor's help, many openly said they would no longer keep their oath of loyalty to him. Instead of returning any land they captured, the Crusaders agreed to keep it for themselves.

2. Why did Emperor Alexius and the Crusaders have a poor relationship? (Use **Source C** and recall.)

3. Describe the capture of Jerusalem in 1099.

[END OF CONTEXT 2]

Marks

HISTORICAL STUDY: EUROPEAN AND WORLD

> **CONTEXT 3: WAR, DEATH AND REVOLT IN MEDIEVAL EUROPE, 1328–1436**

Answer the following questions using recalled knowledge and information from the sources where appropriate.

Source A explains the French defeat at Crecy.

Source A

> The English took up position on a hillside outside the village of Crecy. The French were forced to fight uphill. The French archers used crossbows which fired deadly iron-tipped bolts. However these weapons took time to reload. The first French cavalry charge was met by a hail of arrows. The knights were forced back and many French foot-soldiers were trampled by their own horsemen. The French charged 16 times but by midnight it was all over.

1. Why were the French defeated at Crecy? (Use **Source A** and recall.)   5

2. Describe the Jacquerie risings in France in 1358.   5

Sources B and **C** describe the effects of the Hundred Years War on France.

Source B

> By the end of the war there was not a chateau or a church in northern and western France which had not been destroyed by the English. No proper peace treaty was ever signed. The English regarded their expulsion from France as only temporary. In 1457 Charles VII wrote to the King of Scots that Frenchmen had to watch the coast daily for a new English invasion. The English still had the advantage of controlling Calais from where they could march out to re-conquer lost lands.

Source C

> Although Charles VII was at first worried that the English would return, he ensured that his coasts were well defended and encouraged attacks on English shipping in the Channel. The English were faced with the problem of having to pour resources into the defence of Calais. All in all the French emerged stronger from the war and the English weaker. The recovery by the French of much of their land in the north and west had been easy and had caused little destruction.

3. How far do **Sources B** and **C** disagree about the effects of the Hundred Years War on France?   4

[END OF CONTEXT 3]

Ma

HISTORICAL STUDY: EUROPEAN AND WORLD

CONTEXT 4: NEW WORLDS:
EUROPE IN THE AGE OF
EXPANSION, 1480s–1530s

Answer the following questions using recalled knowledge and information from the sources where appropriate.

1. Describe the improvements in technology which made the voyages of discovery possible.

5

Source A explains the importance of Vasco da Gama's voyage.

Source A

> In 1497–8, Vasco da Gama made the longest voyage that any European vessel had achieved in the open sea. He sailed far out into the South Atlantic before heading east and crossing the Indian Ocean to Calicut. He returned the following year with three quarters of his crew and the first cargo of spices. When the cargo was sold it made a profit sixty times the cost of the voyage. The king of Portugal was delighted that he had found trade routes to Ethiopia, Arabia, Persia and India.

2. Why was Vasco da Gama's voyage important for European trade? (Use **Source A** and recall.)

5

Sources B and **C** describe the impact of Europeans on the native peoples of the New World.

Source B

> Great cities, their culture, their religion and their civilisations were destroyed by the Conquistadors. Kings who had gold and wealth were held captive and their people forced to pay ransoms in gold for them. The native people were used as slaves to make money for their new rulers in many ways such as in silver mines and even on sugar plantations. In return, the Europeans brought them new diseases which wiped them out in hundreds of thousands.

Source C

> The European explorers opened the New World to European settlers. Smallpox and measles spread rapidly and whole populations, such as the people of Hispaniola, had no resistance and died. Both the Spanish and Portuguese were keen to convert the native people to Christianity and their existing religions were harshly discouraged. However, this did not prevent the Europeans from taking gold and riches from the New World by any means, fair or unfair.

3. How far do **Sources B** and **C** agree about the impact of Europeans on the native peoples of the New World?

[END OF CONTEXT 4]

HISTORICAL STUDY: EUROPEAN AND WORLD

Marks

> ### CONTEXT 5: "TEA AND FREEDOM": THE AMERICAN REVOLUTION, 1763–1783

Answer the following questions using recalled knowledge and information from the sources where appropriate.

1. Describe what happened during the *Gaspée* incident in 1772.　　5

Source A explains why many colonists were unhappy with British rule by 1776.

Source A

> The writer Thomas Paine was firmly opposed to British rule. In January 1776, he published a cleverly written pamphlet called "Common Sense". In it, he argued that the British government was abusing the rights of the American people and many colonists were persuaded by his arguments. The answer, Paine believed, was independence. Paine's ideas were very popular and 150,000 pamphlets were sold. The King's rejection of the Olive Branch Petition also moved many colonists towards independence, as did news that the British were hiring mercenary soldiers from Germany to help them control the colonies.

2. Why had many colonists turned against British rule by 1776? (Use **Source A** and recall.)　　5

Sources B and **C** are about the defeat of British forces, led by General Cornwallis, at Yorktown.

Source B

> In 1781, Cornwallis moved into Virginia and began to build a base at Yorktown. By late summer, Cornwallis's position at Yorktown was deteriorating fast. While American forces prevented him from moving inland, a large French fleet carrying 3,000 troops had sailed up from the West Indies to join the siege. The fate of Cornwallis was sealed when the French defeated the British fleet in Chesapeake Bay. On October 19 Cornwallis surrendered his entire army of 7,000 men.

Source C

> To launch his campaign in Virginia, Cornwallis's army carried out raids, harassing the Americans wherever he could. In August 1781, Cornwallis set up camp at Yorktown but this turned out to be a poor position. American troops moved quickly to surround him and keep him there. The British could not help Cornwallis's army to escape or bring in reinforcements. In September, the French defeated the British fleet in a naval battle near Yorktown, giving the allies control over the sea in the area.

3. How far do **Sources B** and **C** agree about the reasons for the defeat of the forces led by Cornwallis at Yorktown?　　4

[END OF CONTEXT 5]

M

HISTORICAL STUDY: EUROPEAN AND WORLD

> ### CONTEXT 6: "THIS ACCURSED TRADE": THE BRITISH SLAVE TRADE AND ITS ABOLITION, 1770–1807

Answer the following questions using recalled knowledge and information from the sources where appropriate.

Source A explains why resistance was difficult on slave plantations in the West Indies.

Source A

> Most slaves in the West Indies were involved in the production of sugar which was hard, heavy work. The life of the slave on the plantation was controlled by strict slave laws, or codes. Some slaves, however, refused to accept their circumstances and attempted to escape or plotted revolt. Those who escaped would be hunted down. Slave owners lived in constant fear of a revolt by their slaves. Slave risings took place throughout the colonies but very few had effective leadership and they were soon crushed by the better armed and organised whites.

1. Why was resistance difficult for slaves on the plantations? (Use **Source A** and recall.)

Sources B and **C** are about the importance of the slave trade for Britain.

Source B

> There were many reasons why it took so long to abolish the slave trade. One reason was that the slave trade had many powerful supporters. Plantation owners and merchants in British ports which relied on the slave trade were well organised and had political influence. They had enough wealth to bribe MPs to support them. They also had the support of King George III. Many people believed that the trade had helped them to make Britain wealthy and prosperous.

Source C

> The Abolitionists faced powerful opposition. The plantation owners allied themselves with important groups to promote the case for slavery and the slave trade. Their case seemed overwhelming. Dozens of British ports and surrounding areas relied on the slave trade. British consumers had become addicted to the products of the slave trade, most notably sugar. The Atlantic slave trade represented a large amount of British trade and seemed vital to the continuing prosperity of Britain and the Caribbean Islands.

2. How far do **Sources B** and **C** agree about the reasons the slave trade continued in Britain throughout the eighteenth century?

3. In what ways did the Abolitionists try to win support for their cause?

[END OF CONTEXT 6]

Marks

HISTORICAL STUDY: EUROPEAN AND WORLD

CONTEXT 7: CITIZENS! THE FRENCH REVOLUTION, 1789–1794

Answer the following questions using recalled knowledge and information from the sources where appropriate.

1. Describe the complaints of the French peasants in 1789.

5

Sources A and **B** describe the supporters of the revolution who were known as the sans-culottes.

Source A

> The sans-culotte is an honest man who wants an honest reward for his work. The sans-culotte is a quiet, humble fellow who wishes only to live in peace with his fellow man. He feels at home in the poorest areas of Paris and lives only for the wife and children he loves so much. He is happy so long as he has a loaf of bread and a glass of wine, for his needs are simple.

Source B

> The main aim of these so-called sans-culottes is to get as much as they can for as little effort as possible. They have adopted a system of politics which puts them at the top of society and they care about little else. Violence is the only method they have to get what they want and the arrogance of these people from the gutter is astonishing.

2. How far do **Sources A** and **B** disagree about attitudes towards the sans-culottes?

4

Source C explains the unhappiness of the French people with the treatment of the Catholic Church.

Source C

> The National Assembly decided it was time to bring the Catholic Church under much tighter state control. The *assignat*, the new currency, was not being accepted and the government needed more money. Church lands were to be sold and the proceeds taken by the Assembly. Priests were to become government agents rather than servants of the Church. Bishops were to be elected which many French Catholics resented because even Protestants would be allowed to vote. However, the Assembly continued to support the teachings of the Church.

3. Why were many French people unhappy with the treatment of the Catholic Church during the French Revolution? (Use **Source C** and recall.)

5

[END OF CONTEXT 7]

M

HISTORICAL STUDY: EUROPEAN AND WORLD

> **CONTEXT 8: CAVOUR, GARIBALDI
> AND THE MAKING OF ITALY,
> 1815–1870**

Answer the following questions using recalled knowledge and information from the sources where appropriate.

Source A explains the influence of Napoleon Bonaparte on Italy.

Source A

> Napoleon proclaimed himself Emperor of France in 1804. He incorporated one third of Italy into the French Empire and created a Kingdom of Italy in the north. In this kingdom he encouraged the Italian language and literature. He took on the title of "King of Italy". Positive changes were introduced by Napoleon such as the abolition of internal customs barriers and the building of roads across the Alps, bringing Italians closer together.

1. Why did Napoleon Bonaparte have an important influence on Italian unification? (Use **Source A** and recall.)

2. Describe the events between 1850 and 1871 which led to the unification of Italy.

Sources B and **C** are about Cavour's contribution to unification.

Source B

> Cavour was not always a supporter of a united Italy. He took advantage of opportunities that came along rather than carrying out a clear plan of his own. He only united Italy to stop the activities of Garibaldi and not because he really believed in Italian unification. Cavour's actions in uniting Italy were a last desperate attempt to protect the power and influence of Piedmont.

Source C

> Cavour was a great diplomat and a brilliant planner. His ambition was always to unite Italy. To do this he raised the prestige of Italy and won the respect of foreign powers. Cavour allowed Garibaldi to win the south for Italy and for King Victor Emmanuel. Cavour himself gained the support of Napoleon III to break the power of Austria and keep Italy free from foreign intervention.

3. How far do **Sources B** and **C** disagree about the contribution of Cavour to the unification of Italy?

[END OF CONTEXT 8]

Marks

HISTORICAL STUDY: EUROPEAN AND WORLD

> **CONTEXT 9: IRON AND BLOOD?**
> **BISMARCK AND THE CREATION OF**
> **THE GERMAN EMPIRE, 1815–1871**

Answer the following questions using recalled knowledge and information from the sources where appropriate.

1. In what ways did German national feeling grow before 1848?   **5**

Source A explains the changing power of Austria and Prussia between 1850 and 1860.

Source A

> The balance of power between Austria and Prussia changed in the 1850s. During this time Austria had never been able to find anyone as skillful as Metternich in controlling the German states. Austria also lost an important alliance with Russia when it failed to help Russia in the Crimean War. In 1859 the French defeat of Austria destroyed her strong military reputation. Although Prussia had been humiliated at Olmutz, Prussian industrialisation led to economic growth and better trade links. This strengthened her position in the German Confederation.

2. Why had Austria lost her leading position in Germany by 1860? (Use **Source A** and recall.)   **5**

Sources B and **C** are about Bismarck's aims for unification.

Source B

> The British Prime Minister, Disraeli, had a conversation with Bismarck in 1862. Disraeli reported Bismarck's first vital task to strengthen Prussia's position in Germany was going to be the re-organisation of the army, with or without the help of the Prussian Parliament. Disraeli then said that Bismarck wanted to seize the first excuse to create war against Austria, control the smaller states and thus unite Germany under Prussian leadership.

Source C

> Bismarck's aims were to remove Austria and extend Prussia's power over the other German states in order to unite them under Prussian leadership. It was Bismarck's decision to reform the army which made Prussia dominant in Germany. After this he planned to force Austria to go to war with Prussia. The triumph of Bismarck's policy was to be seen on the battlefield at Koniggratz in 1866.

3. How far do **Sources B** and **C** agree about Bismarck's aims to unite Germany?   **4**

[END OF CONTEXT 9]

HISTORICAL STUDY: EUROPEAN AND WORLD

Ma

CONTEXT 10: THE RED FLAG: LENIN AND THE RUSSIAN REVOLUTION, 1894–1921

Answer the following questions using recalled knowledge and information from the sources where appropriate.

1. Describe the hardships faced by industrial workers in Russia before 1914.

5

Source A explains why the Russian Royal Family had become increasingly unpopular by 1917.

Source A

> The Romanov dynasty had lasted for 300 years and Nicholas and Alexandra were unwilling to give up autocratic rule. Although the Tsar had been persuaded to set up the Duma he did not let it run the country and largely ignored it. When the Tsar left Alexandra in charge of the government this was a disastrous decision. Alexandra was influenced by Rasputin who advised her to sack many of the competent ministers if he simply disliked them. This made the situation even worse.

2. Why had the Russian Royal Family become increasingly unpopular by 1917? (Use **Source A** and recall.)

5

Sources B and **C** describe Trotsky's leadership in the Civil War.

Source B

> For three years Trotsky lived on his armoured train travelling to all areas of the front. He covered 65,000 miles during the course of the war ensuring that the Red Army was well fed and properly armed. He was an inspirational leader and was dedicated to the cause. He made rousing speeches to the troops and raised morale even when other Bolshevik leaders were not convinced that they would defeat the Whites. Over 5 million men had joined the Red Army by 1920 of their own free will.

Source C

> Trotsky was appointed Commissar for War in early 1919 and quickly established a reputation as a ruthless leader who used strict discipline. He forced people to join the Red Army to raise the numbers of troops and introduced 50,000 former Tsarist officers to train the raw recruits. The death penalty was not only used for deserters. When 200 soldiers deserted at Svyazhsk, Trotsky arrived and ordered the execution of one in every ten men in the regiment, as a warning to the rest.

3. How far do **Sources B** and **C** disagree about Trotsky's leadership in the Civil War?

[END OF CONTEXT 10]

Marks

HISTORICAL STUDY: EUROPEAN AND WORLD

> **CONTEXT 11: FREE AT LAST? RACE RELATIONS IN THE USA, 1918–1968**

Answer the following questions using recalled knowledge and information from the sources where appropriate.

1. Describe the activities of the Ku Klux Klan in the 1920s and 1930s.   **5**

Sources A an **B** describe the results of the Montgomery Bus Boycott.

Source A

> Throughout the boycott a young black preacher inspired the black population of Montgomery. His name was Martin Luther King and this was to be his first step towards becoming the leading figure in the Civil Rights Movement. The boycott lasted over a year until eventually the courts decided that segregation on Montgomery's buses was illegal. On its own the bus boycott only had limited success. Montgomery remained a segregated town. There were still white-only theatres, pool rooms and restaurants.

Source B

> The bus company's services were boycotted by 99% of Montgomery's African Americans for over a year. As a result of the protest, the US Supreme Court announced that Alabama's bus segregation laws were illegal. However, most other facilities and services in Montgomery remained segregated for many years to come. As a result of the boycott, Martin Luther King became involved in the Civil Rights Movement. He went on to become an African American leader who was famous throughout the world.

2. How far do **Sources A** and **B** agree about the results of the Montgomery Bus Boycott?   **4**

Source C explains why Malcolm X opposed non-violent protest.

Source C

> Malcolm X was mistreated in his youth and this gave him a different set of attitudes to Martin Luther King. Later, while in jail, he was influenced by the ideas of Elijah Muhammad who preached hatred of the white race. In his speeches he criticised non-violence. He believed that the support of non-violence was a sign that Black people were still living in mental slavery. However, Malcolm X never undertook violent action himself and sometimes prevented it. Instead he often used violent language and threats to frighten the government into action.

3. Why did Malcolm X oppose non-violent protest? (Use **Source C** and recall.)   **5**

[END OF CONTEXT 11]

Ma

HISTORICAL STUDY: EUROPEAN AND WORLD

CONTEXT 12: THE ROAD TO WAR, 1933–1939

Answer the following questions using recalled knowledge and information from the sources where appropriate.

Source A explains why Hitler wanted to rearm Germany in the 1930s.

Source A

> Hitler claimed that Germany alone was forced to leave herself defenceless as part of the punishment dictated by her enemies in 1919. He never missed an opportunity to attack the Treaty of Versailles. Hitler further stated that Germany was surrounded by hostile countries whose main purpose was to keep her in a weakened position and this could no longer be tolerated. A strong Germany would not only restore the balance of power in Europe but was also necessary to safeguard European civilisation against the threat from the east.

1. Why did Hitler want to rearm Germany in the 1930s? (Use **Source A** and recall.)

Sources B and **C** are about the Germans in the Sudetenland, Czechoslovakia.

Source B

> Germany's justification for interfering in Czechoslovakia was that the Sudetenland wanted to return to the German Fatherland. Ever since 1919 the Sudeten Germans had resented being part of the new state of Czechoslovakia which was based on the medieval kingdom of Bohemia. The German government claimed that the Germans in Czechoslovakia had suffered constant persecution because they were an ethnic minority.

Source C

> Sudeten German unrest grew only after the economic depression began in the early 1930s. Germany seemed to be the only country whose economy was improving. Although they shared the same language and culture, the Sudetenland had never been part of Germany. Since 1919, the Sudeten Germans had been treated with respect in Czechoslovakia because they had contributed greatly to the nation's wealth.

2. How far do **Sources B** and **C** disagree about the Germans living in Czechoslovakia?

3. Describe events in 1939 that led to the outbreak of war between Britain and Germany.

[END OF CONTEXT 12]

Marks

HISTORICAL STUDY: EUROPEAN AND WORLD

> CONTEXT 13: IN THE SHADOW OF
> THE BOMB: THE COLD WAR,
> 1945–1985

Answer the following questions using recalled knowledge and information from the sources where appropriate.

1. Describe the events which led to the formation of the Warsaw Pact in 1955.   **5**

Sources A and **B** are about the Cuban Missile Crisis.

Source A

> Under Fidel Castro, Cuba was a proud example of a Communist country and was a role model to other countries. Khrushchev had the idea of installing a small number of nuclear missiles on Cuba without letting the USA know until it was too late to stop them. Khrushchev said they only wanted to keep the Americans from invading Cuba. He stated they had no desire to start a war.

Source B

> To the American government, placing missiles on Cuba was a warlike act by the Soviets. They believed that the Soviet Union intended to supply a large number of powerful nuclear weapons. Spy photographs proved the offensive purpose of the missiles which were pointed directly at major American cities. It was estimated that within a few minutes of them being fired, 80 million Americans would be dead.

2. How far do **Sources A** and **B** disagree about the Soviet Union's actions during the Cuban Missile Crisis?   **4**

Source C explains why the United States became involved in a war in Vietnam.

Source C

> In its early stages, the war in Vietnam had nothing to do with the USA. American involvement began when it was asked by its ally, France, for assistance. France was fighting to regain control over its former colony. The Americans agreed. They disapproved of French colonialism, but feared Communism more. They believed that they could establish a friendly government in South Vietnam, under the leadership of President Diem. By the early 1960s an increase in Vietcong attacks in South Vietnam led to a fear that a civil war was developing.

3. Why did America become involved in a full scale war in Vietnam by 1964? (Use **Source C** and recall.)   **5**

[END OF CONTEXT 13]

[END OF PART 3: EUROPEAN AND WORLD CONTEXTS]

[END OF QUESTION PAPER]

[BLANK PAGE]

Acknowledgements

Permission has been sought from all relevant copyright holders and Bright Red Publishing is grateful for the use of the following:

An extract from 'The Kings and Queens' by Plantagenent Somerset Fry, published by Dorling Kindersley, 1997. Reproduced by permission of Penguin Books Ltd (2007 page 8);

An extract from 'Immigrants and Exiles: Scotland 1830s–1930s' by Sydney Wood, published by Hodder & Stoughton, 2001 (2007 page 13);

An extract from 'From the Cradle to the Grave: Social Welfare in Britain 1890s–1951' by Simon Wood and Claire Wood, published by Hodder & Stoughton, 2002 (2007 page 14);

An adaptation of a memo from District Inspector Spears to the Minister of Home Affairs, 1923, taken from the Public Records Office of Northern Ireland (2007 page 16);

An extract from 'Nationalist and Unionist: Ireland before the Treaty' by T Gray, published by Blackie & Son Ltd, 1990. Reproduced by permission of T Gray (2007 page 16);

An extract from 'The Crusades' by RR Sellman, published by McHuen & Co Ltd, 1968 (2007 page 18);

Adapted extracts from 'Events and Outcomes The Slave Trade' by Tom Monaghan, published by Evans Brothers Ltd (2007 page 22);

An extract from 'Investigating History: Britain 1750–1900', published by Hodder & Stoughton, 2003 (2007 page 22);

An extract from 'Re-discovering Britain 1750–1900' by Andy Reid, Colin Shephard and Dave Martin, published by John Murray, 2001 (2007 page 22);

An extract from 'Free at Last? Race Relations in the USA 1918–1968' by John A Kerr, published by Hodder & Stoughton, 2000 (2007 page 27);

An extract from 'Konclave in Kokomo by Robert Coughlin, taken from 'The Aspirin Age' by Isabel Leighton, published by Simon & Schuster, 1963 (2007 page 27);

An extract from 'History of Britain' by Andrew Langley. Published by Heinemann Educational Publishers, 1996. Reproduced by permission of Pearson Education (2008 page 11);

Two extracts from 'Immigrants and Exiles: Scotland 1830s–1930s' by Sydney Wood, published by Hodder & Stoughton, 2001 (2008 page 13);

An extract from 'Patterns of Migration', published by Scottish Consultative Council on the Curriculum © Learning and Teaching Scotland 2010 (2008 page 13);

An extract from 'From the Cradle to the Grave: Social Welfare in Britain 1890s–1951' by Simon Wood and Claire Wood, published by Hodder & Stoughton, 2002 (2008 page 14);

An extract from 'The Edwardian Age: Complacency and Concern' by Ian B McKellar, published by Blackie & Son, 1980 (2008 page 14);

Extract from 'Colonialism and Colonies', Microsoft Encarta Online Encyclopedia 2008. Reproduced with permission of Microsoft (2008 page 20);

Adapted extracts from 'Events and Outcomes The American Revolution' by Dale Anderson, published by Evans Brother Ltd (2008 page 21);

An extract from 'Black Ivory' by James Walvin, published by Fontana Press, HarperCollins © James Walvin (2008 page 22);

An extract from 'The Unification of Germany 1815–90' by Andrina Stiles, published by Hodder & Stoughton, 1989 (2008 page 23);

An extract from 'Free at Last? Race Relations in the USA 1918–1968' by John A Kerr, published by Hodder & Stoughton, 2000 (2008 page 27);

An extract from 'The Cold War' published by HarperCollins Publishers Ltd © 1996 Fiona MacDonald (2008 page 28);

An extract from 'History of Britain' by Andrew Langley. Published by Heinemann Educational Publishers, 1996. Reproduced by permission of Pearson Education (2009 page 11);

An extract from 'Scotland: A Concise History' by Fitzroy MacLean. Copyright © 1970, 1993 and 2000 Thames & Hudson Ltd., London. Reproduced by permission of Thames & Hudson (2009 page 11);

An extract from 'Highland News, 8th April 1911, reproduced in 'Adventurers and Exiles: The Great Scottish Exodus' by Marjory Harper, published by Profile Books, 2003 (2009 page 13);

An extract from 'From the Cradle to the Grave: Social Welfare in Britain 1890s–1951' by Simon Wood and Claire Wood, published by Hodder & Stoughton, 2002 (2009 page 14);

A cartoon from the Daily Herald newspaper in 1942 © Daily Herald Archive at the National Media Museum/Science & Society Picture Library (2009 page 14);

A poster produced by the Irish National Party in 1915. Courtesy of the National Library of Ireland (2009 page 16);

An extract from 'Understanding Global Issues 10/92 Columbus and after: The beginnings of Colonisation' edited by Richard Buckley, published by European Schoolbooks, 1992 (2009 page 20);

An extract from http://www.en.wikipedia-org/wiki/AgeofDiscovery (2009 page 20);

An extract from 'The Unification of Italy', by Andrina Stiles, published by Hodder & Stoughton, 2006 (2009 page 24);

An extract from 'Cavour, Garibaldi and the Making of Italy 1815–70', published by Scottish Consultative Council on the Curriculum © Learning and Teaching Scotland, 2000 (2009 page 24);

Two extracts from 'Germany 1815–1939' by Jim McGonigle, published by Hodder Gibson 2006 (2009 page 25);

An extract from 'The Growth of Nationalism: Germany and Italy 1815–1939' by Ronald Cameron, Christine Henderson & Charles Robertson, published by Pulse Publications (2009 page 25);

An extract from 'The Civil Rights Movement' by Mark Newman, published by Edinburgh University Press (BAAS Paperbacks) 2004 (2009 page 27);

Two extracts from 'Free at Last? Race Relations in the USA 1918–1968' by John A Kerr, published by Hodder & Stoughton, 2000 (2009 page 27);
A picture taken from Illustrated London News, December 22, 1849. Public Domain (2011 page 13).

INTERMEDIATE 2 | ANSWER SECTION

SQA INTERMEDIATE 2
HISTORY 2007–2011

PART 1: THE SHORT ESSAY

Scottish and British

Context 1: Murder in the Cathedral: Crown, Church and People, 1154–1173

1. The candidate explains why Henry II quarrelled with Archbishop Becket by referring to evidence such as:
   - Henry and Becket had previously been good friends. When Becket resigned as chancellor and became Archbishop of Canterbury he changed and Henry felt betrayed
   - Becket repeatedly defended the Church's rights against Henry
   - Henry and Becket argued over 'Criminous Clerks'. Henry believed that clergymen suspected of crimes should be tried in the king's court. Becket believed that members of the clergy should be tried in the Church's court
   - Henry and Becket argued over the Constitutions of Clarendon. Henry attempted to trick Becket into signing a document that limited the Church's power
   - Henry asked Becket to answer a charge over his conduct as chancellor at the Northampton trial. He refused to appear and was charged with contempt of court
   - the Archbishop of York crowned Henry's son. Becket responded by excommunicating all the bishops involved.
   - Becket fled to France and was in exile for six years. He was protected by Henry's enemy Louis VII.

Context 2: Wallace, Bruce and the Wars of Independence, 1286–1328

2. The candidate explains why Robert Bruce was successful in making himself King of Scots by referring to evidence such as:
   - he had royal blood
   - he had the support of some Scots from the very beginning
   - Edward I died which removed a powerful enemy
   - Edward II was not a successful king and did not concentrate on defeating Bruce
   - Bruce was able to drive out the English by capturing the castles they held
   - Bruce destroyed his Scottish enemies (eg the Comyns) by ruining their lands
   - Bruce defeated the English at the Battle of Bannockburn
   - Bruce won the support of the Pope and the King of France.

Context 3: Mary, Queen of Scots and The Scottish Reformation, 1540s–1587

3. The candidate explains why Queen Elizabeth ordered the execution of Mary, Queen of Scots in 1587 by referring to evidence such as:
   - Mary claimed that she was the true, Catholic Queen of England
   - Mary was Elizabeth's heir who would take over when Elizabeth died
   - some English Catholics supported Mary's claims to be Queen of England
   - some English Catholics plotted to murder Elizabeth
   - foreign Catholic rulers and the Pope supported these murder plots
   - Mary had been involved in the Babington Plot
   - Mary's son, who was next in line to the English crown, was a Protestant.

Context 4: The Coming of the Civil War, 1603–1642

4. The candidate explains why James I quarrelled with the English Parliament during his reign by referring to evidence such as:
   - James's belief in the Divine Right of Kings deeply offended the House of Commons
   - impeachment of royal ministers such as Bacon and Cranfield
   - quarrels over war with Spain
   - Commons complained about king's extravagance
   - disputes over royal rights to raise taxes
   - quarrels over sale of monopolies by Crown
   - quarrels over king's choice of leading ministers eg Duke of Buckingham
   - quarrels over royal impositions eg on currants
   - Parliament was suspicious of James's perceived Catholic sympathies.

Context 5: 'Ane End of Ane Auld Sang': Scotland and the Treaty of Union, 1690s–1715

5. The candidate explains why the Scottish colony at Darien failed by referring to evidence such as:
   - the climate was unsuitable for Scottish colonists
   - the area was unhealthy – many colonists died from disease
   - the Scots had brought the wrong goods for trading
   - the Scots wanted too much for their goods and could not sell them
   - the colonists argued among themselves
   - the colony was attacked by the native people
   - the colony was attacked by the Spaniards
   - the colony received no help from English colonists.

Context 6: Immigrants and Exiles: Scotland, 1830s–1930s

6. The candidate explains why many Scots left to go overseas between the 1830s and 1930s by referring to evidence such as:
   - the Highland Clearances
   - potato famine in 1840s
   - later clearances due to deer estates and sporting activities
   - poverty and unemployment
   - movement of population from the land/changes in lowland farming
   - activities of emigration societies/assisted passages
   - attractions of overseas countries
   - failure of herring, kelp and whisky industries.

Context 7(a): From the Cradle to the Grave? Social Welfare in Britain, 1890s–1951

7 (a). The candidate explains why the social reforms of the Liberal government 1906–1914 were important in improving the welfare of the British people by referring to evidence such as:
   - reforms tried to deal with the problem of poverty
   - introduced school meals and medical inspection for children
   - introduced old age pensions for those of 70 years and over
   - National Insurance Act provided free medical treatment for workers earning under £160 a year
   - unemployment benefit was given to workers in some industries
   - labour exchanges were set up to help people find work
   - it can be argued the Liberals laid the foundations of a welfare state.

Context 7(b): Campaigning for Change: Social Change in Scotland, 1900s–1979

7 (b). The candidate explains why all women were given the vote by 1928 by referring to evidence such as:
- women had gained many rights in the previous century – rights over property, children, education
- women had been agitating for the vote since before 1900
- the peaceful activities of the NUWSS persuaded many men (and women) to accept female suffrage
- the Pankhursts and the WSPU attempted to force the government into giving women the vote – though the militancy/violence of WSPU was a retrograde step
- women suspended their campaign on the outbreak of the Great War, 1914, in support of the government
- women participated in many aspects of the war effort, largest number in munitions
- married women over 30 given vote in 1918 (either as a reward or out of fear of renewed militant campaign)
- universal male suffrage was introduced in 1918; women were given parity with men in 1928.

Context 8: A Time of Troubles: Ireland, 1900–1923

8. The candidate explains why the Ulster Unionists opposed the Home Rule Bill by referring to evidence such as:
- Unionists felt it would destroy their way of life
- Home Rule threatened Ulster's economic prosperity eg industry
- Ireland would be cut off from markets in Britain and Empire/threatened unity of Empire
- loss of money and business for many
- many felt that Home Rule would destroy improvements made in housing, wages etc
- Unionists believed Ireland was too weak to survive on her own/needed to remain in the Union
- Unionists worried that parliament in Dublin would be strongly influenced by the Roman Catholic Church/worried the Protestant Church would be weakened
- divisions between Catholics and Protestants.

European and World

Context 1: The Norman Conquest, 1060–1153

9. The candidate explains why David I's reign has been called the 'Normanisation' of Scotland by referring to evidence such as:
- rule by Royal Council
- introduction of knight-service eg castle-guard
- creation of Norman feudal baronage
- introduction of sheriffs
- promotion of David's great Norman friends eg the Bruces
- creation of royal burghs
- use of knights in royal army
- building of castles
- founding of monasteries.

Context 2: The Cross and the Crescent: The First Crusade, 1096–1125

10. The candidate explains why the People's Crusade failed by referring to evidence such as:
- the People's Crusade was not well organised or well prepared
- Peter the Hermit was a good spiritual leader but had no military experience
- the People's Crusade got involved in a number of incidents in Germany where they massacred Jews

- the People's Crusade gained a bad reputation because of their behaviour across Europe
- the People's Crusade ran into trouble in Hungary because they were too few to avoid attack
- they were unable to defend themselves/they were poorly armed and trained
- the different nationalities amongst the People's Crusade split and elected their own leaders
- when the Crusaders arrived at Constantinople, Alexius was not ready for them; this led to rioting
- Peter the Hermit did not take Alexius's advice to wait for the support of the knights
- Peter the Hermit was in Constantinople when the People's Crusade was finally defeated at Nicaea.

Context 3: War, Death and Revolt in Medieval Europe, 1328–1436

11. The candidate explains why Joan of Arc was executed in 1431 by referring to evidence such as:
- she was condemned as a heretic after trial by a Church court
- she refused to deny that she had been an instrument of God
- English hatred for Joan
- she contributed to the revival of French spirits in the Hundred Years' War
- she contributed to the war effort eg she raised the siege of Orleans
- Charles VII refused to ransom Joan or save her.

Context 4: New Worlds: Europe in the Age of Expansion, 1480s–1530s

12. The candidate explains why Portugal was able to discover new trade routes to the East in the late fifteenth and early sixteenth centuries by referring to evidence such as:
- patronage of Henry the Navigator
- influence of college at Sagres in teaching navigational skills
- improvements in map-making
- Portugal was well placed geographically to make voyages to the East
- better ships such as the carrack/caravel were available
- improved navigational aids such as the compass/quadrant/astrolabe were available
- Diaz's success in rounding Africa encouraged further voyages
- Da Gama's opening up of a route to India encouraged further routes to be opened up.

Context 5: 'Tea and Freedom': The American Revolution, 1763–1783

13. The candidate explains why the defeat of the French created tensions in the American colonies by referring to evidence such as:
- the French War had hidden developing problems/the end of the war brought them to the surface
- the French were no longer a threat so the colonists did not need British protection
- British believed troops were still needed in the colonies, eg threat of Indian risings and from French settlers
- British soldiers displayed a dangerous contempt for the colonists' fighting ability/believing they were not able to defend themselves
- Britain had financial problems as a result of the French wars/thought it was fair that the American colonists paid for their own defence/the colonists did not like this
- the king wished to have a tighter control of his Empire/the colonists resented this
- victory in 1763 had made Britain prouder of her Empire
- the British wished to stop the colonists moving west/colonists eager to push west.

Context 6: 'This Accursed Trade': The British Slave Trade and its Abolition, 1770–1807

14. The candidate explains why slave resistance on the plantations was mainly unsuccessful by referring to evidence such as:
    - the slaves had no weapons
    - the slaves had no leaders
    - the slaves didn't think they could succeed
    - the slaves were brainwashed to obey
    - the white masters were united
    - punishments were very severe
    - the fear of being separated from their families by being sold off
    - most West Indian Islands are quite small and made hiding and planning difficult
    - some successes however eg Haiti.

Context 7: Citizens! The French Revolution, 1789–1794

15. The candidate explains why the Terror gave Robespierre complete control of France by referring to evidence such as:
    - freedom of speech and demonstrations were curtailed
    - opponents of the Jacobins were labelled as 'traitors' to France
    - the Terror enabled Robespierre to defeat his enemies very quickly
    - opponents could be persecuted by lists under the Law of Suspects
    - trials and executions were quick and uncontested
    - accused were not entitled to lawyers or right of appeal
    - accusation meant the assumption of guilt in vast majority of cases
    - death was the only sanction available to the Revolutionary Tribunals
    - revolts in the Vendee and other provinces were put down with great brutality
    - the Terror gave Robespierre control of all French cities
    - economic measures, such as wage cuts, could be enforced.

Context 8: Cavour, Garibaldi and the Making of Italy, 1815–1870

16. The candidate explains why Italian unification had not been achieved by 1850 by referring to evidence such as:
    - Congress of Vienna 1815 restored autocratic leaders of the Italian states
    - Italian states were under Austrian domination
    - role of Metternich in controlling nationalism eg risings of 1830
    - ineffectiveness of nationalist organisations, especially the Carbonari
    - population of the Italian states were largely indifferent to nationalism
    - divisions within the nationalist cause
    - failure of the revolutions of 1848.

Context 9: Iron and Blood? Bismarck and The Creation of the German Empire, 1815–1871

17. The candidate explains why there was a growth of German nationalism between 1815 and 1850 by referring to evidence such as:
    - influence of Napoleon's creation of a Confederation of the Rhine
    - effects of common language and culture eg German music, literature
    - enthusiasm of students who would become future leaders
    - growth of Zollverein which increased economic unity
    - improved transport and communication
    - outbreak of revolution in 1848
    - decline of Austria leading to reduced influence over German states
    - weakness of the Bund as Prussian influence increased.

Context 10: The Red Flag: Lenin and the Russian Revolution, 1894–1921

18. The candidate explains why there was a revolution in Russia in January 1905 by referring to evidence such as:
    - economic problems during the war with Japan
    - feeling that the people and their problems were being ignored
    - social problems of the people of Russia in cities and countryside due to effects of war
    - public anger over the defeats by Japan
    - aftermath of Bloody Sunday – public opinion
    - counterproductive effects of Tsar's repression
    - workers and liberal middle classes united against Tsar.

Context 11: Free at Last? Race Relations in the USA, 1918–1968

19. The candidate explains why a civil rights movement grew in the USA in the 1950s and 1960s by referring to evidence such as:
    - existence of Jim Crow laws in southern states
    - existence of segregation – examples such as schools, waiting rooms
    - concern at inequalities of Black Americans eg extreme poverty, poor housing
    - refusal of southern states to desegregate eg Brown v Topeka
    - success of the bus boycott in Montgomery
    - leadership of Martin Luther King eg 'I have a dream' speech
    - the belief that a non-violent campaign would succeed
    - reaction of groups like the Ku Klux Klan
    - growing support from Whites eg students and groups like CORE.

Context 12: The Road to War, 1933–1939

20. The candidate explains why Germany's neighbours felt threatened by Hitler's foreign policy by referring to evidence such as:
    - Nazi ideas on racial superiority – the idea of Master Race justified the policies of Lebensraum and Greater Germany
    - withdrawal from the League of Nations was seen as unfriendly
    - breaking the Treaty of Versailles might lead to conflict
    - Germany's decision to rearm increased tension in Europe, especially France
    - the aim of a Greater Germany was a threat to countries with German minorities
    - the policy of Lebensraum was a threat to eastern Europe, especially Russia
    - the reoccupation of the Rhineland made France and Belgium feel less secure
    - Austria was annexed after being invaded
    - the breaking of treaties eg Locarno increased tension.

Context 13: In the Shadow of the Bomb: The Cold War, 1945-1985

21. The candidate explains why views on the Vietnam War changed in the United States by referring to evidence such as:
    - the growing number of American casualties
    - the horror of the war itself was relayed to the world on television
    - demoralising effect on the American people by the media coverage of the war
    - the draining of funds that prevented domestic improvements the President had promised
    - growing criticism from abroad
    - more and more people felt that the USA could not win the war

- the unpleasant racial overtones of the war – Oriental life was cheap
- protestors increased first among students then professional classes/intellectual opposition to the war
- growing opposition in Congress
- lack of support from foreign governments.

PART 2: HISTORICAL STUDY

Scottish and British

Context 1: Murder in the Cathedral: Crown, Church and People, 1154–1173

1. The candidate explains why Henry II had to reform the legal system when he became king by referring to evidence such as:

   from the source
   - Henry needed to regain control of his country
   - barons had set up their own law courts
   - sheriffs had become corrupt
   - needed to remove barons' armies.

   from recall
   - barons were stealing land from one another and many were getting richer
   - barons had built castles illegally to protect the land they stole
   - barons were keeping fines paid by convicted criminals and not giving them to the king
   - the Church had gained more power and its clergy were not tried in the king's court if they were suspected of a crime.

2. The candidate describes the use of castles by referring to evidence such as:
   - castles were used to defend and protect the Lord's lands and the people who lived on them
   - castles were a symbol of power and showed how important the lord or baron was
   - castles were used as administrative centres and controlled all the business for the local village
   - castles were used as store rooms. Peasants' taxes would be paid in produce and this was often stored in the grounds of the castle
   - castles were centres of entertainment eg feasts and banquets
   - castles were used as barracks for soldiers
   - castles were used as courts of law.

3. The candidate evaluates the usefulness of the source by referring to evidence such as:
   - contemporary/primary source written during the twelfth century at the time of monasticism
   - author was an Abbot and actually lived in a monastery. He had first hand experience of monastic life
   - purpose: to show what life was like for a medieval monk
   - content: a monk ate simple food/no moment of idleness

   Maximum of one mark for commenting on content omission such as:
   - monks took a vow of chastity, poverty and obedience
   - monks worked the land, looked after the sick, educated local children.

Context 2: Wallace, Bruce and The Wars of Independence, 1286–1328

1. The candidate evaluates the usefulness of the source by referring to evidence such as:
   - primary source written at the time of the Maid's death
   - author was the Bishop of St Andrews so he would be well informed
   - purpose: to inform Edward of events as they were happening
   - content: indicates the uncertainty that there was at the time about the Maid's health.

Maximum of one mark for commenting on content omission such as:
- Robert Bruce's supporters were gathering their armies and threatening civil war.

2. The candidate describes what happened at the Battle of Falkirk in 1298 by referring to evidence such as:
   - Wallace gathered his army between a loch and forested hills
   - Wallace positioned his men in schiltrons
   - King Edward's first attack on the schiltrons was unsuccessful
   - the Scottish cavalry (knights) fled when Edward advanced
   - King Edward's men massacred the Scottish archers
   - English archers fired into the Scottish schiltrons and killed many men
   - Edward's men then killed the survivors in the Scottish schiltrons
   - the Scots were heavily defeated.

3. The candidate explains why the Scots had recognised King Edward's authority by 1305 by referring to evidence such as:

   from the source
   - Edward invaded and made an armed progress through Scotland
   - Edward stayed in Scotland over the winter of 1303–4
   - Edward punished the Scottish nobles by fines or exile
   - Edward executed only one person.

   from recall
   - Edward captured Stirling Castle
   - Edward travelled to the north of Scotland which demoralised the Scots
   - Edward's long stay also demoralised the Scots
   - Edward was reasonably lenient in his fines and punishments which won the Scots over
   - Edward executed Wallace
   - Edward issued an Ordinance sharing power between the Scots and the English.

Context 3: Mary, Queen of Scots and the Scottish Reformation, 1540s–1587

1. The candidate explains why Scottish Protestants rebelled against Mary of Guise in 1559 by referring to evidence such as:

   from the source
   - Mary, Queen of Scots being Queen of France worried the Protestant Scottish nobles
   - Scotland was controlled by a French Regent
   - Mary of Guise was using more French officials and soldiers
   - Mary of Guise took action against Scottish Protestants.

   from recall
   - the marriage treaty said that Scotland was to become part of France
   - the Protestants wanted to defend their religion against Mary of Guise
   - the Protestants were encouraged by Queen Elizabeth
   - the Protestants were encouraged by John Knox.

2. The candidate evaluates the usefulness of the source by referring to evidence such as:
   - primary source written in the exact year
   - Mary's own orders so they reflect her support
   - purpose: to ensure that ministers were paid
   - content: £10,000 was to be used to pay ministers.

   Maximum of one mark for commenting on content omission such as:
   - Mary remained a Roman Catholic
   - Mary wanted support from the Church at a difficult time in her reign

3. The candidate describes the events which led to Mary, Queen of Scots being made a prisoner in Loch Leven Castle by referring to evidence such as:
   - Mary was blamed by many for the death of Darnley

- Mary had allowed the trial of Bothwell to be disrupted
- Mary had married Bothwell
- people thought that Mary wanted Darnley dead so she could marry his killer
- Scottish nobles (mainly Protestant) rebelled against Mary
- Mary had surrendered to the rebels at Carberry.

Context 4: The Coming of the Civil War, 1603–1642

1. The candidate evaluates the usefulness of the source by referring to evidence such as:
   - primary source produced by Parliament during the breakdown of good relations with the king
   - biased account produced by Parliament against the king
   - purpose: to highlight and curb abuses of royal prerogative
   - content: shows key areas of dispute between Crown and Parliament eg taking forced loans without Parliament's consent.

   Maximum of one mark for commenting on content omission such as:
   - religious grounds of dispute between Crown and Parliament.

2. The candidate explains why Charles I encountered difficulties with the Presbyterians in Scotland by referring to evidence such as:

   from the source:
   - coronation service employed Anglican forms
   - clergy in Scotland were told to wear Anglican surplices
   - General Assembly was in abeyance
   - presbyteries were threatened with dissolution.

   from recall:
   - Charles attempted to force a revised version of the Prayer Book on Scotland
   - bishops were to be introduced into the Scottish Church
   - Charles's policy of Anglicisation provoked the signing of the National Covenant.

3. The candidate describes the main activities of the Long Parliament against the king from 1640 until the outbreak of war in 1642 by referring to evidence such as:
   - impeachment of Strafford and Laud
   - passing of Triennial Act ensuring regular parliaments even without the king's consent
   - Act forbidding dissolution of the Long Parliament without its own consent
   - Tonnage and Poundage were forbidden to be levied without Parliament's consent
   - Ship Money was declared illegal
   - abolition of prerogative courts such as Star Chamber
   - Grand Remonstrance adopted.

Context 5: 'Ane End of Ane Auld Sang': Scotland and The Treaty of Union, 1690s–1715

1. The candidate explains why many Scots opposed the Union of 1707 by referring to evidence such as:

   from the source
   - they argued that Scotland would become poorer than ever
   - they felt that Scots MPs would spend all the country's money in London
   - they felt MPs would take too much money to England
   - they felt that Scottish nobles would move to London permanently
   - they felt Scottish industries would be ruined.

   from recall
   - they did not want to give up their independence
   - they did not want to lose the Scottish Parliament
   - they felt their religion was threatened
   - they felt England's interests would overwhelm Scotland.

2. The candidate evaluates the usefulness of the source by referring to evidence such as:

- primary source written at the time union was being debated
- written by a member of the government who knew about the bribes
- purpose: to try to keep information about the bribes confidential
- content: names several of the nobles who were bribed/considerable amounts were paid to some nobles.

Maximum of one mark for commenting on content omission such as:
- other forms of bribery were used eg titles, jobs.

3. The candidate describes the events that led to the Jacobite Rising of 1715 by referring to evidence such as:
   - James VII had been deposed in 1689 and replaced by William and Mary and then Queen Anne
   - the Act of Union was unpopular and the Jacobites promised to repeal it
   - the Act of Succession angered Jacobites who did not want a Hanoverian Succession
   - the succession of George I in 1714 angered the Jacobites
   - the Earl of Mar joined the Jacobites when King George I ignored him
   - indications of support for the Jacobites from France.

Context 6: Immigrants and Exiles: Scotland, 1830s–1930s

1. The candidate explains why many Irish people came to Scotland in the nineteenth century by referring to evidence such as:

   from the source
   - places like Ayrshire were close to Ireland
   - cheap fares were available to Glasgow
   - work was available in factories such as Dundee jute mills
   - some Irish folk only came for temporary farm work and returned to Ireland.

   from recall
   - wages were higher in Scotland
   - housing was available in growing towns and cities
   - poverty of Irish tenants encouraged them to leave home
   - many relatives and friends had settled in Scotland
   - potato famine of the 1840s.

2. The candidate evaluates the usefulness of the source by referring to evidence such as:
   - primary source from 1836 when many Irish immigrants were coming to Scotland
   - author is a Glasgow manufacturer who would employ many Irish
   - purpose: to defend the Irish: they arrived as decent people
   - content: their behaviour deteriorated as a result of mixing with Scots.

   Maximum of one mark for commenting on content omission such as:
   - most Scots had the opposite opinion
   - many Scots thought the Irish stole their jobs.

3. The candidate describes the ways Scottish immigrants helped develop countries where they settled by referring to evidence such as:
   - helped to develop farming in Canada, Australia, New Zealand
   - reputation for industry and hard work
   - contribution to education
   - exploration of new countries
   - developed businesses, banks and trading companies
   - reference to individuals eg Donald Mackay (Boston shipyards); Carnegie (steel)
   - held important government positions eg Governor-General of Canada.
   - Scottish customs changed the culture of the new homeland.

Context 7: (a) From the Cradle to the Grave?
Social Welfare in Britain, 1890s–1951

1. The candidate evaluates the usefulness of the source by referring to evidence such as:
   - primary source from late 19th century when poverty was extensive
   - author was campaigner against poverty so possible bias/eyewitness account
   - purpose: to show the dreadful conditions people were living in/to encourage reform
   - content: several examples of poverty eg man with smallpox.
   Maximum of one mark for commenting on content omission such as:
   - only one study of poverty; others came from Booth and Rowntree
   - only London referred to.

2. The candidate describes how the Second World War changed people's attitude to poverty by referring to evidence such as:
   - evacuation led to increasing awareness of problems of inner-city deprivation
   - houses destroyed; sharing shelters/temporary accommodation
   - greater sense of 'community' was created
   - food rationing caused rich and poor to share more equally
   - Beveridge Report was published encouraging the demand for reform
   - social welfare reforms came during war eg provision of free milk and vitamins
   - suffering created a determination to deal with welfare problems when the war ended
   - the government became more involved in all areas of peoples lives
   - conscription broke down attitudes/common experiences

3. The candidate explains why Labour welfare reforms were thought to be a great success by referring to evidence such as:
   from the source:
   - everyone was given help from the cradle to the grave
   - free medical care was given to all
   - 200,000 homes a year were built between 1948–51
   - ambitious school building programme was started.
   from recall:
   - huge improvement in health of people/free spectacles, false teeth, prescriptions
   - policy of full employment was promoted
   - nationalisation of industries helped full employment
   - real progress in housing despite shortages of materials and labour
   - attempted to deal with the 'five giants' identified by Beveridge.

Context 7: (b) Campaigning for Change: Social Change in Scotland, 1900s–1979

1. The candidate explains why some people feared that revolution was breaking out on Clydeside by referring to evidence such as:
   from the source:
   - there was a wave of working class protest
   - suspicion that some wanted to copy the Bolshevik revolution
   - there was a great deal of political unrest
   - there was a call for a Scottish Workers' Republic.
   from recall:
   - 40,000 workers went on strike
   - huge demonstration in Glasgow turned into a riot
   - troops and tanks were ordered to Clydeside.

2. The candidate evaluates the usefulness of the source by referring to evidence such as:
   - primary source from the period when radio was popular
   - author is an eyewitness/has first hand knowledge
   - purpose: to show how important radio was for people as they were willing to pay a lot of money
   - content: repairman was regarded with respect 'like doctor'

Maximum of one mark for commenting on content omission such as:
- almost every home had a radio set
- other forms of entertainment, such as the cinema, rivalled radio.

3. The candidate describes changes in Scottish industry after 1945 by referring to evidence such as:
   - decline of Scottish shipbuilding industry from 1950s onwards
   - decline of mining and steel industries because of this
   - decline in textile industry
   - discovery of North Sea oil rejuvenated industry eg oil rig building
   - new industries such as light engineering and computing
   - growth in service industries such as teaching and NHS
   - growth in banking and financial services, especially in Edinburgh.

Context 8: A Time of Troubles: Ireland, 1900–1923

1. The candidate explains why support for Sinn Fein increased between 1916 and 1918 by referring to evidence such as:
   from the source
   - De Valera reorganised Sinn Fein
   - Sinn Fein became leading Irish party
   - public began to view Sinn Fein as main opposition to British.
   from recall
   - execution of rebel leaders in the Easter Rising caused resentment against the British
   - Sinn Fein opposed the war eg organised strikes against conscription
   - Sinn Fein's tactics were supported by the Catholic Church
   - De Valera's leadership encouraged support.

2. The candidate describes the terms of the Anglo-Irish Treaty by referring to evidence such as:
   - Ireland was to be given the same legal status within the British Commonwealth as Canada, Australia/known as Irish Free State
   - the British king was to be represented in Ireland by a Governor-General
   - all members of the Dail were to swear an oath of allegiance to the British king
   - Britain would still use three Irish ports for the Royal Navy
   - a Boundary Commission was set up to decide the exact boundary between Northern Ireland and the Irish Free State
   - a Council of Ireland was to be set up if and when Northern Ireland decided to join the Irish Free State.

3. The candidate evaluates the usefulness of the source by referring to evidence such as:
   - primary source written at the time of partition in Ireland
   - author was in a position of authority at the time and knew what was happening in Ireland. No bias
   - purpose: to alert authorities of concerns over violence in Ireland
   - content: detail of the source eg 'No-one obeys the law'.
   Maximum of one mark for commenting on content omission such as:
   - special powers act introduced by Dail.

PART 3: HISTORICAL STUDY

European and World

Context 1: The Norman Conquest, 1060–1153

1. The candidate explains why King Harold lost the Battle of Hastings by referring to evidence such as:
   from the source
   - Harold was rash in moving south to meet William
   - Harold did not have all his men available to him

- the English broke their own battle-line
- the English mistakenly thought the Normans were retreating.

from recall

- Harold's men were tired by their forced march from the north
- William's landing took the English by surprise
- Normans pretended to retreat and the English broke the shield wall to chase them
- Harold's death in the battle demoralised the English.

2. The candidate describes William I's methods of controlling England after 1066 by referring to evidence such as:

- severe taxation was applied
- Harrying of the North following rebellion there
- replacing Saxon lords killed at Hastings with Norman barons
- creation of royal castles to control the countryside
- Tower of London built to intimidate the capital
- creation of royal feudal army
- enforcing feudal obligations of knight-service on nobles
- set up Norman-dominated Royal Council of nobles to advise the king
- Domesday Book used to increase king's control.

3. The candidate makes an accurate comparison of the sources by referring to evidence such as:

The sources mainly disagree:

Source B	Source C
primary source written near time of the Conquest by a medieval chronicler	secondary source written by a modern historian with the benefit of hindsight
castles meant the English could only put up weak resistance	knocking out the Anglo-Saxons in battle was more important than castle-building
castles meant men suffered great oppression and much injustice.	castles were only symbols of lordship and not weapons of conquest

But agree:

Source B	Source C
castles were hardly known in England	the building of castles was a new technical idea

Context 2: The Cross and the Crescent: The First Crusade, 1096–1125

1. The candidate explains why people joined the First Crusade by referring to evidence such as:

from the source

- wanted to serve God
- believed it was their duty to help Christians in the east
- famine and plague meant people wanted to leave Europe
- recapturing Jerusalem was an attractive idea.

from recall

- many peasants were influenced by preachers like Peter the Hermit
- the Church promised that sins would be forgiven if the journey to Jerusalem was undertaken
- some people wanted to avoid paying their debts which were suspended whilst people were on crusade
- motivated by religious zeal eg Raymond of Toulouse
- motivated by economic reasons, desire for land eg Bohemond/Baldwin
- desire for adventure and opportunity to use military skills eg Tancred
- on crusade because of peer pressure eg Hugh of Vermandois.

2. The candidate makes an accurate comparison of the sources by referring to evidence such as:

The sources mainly disagree:

Source B	Source C
author travelled with Bohemond, biased in favour of him	author was Alexius's daughter and disliked Bohemond, biased against him
Alexius feared Bohemond	Alexius did not trust Bohemond
Alexius tried to trick Bohemond but his plan failed	Bohemond tried to trick Alexius but his plan failed

But agree:

Source B	Source C
Alexius insisted Bohemond take an oath of loyalty	Alexius insisted Bohemond take an oath of loyalty

3. The candidate describes the problems faced by the Crusaders after the capture of Jerusalem by referring to evidence such as:

- only a small number of knights remained in Jerusalem to protect it/most knights had returned home having fulfilled their vow or had been killed
- the Crusaders were surrounded by hostile Muslim neighbours
- after the death of Baldwin the Crusaders lost land to the Muslims
- due to these defeats the Crusaders had to make treaties with the Muslims – this upset new Crusaders who were arriving from the west
- the Crusaders did not have the appropriate supplies needed to sustain their lives in the east/Italian merchants had to be invited to settle in the east in return for furs, timber, woollen cloths
- there were no Christian peasants in the east so the establishment of the feudal system was under threat
- Crusaders had to negotiate with Muslim peasants so that they could get them to farm the land
- castles had to be built to protect the Latin states/knights such as the Templars and Hospitallers had to stay in the east to protect Jerusalem.

Context 3: War, Death and Revolt in Medieval Europe, 1328–1436

1. The candidate explains why England was preparing for war with France by 1337 by referring to evidence such as:

from the source

- Edward III wanted to extend his lands in France
- Edward III claimed he was rightful King of France
- The French denied that Edward had a legitimate claim to the throne
- English anger at French interference with Flemish trade.

from recall

- French claims to overlordship of English possessions in France
- English reaction to continuance of French alliance with Scotland
- English anger at the activities of French pirates
- King Philip declared Edward's lands in France forfeit
- King Philip invaded Gascony.

2. The candidate makes an accurate comparison of the sources by referring to evidence such as:

The sources agree:

Source B	Source C
Black Death led to a lack of shepherds/farm workers	Black Death led to a shortage of labour/peasants
livestock perished	farm animals died
no-one could be hired for less than 4 pennies plus meals	Lords forced to pay more/wages rose

3. The candidate describes Henry V's campaign in France between 1415 and 1420 by referring to evidence such as:
   - sailed to France in the spring of 1415
   - successful siege of Harfleur
   - turned his army towards Calais
   - large French force blocked his path
   - defeated the French at Agincourt
   - marched into Normandy
   - attacked Rouen
   - made peace in 1420 under Treaty of Troyes

Context 4: New Worlds: Europe in The Age of Expansion, 1480s–1530s

1. The candidate describes Columbus's first voyage to the New World by referring to evidence such as:
   - expedition was sponsored by Ferdinand and Isabella of Spain
   - set sail from Palos in Spain
   - expedition consisted of three ships, the Santa Maria, the Pinta and the Niña
   - put in at the Canary Islands for repairs and supplies
   - crew threatened mutiny because they had sailed so far west out of sight of land
   - San Salvador in the Bahamas group was their landfall
   - the Santa Maria was lost during the expedition.

2. The candidate makes an accurate comparison of the sources by referring to evidence such as:

The sources agree:

Source A	Source B
primary source from map-maker enabling voyages to take place	primary source from leading patron who helped voyages occur
Columbus had great desire to explore	Magellan's greatest desire is to discover new lands
a map is sent to show Columbus the route	the king says he has seen maps of the journey
spices are the object of the voyage	spices are to be found/ordered to seek out spices

3. The candidate explains why the native peoples of the New World were unable to defeat the Spanish Conquistadors by referring to evidence such as:
   from the source:
   - Spanish artillery and musketeers did much damage
   - Spanish sword-play forced the enemy back
   - skilful cavalrymen of the Spanish were their greatest asset
   - Spanish maintained their battle formation.
   from recall:
   - native peoples lacked guns and gunpowder
   - native peoples did not unite against the Spanish
   - native peoples had no horses and therefore no cavalry
   - native peoples had no metal armour.

Context 5: 'Tea and Freedom': The American Revolution, 1763–1783

1. The candidate describes the events in Boston in 1770 by referring to evidence such as:
   - the introduction of British troops in Boston made a clash inevitable
   - it was a riot between British soldiers and Boston citizens
   - a crowd of 60 townspeople surrounded British sentries guarding the customs house
   - soldiers were jeered and taunted, snowballs were thrown at the sentries
   - a shot rang out, followed by several others
   - eleven colonists were hit and five were killed
   - Crispus Attucks, a former slave, was one of the dead
   - at the trial the soldiers were defended by John Adams, cousin of Sam Adams
   - the soldiers were acquitted.

2. The candidate makes an accurate comparison of the sources by referring to evidence such as:

The sources mainly disagree:

Source A	Source B
George III, King of Britain, defends British rule	Tom Paine criticises British rule
Britain helped these colonies become successful	America would have flourished had no European nation taken notice of her
Britain has established the colonies with great care	Britain's actions are not out of concern but for trade and power

But agree:

Source A	Source B
the British have protected and defended the colonies at great cost	she has defended the American continent at not only her own expense but also that of the colonists

3. The candidate explains why French support was important to the colonists by referring to evidence such as:
   from the source:
   - lent the American government money to keep the war going
   - army equipped and supplied by the French
   - the majority of Washington's army at Yorktown were French
   - the French navy trapped Cornwallis's soldiers in Yorktown.
   from recall:
   - the French sent arms, ammunition and clothing
   - French navy denied Britain command of the seas/disrupted communications and supplies
   - the French spread the war to other British colonies therefore diverting British navy's attention from the American colonies
   - increased activity by the French played a large part in Britain seeking peace in 1783.

Context 6: 'This Accursed Trade': The British Slave Trade and its Abolition, 1770–1807

1. The candidate describes the ways Britain profited from the slave trade by referring to evidence such as:
   - growth of major ports and cities: Liverpool, Bristol and London
   - government income increased dramatically as a result of the trade
   - huge fortunes were made by individuals eg planters
   - provided employment for many people
   - banks and finance houses grew rich

- British sailors were kept in work by the slave trade
- industry developed/Manchester grew into a large city of mills making cloth from slave grown cotton
- canals were built as a result of money coming from the trade
- financed Britain's industrial revolution.

2. The candidate makes an accurate comparison of the sources by referring to evidence such as:
   The sources mainly agree:

Source A	Source B
Atlantic slave trade was a terrible ordeal for Africans	Atlantic slave trade spelled disaster for Africa's people
for four centuries millions of healthy Africans were torn from their homeland	for four hundred years millions of the healthiest young people were stolen from their homeland
no way to work out how many people perished	no-one is exactly sure how many were sold into slavery

But disagree:

Source A	Source B
about 10 million survived the Middle Passage	11 million arrived in the New World

3. The candidate explains why it took so long to persuade parliament to abolish the slave trade by referring to evidence such as:
   from the source:
   - the supporters were well organised and influential
   - some of the plantation owners were MPs
   - they had the support of the king
   - supporters of the trade created many difficulties.
   from recall:
   - many people believed the Abolitionists had exaggerated their claims
   - many people such as ship owners, bankers and manufacturers believed the slave trade had made Britain wealthy and prosperous
   - the French Revolutionary Wars had delayed the abolition
   - the trade provided much needed money to finance the wars.

Context 7: Citizens! The French Revolution, 1789–1794

1. The candidate describes the problems faced by Louis XVI's government by referring to evidence such as:
   - the government was deeply in debt and almost bankrupt
   - the government had to borrow money at high rates of interest
   - tax gathering was very inefficient
   - government officials often bought their posts and were very inefficient
   - the nobility and Church were unwilling to pay taxes
   - there was increased opposition from the *parlements* concerning taxation.

2. The candidate makes an accurate comparison of the sources by referring to evidence such as:
   The sources agree:

Source A	Source B
the soil is barren	the land is unproductive
they are heavily burdened by feudal dues/find a way to relieve our poverty	our burdens should be lightened
the landlords pay no taxes	all citizens should pay taxes
they don't understand what they are paying for	they should be told what happens to taxes

3. The candidate explains why many French people were disappointed in the revolution by referring to evidence such as:
   from the source:
   - the revolution seemed to be a victory only for the middle class
   - aristocracy were to be compensated for loss of feudal rights
   - it was difficult for poor peasants to buy Church lands
   - workshops for the unemployed were closed.
   from recall:
   - only the bourgeoisie could vote
   - only the very well off could elect members of the Assembly
   - most working men and artisans were declared 'passive citizens'
   - only 'active citizens' could join the National Guard.

Context 8: Cavour, Garibaldi and The Making of Italy 1815–1870

1. The candidate makes an accurate comparison of the sources by referring to evidence such as:
   The sources mainly agree:

Source A	Source B
Austria lost the friendship of Russia	Austria lost her great ally – Russia
Austria was isolated	Austria was now isolated diplomatically
Austria could not expect help from Britain and France when it came to controlling the Italian states	Neither France nor Britain would be sympathetic to maintaining Austrian power in northern Italy

2. The candidate explains why Guiseppe Mazzini was important to Italian unification by referring to evidence such as:
   from the source:
   - did much to publicise the aim of unification
   - active member of the Carbonari
   - formed Young Italy
   - spent most of his life plotting against the rulers of Italian states.
   from recall:
   - played prominent role in Roman republic of 1849
   - edited prominent nationalist journal – 'La Giovine Italia' (Young Italy)
   - inspirational leader, eg during the Roman Republic
   - Mazzini inspired important nationalists – especially Garibaldi.

3. The candidate describes the contribution of Guiseppe Garibaldi to Italian unification by referring to evidence such as:
   - Garibaldi inspired Italians with his actions eg Roman Republic 1849
   - he was a successful military leader who inspired the Red Shirts to victories – often against stronger opponents
   - his role in the southern campaign when unification movement had stalled in 1859
   - conquest of Sicily
   - he won the support of peasants in Sicily and Naples
   - his role in the conquest of Naples
   - he handed over the south to King Victor Emmanuel at Teano.

Context 9: Iron and Blood? Bismarck and The Creation of the German Empire, 1815–1871

1. The candidate describes the 1848 Revolution in Germany by referring to evidence such as:
   - demonstrations in Berlin in March 1848
   - king used force against demonstrations
   - revolutionaries built barricades
   - Frederick William changed his mind and agreed to call a National Assembly

- formation of Frankfurt Parliament
- refusal of Frederick William to accept invitation to become king
- failure of Frankfurt Parliament.

2. The candidate makes an accurate comparison of the sources by referring to evidence such as:
The sources mainly agree:

Source A	Source B
Prussian leaders prepared carefully	Bismarck's leadership was crucial
we ensured the support of other countries	agreements were made with France and Italy before the war
no land was to be taken by Prussia from Austria	not a bit of territory should be annexed by Prussia from Austria
Austria was forced to give up her control over the north German states	Prussia gained supremacy over the north German states

3. The candidate explains the growing hostility between Prussia and France between 1868 and 1870 by referring to evidence such as:
from the source:
- France believed that a Hohenzollern King on the Spanish throne would alter the balance of power to her disadvantage
- announcement of Hohenzollern candidature was greeted with hostility in Paris
- French government demanded that Hohenzollerns would never again claim the Spanish throne
- Prussian king refused to give such a guarantee.
from recall:
- French pressure forced Leopold to withdraw his candidature
- Bismarck altered King Wilhelm's account of his meeting with the French to make it more insulting to France (Ems Telegram)
- Publication of Ems Telegram caused outrage against Prussia in France
- Napoleon III felt he had no alternative but to declare war on Prussia.

Context 10: The Red Flag: Lenin and the Russian Revolution, 1894–1921

1. The candidate describes the methods used by the Tsar to maintain his control over Russia before 1914 by referring to evidence such as:
- the use of secret police to spy on cities
- the nature of government bureaucracy
- use of the army to control demonstrations
- control and use of the Orthodox Church to keep peasants obedient
- used control over Dumas to limit reform granted
- use of executions and exile of opponents

2. The candidate makes an accurate comparison of the sources by referring to evidence such as:
The sources disagree:

Source A	Source B
trouble comes from a few idlers	discontent is general and on the increase
stories of shooting in the streets are all lies	there is wild shooting in the streets
transport workers are on strike	transport system has broken down
people still worship the Tsar – no sign of revolution	urgent need to change government – people do not trust the existing government

3. The candidate explains the victory of the Red Army in the Civil War by referring to evidence such as:
from the source:
- had good commanders who were experienced fighters
- inclusion of communists who would make any sacrifice for the revolution
- soldiers were well supplied (boots, food, tobacco)
- energetic propaganda campaign.
from recall:
- Trotsky and Lenin were great leaders who could be ruthless when required
- Red Army had good communications
- Reds controlled industrial areas which gave them good access to supplies
- peasants were afraid that if the Whites won they would lose their land
- White armies were divided/did not always act together.

Context 11: Free at Last? Race Relations in the USA, 1918–1968

1. The candidate makes an accurate comparison of the sources by referring to evidence such as:
The sources agree:

Source A	Source B
immigrants being problems – crooks, kidnappers	foreigners were ruining our country
a menace and danger to us everyday	anything foreign is un-American and a menace
thousands come here	Americans believed they were in danger of being overrun
pay allegiance to another country and flag/do not respect what our flag represents	(Klan) use of American flag and slogans

2. The candidate describes the events of the Montgomery bus boycott by referring to evidence such as:
- Rosa Parks refused to move seats on the bus
- Rosa Parks was arrested and fined
- black population refused to use city buses
- people walked to work or organised car pools
- established Martin Luther King as a civil rights leader
- bus company faced bankruptcy
- after a year courts decided segregation on buses was unconstitutional.

3. The candidate explains why the Black Panthers gained support from many Black Americans by referring to evidence such as:
from the source:
- Black Panthers argued it was time to defend Black Americans from white aggression
- Blacks distrusted the police and had no faith in them
- Black Panthers organised self-help programmes
- Black Panthers had a ten-point programme demanding freedom and release of Black prisoners.
from recall:
- Black Panthers condoned use of violence
- had programmes to give free breakfasts to children and free health clinics
- Black Panthers attracted support from sportsmen eg Olympic salute.

Context 12: The Road to War, 1933-1939

1. The candidate explains why the reoccupation of the Rhineland was important for Hitler by referring to evidence such as:
from the source:
- Germany scored an important victory without force

- Hitler was held in greater respect abroad
- France's eastern allies saw Germany as stronger
- Belgium became neutral.

from recall:
- Hitler made progress towards one of his key aims, undoing the Treaty of Versailles.
- Hitler's popularity was greatly increased at home
- Germany could now station troops in the Rhineland
- France lost control of the Rhine bridges
- France could no longer launch an attack through the Rhineland

2. The candidate describes the events of the Czechoslovakian crisis leading to the Munich Settlement by referring to evidence such as:
- Hitler ordered an attack on Czechoslovakia in May 1938 (Operation Green)
- Britain and France warned Germany off – the 'May Crisis'
- Runciman mission failed to persuade Czechoslovakia to surrender Sudetenland to Germany
- Hitler and Chamberlain met after a further threat to attack Czechoslovakia
- agreement was reached, but war became likely after demands at second meeting – 'Black Wednesday'
- third meeting: UK, France, Germany and Italy at Munich
- Czechoslovakia was pressurised into ceding Sudetenland to Germany.

3. The candidate makes an accurate comparison of the sources by referring to evidence such as:
The sources mainly disagree:

Source B	Source C
appeasement was a practical solution	appeasement was a surrender of principles
appeasement followed because Germany had been unfairly treated at Versailles	appeasement was due to the belief that Nazism was here to stay
the French and British did not appease because of cowardice	under Chamberlain it was a policy of cowardice and dishonour

But agree:

Source A	Source B
appeasement was a policy of preventing another terrible war	appeasement gained short term peace at someone else's expense

Context 13: In the Shadow of the Bomb: The Cold War, 1945–1985

1. The candidate describes what was meant by 'the Cold War' by referring to evidence such as:
- developed after 1945
- rivalry between the USA (and her allies) and the Soviet Union (and her allies)
- did not lead to actual armed conflict between the two superpowers – no hot war
- led to nuclear arms race
- waged by means of economic pressures, selective actions and diplomatic manoeuvres
- involved or led to a number of small wars but not involving the two superpowers fighting each other, eg Korea, Vietnam and Afghanistan
- led to a number of serious incidents, eg Berlin Crisis and the Cuban Missile Crisis
- so named as a result of the Truman doctrine in 1947.

2. The candidate makes an accurate comparison of the sources by referring to evidence such as:
The sources disagree:

Source A	Source B
American view by the US President	Soviet view by the leader of the Soviet Union
a strict quarantine	not declaring a quarantine but an ultimatum/threat
we are not denying the necessities of life as the Soviets attempted to do in Berlin	by yielding to tyranny – you are not appealing to reason: you want to intimidate us.

But agree:

Source A	Source B
America will turn back the ships	you will then use force to turn back the ships

3. The candidate explains why both sides wanted détente by the late 1960s by referring to evidence such as:
from the source:
- in the 1960s they came to the brink of nuclear war
- Brezhnev felt the economic burden of the nuclear arms race was too great
- the American economy was also in financial trouble as a result of the Vietnam war
- war and the arms race had made funding of welfare reform in USA difficult.

from recall:
- Soviet hopes for better relations with Western Europe, perhaps detaching them from the USA
- the Sino-Soviet split had caused concern in the Soviet Union
- Soviet leadership was terrified of a possible Sino-American alliance
- rough parity in nuclear arms
- a state of mutually assured destruction had been reached
- both Brezhnev and Nixon thought that it would boost their domestic popularity.

HISTORY INTERMEDIATE 2 2008

PART 1: THE SHORT ESSAY

Scottish and British

Context 1: Murder in the Cathedral: Crown, Church and People, 1154-1173

1. The candidate explains why the Church was important in the Middle Ages by referring to evidence such as:
   - provided centres of worship for communities
   - provided spiritual help for parishioners
   - Church provided guidelines on how people should live their lives
   - Church provided services eg baptism, marriage, last rites
   - Church trained local boys for a career in the priesthood
   - Church kept one third of its tithe/crops to give to the parish in times of need
   - canon law impacted on people's lives eg whom you could marry, holidays
   - Church had political power, it could excommunicate a king or place a country under interdict
   - Church had great economic power; it owned land and made a profit from this.

Context 2: Wallace, Bruce and the Wars of Independence, 1286–1328

2. The candidate explains why there was a succession problem in Scotland between 1286 and 1292 by referring to evidence such as:
   - Alexander III's sons had all died before him
   - Alexander's heir was an infant girl (the Maid of Norway)
   - some did not think a female could rule
   - the Maid of Norway died on her way to Scotland
   - many men thought that they should be the next ruler of Scotland, eg thirteen competitors
   - Bruce and Balliol thought they had a better claim to the throne than the others
   - there was a danger of a civil war in Scotland.

Context 3: Mary, Queen of Scots and the Scottish Reformation, 1540s-1587

3. The candidate explains why her marriage to Darnley caused problems for Mary Queen of Scots by referring to evidence such as:
   - the Scottish nobles disliked Darnley
   - many of Mary's ministers left her government because of Darnley (Chaseabout)
   - Queen Elizabeth did not approve of the marriage
   - Darnley did not help Mary to rule Scotland
   - Darnley humiliated Mary by his bad behaviour
   - Darnley was involved in the murder of Riccio
   - Darnley left Mary and threatened to leave Scotland
   - Darnley demanded to be made king (given the Crown Matrimonial)
   - Mary was blamed for the murder of Darnley
   - Darnley's murder led to her captivity and abdication.

Context 4: The Coming of the Civil War, 1603-1642.

4. The candidate explains the reasons why Charles I declared war on Parliament by referring to evidence such as:
   - religious disagreements with Parliament eg Puritans versus High Anglicans
   - disagreements with Parliament over money eg wars, forced loans, customs duties
   - constitutional disagreements with Parliament about his authority
   - failure of the Short Parliament 1640
   - arrest and imprisonment of Laud angered king
   - impeachment and execution of Strafford in 1641 angered king
   - Pym's Triennial Act 1641 restricted power of king
   - nineteen Propositions 1642 rejected by Charles I
   - grand Remonstrance divided Parliament.

Context 5: "Ane End of Ane Auld Sang": Scotland and the Treaty of Union, 1690s-1715

5. The candidate explains why some Scots thought a Union with England would make Scotland richer by referring to evidence such as:
   - Scots would gain entry to England's colonies
   - Scots would gain entry to England's markets
   - English capital would benefit Scottish industry
   - rivalry between English and Scottish trading companies would end (eg Company of Scotland and East India Company)
   - rivalry between the Scottish and English governments would end
   - Scotland would benefit from peace treaties at the end of wars
   - Scots would gain compensation for Darien
   - Scots would gain business opportunities in London.

Context 6: Immigrants and Exiles: Scotland, 1830s-1930s

6. The candidate explains why many Scots resented immigrants from Ireland in the nineteenth century by referring to evidence such as:
   - Scots complained the Irish took their jobs
   - cost of housing increased – competition for housing
   - religious differences – Irish immigrants were mainly Catholic
   - Irish immigrants did not mix – stayed in their own communities
   - many Irish were poor – considered inferior
   - complaints about behaviour – drunkenness, violence
   - blamed Irish for weakening traditional Scottish standards
   - employers preferred Irish – Irish depressed wages; were used as strike breakers.

Context 7 (a): From the Cradle to the Grave? Social Welfare in Britain, 1890s-1951

7. (a) The candidate explains why the Labour welfare reforms after 1945 were successful in meeting the needs of the people by referring to evidence such as:
   - National Insurance Act gave benefits from cradle to grave
   - National Insurance Act provided for the worst off in society
   - there was free health care for all with National Health Service
   - Government continued war government's education policy eg secondary education for all, leaving age 15
   - attempted massive house building scheme
   - shortage of materials meant housing targets not met
   - by 1951 charges had been introduced for some health services.

Context 7 (b): Campaigning for Change: Social Change in Scotland, 1900s-1979

(b) The candidate explains why many Scottish women were able to lead better lives in the period 1918-1939 by referring to evidence such as:
   - impact of the war in changing attitudes to women
   - women were given the right to vote and could now participate in politics
   - women could now become MP's and campaign for fairer laws for women
   - women had greater access to professions such as law, medicine and civil service

- their legal status improved as women got the same rights as men in divorce proceedings
- widows' pensions gave women greater financial security
- young women had a greater degree of personal freedom in leisure eg the Flappers of the 1920s, dance halls, cinema
- working class girls had more job opportunities eg in light industry and office work
- improved contraceptive advice often led to women avoiding 'constant pregnancy'
- labour saving devices made housework easier/increased leisure time for middle class women.

Context 8: A Time of Troubles: Ireland, 1900-1923

8. The candidate explains why the Easter Rising failed by referring to evidence such as:
   - the rebels did not have enough guns/ammunition
   - the rebels were not well organised
   - only 1,500 armed men took part, few of the leaders were trained soldiers
   - the general public were puzzled by events and indifferent to them
   - the plan to capture the centre of Dublin and Dublin castle failed
   - the British army was able to cut the city in half
   - the British army threw a military cordon around the city
   - reinforcements brought in from England, easily outnumbered the rebels
   - the British army brought in artillery and a gunboat, Helga
   - the rebels surrendered after a week: leaders were executed.

European and World

Context 1: The Norman Conquest, 1060-1153

9. The candidate explains why Anglo-Saxon opposition to William was ineffective after 1066 by referring to evidence such as:
   - Anglo-Saxons lacked a native king
   - lack of leadership because most Anglo-Saxon nobles died at Hastings
   - Anglo-Saxon opposition lacked unity
   - Anglo-Saxon opposition was weak/scattered
   - William's ruthlessness in crushing rebels eg harrying of the North
   - Norman military strength especially knights
   - Normans replaced Saxons in key positions eg among the clergy.

Context 2: The Cross and the Crescent: The First Crusade, 1096–1125

10. The candidate explains why the First Crusade was able to achieve its aims by referring to evidence such as:
    - Crusaders had effective leaders in Bohemond of Taranto and Raymond of Toulouse who were experienced knights
    - Crusaders were motivated by the crusading ideal eg visions at Antioch and Jerusalem, discovery of the Holy Lance
    - Crusaders were helped by emperor Alexius eg provided the knights with supplies at Constantinople/gave the Crusaders boats at Nicaea/supplied a regiment of soldiers
    - Crusaders used effective tactics to defeat the Muslims eg bribery at Antioch, siege towers used at Jerusalem
    - Crusaders helped by Muslim disunity. This was evident at Nicaea, Antioch and Jerusalem
    - Crusaders achieved their aim and recaptured Jerusalem
    - after the capture of Jerusalem, the Crusaders were aided by the knights Templar and built castles to protect the land they had taken
    - trade routes were established with the Italian ports to provide supplies.

Context 3: War, Death and Revolt in Medieval Europe, 1328-1436

11. The candidate explains why the French were eventually successful in the Hundred Years' War by referring to evidence such as:
    - improved tactics eg avoiding large pitched battles
    - death of Henry V meant that the English had lost a great military leader
    - succession of the infant Henry VI
    - Joan of Arc raised the siege of Orleans
    - defeat of English forces at Patay
    - Charles VII was crowned king of France at Rheims
    - Charles made peace with the Burgundians at Arras
    - English armies were forced out of Normandy and Guyenne.

Context 4: New Worlds: Europe in the Age of Expansion, 1480s-1530s

12. The candidate explains why developments in technology were important in encouraging voyages of exploration by referring to evidence such as:
    - new types of ships were developed eg carrack and caravel
    - longer and faster voyages were possible because of improvements in ship design eg lateen sails
    - sailors were able to find position/direction eg quadrants, compass, cross-staff
    - sailors were able to calculate their speed eg log-lines, hourglass
    - ships could carry more men and goods
    - improvements in cartography made it easier to find their way home.

Context 5: "Tea and Freedom": The American Revolution, 1763-1783

13. The candidate explains why some American colonists remained loyal to Britain by referring to evidence such as:
    - fear of some of the revolutionary ideas spreading
    - the monarchy was important
    - religious prejudices against New England
    - merchants feared damage to their trade
    - feared the breakdown of law and order
    - loyalists were mainly conservative and feared change
    - they believed in the importance of the Empire
    - individuals like Flora MacDonald used fellow Scots to support the King
    - some sought to win favour with the British Government.

Context 6: "This Accursed Trade": The British Slave Trade and its Abolition, 1770–1807

14. The candidate explains why many people were in favour of the Slave Trade in the eighteenth century by referring to evidence such as:
    - huge fortunes were made by merchants/ship- owners/planters
    - many people gained their livelihood from the trade
    - banks and finance expanded as a result of the trade and many grew rich
    - British sailors were kept in work by the slave trade
    - industry developed/Manchester grew into large city of mills making cloth from slave grown cotton
    - canals and railways were built as a result of money coming from the trade
    - growth of major ports and cities/Liverpool, Bristol and London.

Context 7: Citizens! The French Revolution, 1789-1794

15. The candidate explains why France became a republic in 1792 by referring to evidence such as:
    - the king came under suspicion after the attempt to escape from Paris – flight to Varennes
    - the war with Austria and Prussia made the monarchy unpopular

- Marie Antoinette was suspected of encouraging invasion
- political clubs calling for a republic became more popular – Jacobins, under Robespierre, and Cordeliers
- political clubs organised petitions to remove the monarchy
- Republicanism was popular among the sans-culottes
- the Brunswick Manifesto made the monarchy even more unpopular
- the storming of the Tuileries showed popular contempt for the monarchy
- the newly elected Convention proclaimed the French Republic in August 1792.

Context 8: Cavour, Garibaldi and the Making of Italy, 1815-1870

16. The candidate explains why Italy became a unified country by 1870 by referring to evidence such as:
    - Cavour's pact with France (Plombieres) gained support from the French army in the war against Austria
    - defeats of Austrian army at Magenta and Solferino
    - the Austrians were driven out of Lombardy
    - plebiscites in the duchies supported unification
    - Garibaldi's leadership in the campaign in Sicily and Naples
    - Garibaldi's ability to attract support of peasants in the south
    - support from Britain for Garibaldi's landing in Naples
    - meeting at Teano united north and south
    - French evacuation of Rome in 1870.

Context 9: Iron and Blood? Bismarck and The Creation of the German Empire, 1815-1871

17. The candidate explains why Prussia succeeded in uniting Germany by 1871 by referring to evidence such as:
    - restructuring of army following reforms
    - economic strength of Prussia
    - annexation of Schleswig-Holstein in 1862
    - disputes over Schleswig-Holstein gave Prussia an opportunity to wage war on Austria
    - Austria was excluded as a result of the Austro-Prussian war
    - North German Confederation was formed
    - Prussia treated Austria leniently to keep on friendly terms
    - Bismarck's diplomacy eg Ems Telegram
    - Franco-Prussian war united South German states.

Context 10: The Red Flag: Lenin and the Russian Revolution, 1894-1921

18. The candidate explains why there was discontent among Russian industrial workers in the years leading up to 1914 by referring to evidence such as:
    - harsh conditions in factories eg long hours of work, dangerous machinery
    - harsh living conditions eg barracks or slum housing
    - no rights – eg no right to form unions
    - protests were harshly dealt with – eg Bloody Sunday
    - lived in cities where they could see the better standards of living enjoyed by upper classes
    - opposition parties and Soviets stirred up discontent among industrial workers
    - many were peasants who had been forced to leave the land.

Context 11: Free at Last? Race Relations in the USA, 1918-1968

19. The candidate explains why the Ku Klux Klan was feared in the 1920s and 1930s by referring to evidence such as:
    - Klan campaigned against immigrant groups such as Jews, Catholics and Black Americans
    - Klan was a secret terrorist organisation – members wore robes and masks
    - Klan burned large crosses on hillsides to frighten people
    - they kidnapped, whipped, mutilated people if they did not do what the Klan wanted
    - Klan lynched many Black Americans
    - important members of the community such as police, judges and politicians were members of Klan
    - ability to hold marches in cities such as Washington implied a powerful organisation.

Context 12: The Road to War, 1933-1939

20. The candidate explains why Britain allowed Germany to ignore the Treaty of Versailles during the 1930s by referring to evidence such as:
    - there was a reassessment of Versailles – British opinion felt it had been too harsh
    - Britain accepted German rearmament as justified for defence especially as France had not disarmed
    - the Rhineland reoccupation was accepted as fair – "only going into his own back garden"
    - Anschluss was regarded as natural as it seemed to be what the Austrians wanted
    - Chamberlain believed that Hitler's demands were limited and that Hitler could be negotiated with
    - there was a strong pacifist movement in Britain and war was unpopular – "The bomber will always get through"
    - Chiefs of Staff warned government that Britain's forces were unprepared
    - Britain had no reliable allies – Empire unwilling, USA neutral and France unstable
    - war in Europe would open the door to communism.

Context 13: In the Shadow of the Bomb: The Cold War, 1945-1985

21. The candidate explains why a Cold War developed after the Second World War by referring to evidence such as:
    - the only thing that kept them together was over – the Second World War
    - disagreements at Potsdam eg over Poland
    - the Americans had developed the atomic bomb
    - Soviet troops were occupying most of Eastern Europe
    - Truman, the new American President was more anti-communist than Roosevelt
    - an arms race developed
    - different ideas – capitalism versus communism.

PART 2: HISTORICAL STUDY

Scottish and British

Context 1: Murder in the Cathedral: Crown, Church and People, 1154-1173

1. The candidate explains why Henry II was forced to increase his power when he became king by referring to evidence such as:

    from the source
    - castles had been built without permission
    - barons had increased their power/king's authority had been reduced
    - sheriffs decided the laws in their own areas
    - sheriffs were corrupt/could not be trusted

    from recall
    - barons had private armies/hired mercenaries
    - barons were stealing land from their weaker neighbours and increasing their power
    - barons were keeping the fines collected from criminals, instead of giving them to the king.

2. The candidate describes the role of a knight in medieval society by referring to evidence such as:
    - they were an important part of a feudal army
    - they were part of the feudal system and gave part of their land to peasants
    - they were used in local government/members of a jury

- they protected the weak, young and old in society
- they fought for the Church against non-Christians eg crusade
- their behaviour made them role models for the rest of society
- they performed services such as castle-guard for their land.

3. The candidate makes an accurate comparison of the sources by referring to evidence such as:
   The sources agree fully:

Source B	Source C
Becket refused to allow the clergy to be tried in the king's court.	Becket would not agree to the clergy being tried in the king's court.
Only God could judge the clergy	King had no authority to judge clergymen.
Henry felt betrayed by Becket's defence of the Church.	Henry expected Becket to support him and not the Church.
Henry threatened Becket.	Henry threatened and bullied Becket.

Context 2: Wallace, Bruce and the Wars of Independence, 1286-1328

1. The candidate describes what happened when Edward I attacked Berwick in 1296 by referring to evidence such as:
   - Balliol built a new fence round Berwick
   - Balliol moved men from Fife into Berwick to reinforce it
   - Edward surrounded the town by land and sea
   - Edward demanded a surrender within three days
   - the people of Berwick mocked King Edward
   - Edward's ships sailed into the harbour to be attacked and burned
   - Edward's men stormed over the walls
   - everyone in Berwick was killed.

2. The candidate makes an accurate comparison of the sources by referring to evidence such as:
   The sources largely agree:

Source A	Source B
Bruce accused Comyn of betraying him.	Bruce accused Comyn of telling Edward about him.
Comyn denied this.	Comyn said this was a lie.
Bruce hit Comyn with a sword	Comyn was stabbed.
Some evil folk told Bruce that Comyn would live.	He (Comyn) said he thought he would live.
Bruce ordered Comyn's death beside the high altar.	His enemies hit him again beside the altar.

3. The candidate explains why the Scots were able to win at the Battle of Bannockburn by referring to evidence such as:
   from the source
   - the English had no room to move/the English were surrounded by marshes and streams
   - Bruce took advantage of the English mistake
   - the English leaders struggled to organise their men for an attack
   - the English lost confidence in Edward II
   from recall
   - the English had been arguing among themselves
   - the English cavalry could not charge
   - the English bowmen were defeated by the Scots

- many English were trapped by the ditches by the Pelstream and Bannock burns.

Context 3: Mary, Queen of Scots and the Scottish Reformation, 1540s-1587

1. The candidate describes the events which forced Mary, Queen of Scots to leave Scotland in 1548 by referring to evidence such as:
   - the English wanted Mary to marry Edward, son of Henry VIII
   - the Scots broke the treaty of Greenwich and did not send Mary to England
   - English armies invaded Scotland
   - the English destroyed Scottish towns and cities
   - the English defeated the Scots at the Battle of Pinkie
   - there were fears that Mary would be captured by the English and taken to England
   - the Scots and French agreed that Mary was to marry the Dauphin.

2. The candidate explains why many Scots disliked Riccio by referring to evidence such as:
   from the source
   - Darnley blamed Riccio for Mary's refusal to make him king
   - Darnley was jealous of his friendship with Mary
   - Riccio was a low born Italian
   - some people thought Riccio was a secret agent of the Pope
   from recall
   - Riccio was dressing up like a nobleman and acting like a noble
   - Riccio was rude to the Scottish nobles
   - Riccio made the Scottish nobles plead for appointments with Mary
   - some people thought Riccio was having a love affair with Mary.

3. The candidate makes an accurate comparison of the sources by referring to evidence such as:
   The sources fully agree:

Source B	Source C
Two very wicked men were her guards.	Two evil young thugs were to guard her.
People shouted "Burn her! Drown her!".	People shouted "Burn her! Drown her!".
Shouted abuse calling her a murderer.	They insulted her.
The Queen was weeping.	The Queen allowed tears to pour down her face.

Context 4: The Coming of the Civil War, 1603-1642

1. The candidate makes an accurate comparison of the sources by referring to evidence such as:
   The sources mainly disagree/do not agree much:

Source A	Source B
Stuarts lost interest in Scotland/only cared about Scotland when they needed men and money.	The Stuarts remained vitally interested in Scottish affairs.
Stuarts only concerned with England which was richer and more powerful.	Not true to say that Scotland was neglected because England was richer/Scotland and England were much closer in size and wealth.
Scotland was governed like a distant province.	Scotland was their original power base.

But agree:

Source A	Source B
they were glad to escape from a country with its troublesome Presbyterians	They saw the Presbyterians as a threat to their authority.

2. The candidate explains why James VI and I was unpopular with Parliament between 1603 and 1625 by referring to evidence such as:

from the source
- gave money and power to his favourites at court
- spent lavishly eg coronation cost £20,000
- raised taxes without consent of Parliament
- Parliament's anger over monopolies

from recall
- King James believed in the Divine Rights of Kings
- Impositions and the 'Bates Case' 1606
- failure of the 'Great Contract' 1610
- failure of the 'Addled' Parliament
- debates with Parliament over war with Spain 1621.

3. The candidate describes the ways the Scots opposed Charles I over religion by referring to evidence such as:
- Scots resented having Bishops placed over them
- they refused to accept the new Prayer Book 1637
- Scots' riots took place eg St Giles Riot
- the National Covenant 1638 rejected the canons
- Covenanters took over Government of Scotland
- the Scots raised an army and invaded England.

Context 5: "Ane End of Ane Auld Sang": Scotland and the Treaty of Union, 1690s-1715

1. The candidate describes the events leading up to the execution of Captain Green of the Worcester in 1705 by referring to evidence such as:
- the English had seized the Annandale, the last of the Company of Scotland's ships
- the Speedy Return failed to return
- the Scots seized the Worcester and accused its crew of piracy against the Speedy Return
- the Scots found Captain Green and two of his crew guilty and sentenced them to death
- Queen Anne wanted the Scottish government to reprieve Green and his crew
- the Edinburgh mob rioted at the news
- the Scottish government allowed the execution to happen.

2. The candidate explains why Queen Anne wanted a Union between England and Scotland by referring to evidence such as:

from the source
- governing Scotland from Westminster was difficult
- Union would secure the Protestant Succession/avoid arguments about the succession
- Union would create a more powerful state
- Union would protect England from any French threat/prevent the revival of the Auld Alliance

from recall
- the Jacobites would find it more difficult to place a Jacobite monarch on the throne
- the Jacobites could separate Scotland from England
- Scotland and England had been at loggerheads eg Act of Security, Wine Act, Act anent War and Peace.

3. The candidate makes an accurate comparison of the sources by referring to evidence such as:

The sources mainly agree:

Source B	Source C
Scots were soon disillusioned because Union did not bring immediate prosperity.	Some soon became disappointed matters were unchanged.
Appeared to many Scots that politicians in London had the power to re-write the Treaty.	Significant changes were made which they thought broke the terms of the Treaty of Union.
Church of Scotland was outraged when patronage was reintroduced.	Church Patronage angered Church of Scotland ministers.
Many were angry the Malt Tax broke the treaty.	They were unhappy at the introduction of the Malt Tax which would have had serious consequences.

Context 6: Immigrants and Exiles: Scotland, 1830s-1930s

1. The candidate makes an accurate comparison of the sources by referring to evidence such as:
The sources fully agree:

Source A	Source B
Potato famine led to sharp increase in immigration.	Potato crops destroyed by blight led many to leave.
Landlords evicted those who could not pay their rent.	Many landlords used the crisis to take away people's homes.
Transport costs were cheap.	Plenty of ships, so cost was cheap.
Wages in the west of Scotland were higher than those in Ireland.	Higher wages in Scotland were attractive.

2. The candidate describes the ways Scots were encouraged to emigrate between the 1830s and 1930s by referring to evidence such as:
- advertisements extolled virtues of life overseas
- colonial governments appointed agents to tour giving talks
- landowners, especially in Highlands, were willing to help with costs
- charities such as Barnardos, Quarriers and the YMCA assisted with passage
- Government gave help after First World War to reduce level of unemployment
- 1922 Emigrant Settlement Act – money for travel, training and land purchase
- letters sent home told of better life abroad
- successful emigrants paid relatives' fares.

3. The candidate explains why many Scots emigrants, like Andrew Carnegie, became successful abroad by referring to evidence such as:

from the source
- prospered because of energy and ability
- set up new branches like the Company's sleeping car service
- had great financial skills
- invested in businesses successfully
- sold businesses for large sums of money

from recall
- Scots were imaginative and came up with new ideas
- Scots were often relatively well educated

- Scots brought skills in farming, banking, mining
- Scots were willing to venture into interior
- Scots had a reputation for hard work.

Context 7 (a): From the Cradle to the Grave? Social Welfare in Britain, 1890s-1951

1. The candidate makes an accurate comparison of the sources by referring to evidence such as:
   The sources fully agree:

Source A	Source B
Man's earnings were not enough to support himself and family.	Two-thirds were poor because of low pay or irregular earnings.
Men not able to obtain employment for economic reasons.	There was increasing unemployment.
Men could not work due to sickness.	A quarter were poor because of illness.
Bad habits, such as drinking and gambling caused problems.	Only about one-tenth were poor because of personal failings such as drunkenness or gambling.

2. The candidate describes the social reforms of the Liberal government between 1906 and 1914 by referring to evidence such as:
   - provision of school meals 1906 provided free meals for poor children
   - free medical inspections in schools were introduced in 1907
   - old age pensions were given to over 70s in 1908
   - labour exchanges helped the unemployed find work
   - National Insurance Act 1911 gave sick pay
   - National Insurance Act gave support to a limited number of trades when they were unemployed.

3. The candidate explains why the Second World War led people to expect improvements in social welfare by referring to evidence such as:
   from the source
   - Government ensured everyone had a fair share
   - Ministry of Food ensured nation's health and safe food supply
   - free medical treatment was provided for bomb victims
   - the public expected the Government to do more for them
   from recall
   - recognition of scale of poverty because of evacuation
   - bombing destroyed large amounts of housing
   - provision of milk, cod liver oil and orange juice to mothers
   - price of milk/school meals were subsidised – free food to children who needed it.

Context 7 (b): Campaigning for Change: Social Change in Scotland, 1900s-1979

1. The candidate describes the methods used by women to campaign for the vote by referring to evidence such as:
   - NUWSS led a campaign of peaceful methods
   - suffragists attempted to win the support of men to support the cause
   - they held marches and demonstrations to publicise their cause
   - they sent letters and petitions to the government to ask for the vote
   - WSPU formed in 1903 – suffragettes took more radical action
   - details of early activities such as heckling and vandalism
   - details of more extreme activities such as arson attacks
   - hunger strikes and 'Cat and Mouse' strategy.

2. The candidate makes an accurate comparison of the sources by referring to evidence such as:
   The sources mainly agree:

Source A	Source B
Cost – 2 jam jars amounted to one penny.	Cost was a penny.
Films were violent.	Plenty of fighting in films
Seating plain wooden seats.	Seating was benches/some theatres had individual seats.
It was basic and in poor condition.	It was a fleapit.

3. The candidate explains why Scotland's industries found it difficult to compete by referring to evidence such as:
   from the source
   - the railway network was out of date and road building too slow
   - factory buildings needed modernising
   - there was a shortage of skilled workers
   - there was not enough scientific and technical training to compete abroad
   from recall
   - new production techniques were not being introduced
   - lack of investment in industry
   - management was often very amateurish
   - bad labour relations – strikes in many industries, such as shipyards.

Context 8: A Time of Troubles: Ireland, 1900-1923

1. The candidate makes an accurate comparison of the sources by referring to evidence such as:
   The sources completely disagree/do not agree at all:

Source A	Source B
It's in Ireland's interests to go to war/it is your duty to fight against Germany.	Our interests lie in an independent Ireland/your duty is to fight for Ireland not for an empire we do not want to belong to.
It is not time for rebellion.	Now is the moment for rebellion.
By helping Britain we help ourselves.	We gain nothing by helping the British fight this war.
It is brave and courageous to volunteer for war.	It is foolish and misguided to volunteer for war.

2. The candidate describes the actions of both sides in the Anglo-Irish War by referring to evidence such as:
   - IRA used guerrilla tactics, attacking small groups of police or soldiers
   - IRA wore no uniform and so could disappear into the countryside and act like ordinary civilians
   - spy network was used to pass on information to the IRA
   - IRA carried out assassinations of key members of British government/army
   - Black and Tans used stop and search tactics
   - Black and Tans arrested suspects
   - Black and Tans burnt Catholic homes/areas eg centre of Cork.

3. The candidate explains why some Irish nationalists refused to accept the 1921 Treaty by referring to evidence such as:

   from the source
   - De Valera encouraged people to reject the Treaty
   - British were still in Ireland/not driven out
   - anti-treaty forces believed Ulster should not be partitioned
   - De Valera objected to the oath of allegiance to the king

   from recall
   - sacrifices by IRA men and their families would have been in vain
   - they demanded complete independence
   - they did not trust the British to keep their promises
   - they were not aware how near they were to being defeated by the British.

PART 3: HISTORICAL STUDY

European and World

Context 1: The Norman Conquest, 1060-1153

1. The candidate describes the advantages that William had over his enemies at Hastings by referring to evidence such as:
   - advantage of surprise
   - Normans fought on horseback
   - Norman tactics were better eg feigned retreat
   - Norman soldiers were fresher than Saxons who were tired from long march
   - Norman archers were able to weaken the enemy
   - Norman weapons were superior eg large shield and lance of the knights
   - Saxons had already suffered casualties at Stamford Bridge.

2. The candidate explains why David I was influenced by Norman England by referring to evidence such as:

   from the source
   - David agreed that his father had accepted William as overlord
   - he married an Anglo-Norman
   - he had estates in England
   - he saw how the Anglo-Norman king was able to keep a tight grip over his kingdom

   from recall
   - David had spent 17 years in Norman England before becoming king
   - he was brother-in-law of the English King
   - he had a close friendship with many Anglo-Norman families
   - he could use the feudal system to increase royal control.

3. The candidate evaluates the usefulness of the source by referring to evidence such as:
   - primary source taken from the time when Bruce was given his lands in Scotland
   - source was written in the name of the Scottish King
   - the charter was granted to create the lordship of Annandale
   - source shows what the lordship of Annandale included/Bruce had to provide knights for the king's army.

   Maximum of one mark for commenting on content omission such as:
   - the Bruces were now tenants-in-chief
   - the Bruces acted as the king's representatives in Annandale.

Context 2: The Cross and the Crescent: The First Crusade, 1096-1125

1. The candidate evaluates the usefulness of the source by referring to evidence such as:
   - contemporary/primary source written during the time of the First Crusade or secondary source based on interviews
   - author lived in France/observed/recorded these events
   - written to show the popularity of Peter the Hermit
   - says that Peter the Hermit was held in high regard/was seen as being holy.

   Maximum of one mark for commenting on content omission such as:
   - Peter's popularity and authority declined once the Crusaders reached the east.

2. The candidate describes the problems faced by the Crusaders on their journey from Europe to Jerusalem by referring to evidence such as:
   - the peasants were not well prepared and did not bring enough money or food
   - the peasants were attacked before they reached Constantinople because they had stolen food/many peasants were killed
   - Peter the Hermit was a weak military leader/the peasants were easily defeated on several occasions eg Nis
   - the knights did not have the material/supplies needed to build siege machines eg timber
   - the weather caused the peasants and knights problems; many died from dehydration/others were swept away by flash floods
   - the peasants and knights argued among themselves, they did not always work together eg Antioch, Jerusalem
   - many knights became dispirited. They left the Crusade eg Stephen of Blois/Crusaders were out numbered eg Antioch.

3. The candidate explains why the First Crusade found it difficult to capture Jerusalem by referring to evidence such as:

   from the source
   - Jerusalem had massive walls and flanking towers
   - those inside had prepared well for an attack
   - they used drainage systems to reduce the possibility of disease
   - they had water cisterns to provide a good supply of water

   from recall
   - spring/wells had been poisoned to stop Crusaders getting water
   - the north and south-east sides of the city were built on slopes and were difficult to surround
   - it had a large citadel – David's towers which coordinated the defence of the city
   - all Christians had been expelled from the city, preventing treachery
   - there was a lack of material; wood had to be shipped in from Europe.

Context 3: War, Death and Revolt in Medieval Europe, 1328-1436

1. The candidate describes the campaigns of the Black Prince in France by referring to evidence such as:
   - commanded part of the English army and fought bravely at Crecy when 16 years old
   - led English forces to victory at Poitiers despite being outnumbered
   - captured King John II at Poitiers
   - made good use of the longbow
   - encouraged his soldiers to rape and pillage
   - he was given control of Aquitaine in 1362
   - ordered the slaughter of 3,000 civilians at Limoges in 1370.

2. The candidate explains why the French peasants revolted in 1358 by referring to evidence such as:

   from the source
   - France had suffered a humiliating defeat in 1358 (Poitiers)
   - English forces pillaged the countryside
   - French nobles demanded heavier payment of feudal dues
   - the Dauphin ordered peasants to refortify castles

   from recall
   - French nobles were blamed for the series of defeats by English
   - nobles were blamed for failure to protect the peasants
   - weakness of the French government at the time.

3. The candidate evaluates the usefulness of the source by referring to evidence such as:
    *   primary source written at the time of the Peasants' Revolt
    *   author is a monk and is opposed to John Ball and the Peasants' Revolt
    *   source written to condemn aims of revolt
    *   source says that John Ball's aims were to get rid of lords, archbishops etc.
    Maximum of one mark for commenting on content omission such as:
    *   other important aims of the revolt eg disrupt taxation.

Context 4: New Worlds: Europe in the Age of Expansion, 1480s-1530s

1. The candidate explains why European countries wanted to explore overseas by referring to evidence such as:
    from the source
    *   to increase their wealth through trade
    *   to discover new fishing grounds
    *   to search for spices to preserve the meat they ate
    *   to avoid customs duties/taxes
    from recall
    *   to spread Christianity
    *   competition between Spain and Portugal
    *   desire for increased knowledge about the world
    *   searching for slaves.

2. The candidate evaluates the usefulness of the source by referring to evidence such as:
    *   primary source from the time of Portuguese explorations
    *   letter from an African King who is an eyewitness
    *   to complain about Portuguese activities
    *   tells of the capture of African people.
    Maximum of one mark for commenting on content omission such as:
    *   reference to positive effects eg peaceful trading.

3. The candidate describes the methods used by the Spanish Conquistadors to defeat either the Aztecs or the Incas by referring to evidence such as:
    *   Cortez/Pizarro used few soldiers: 600/180
    *   made alliances with enemies of Aztecs/Incas
    *   had better weapons eg guns, steel swords
    *   Spanish Conquistadors used horses
    *   Spanish used element of surprise
    *   Spanish captured leaders of Aztec/Inca states
    *   Spanish metal armour
    *   Spanish took advantage of superstitious beliefs of Aztecs/Incas.

Context 5: "Tea and Freedom": The American Revolution, 1763-1783

1. The candidate describes the complaints of the American colonists against British rule by referring to evidence such as:
    *   Britain had insisted on keeping troops in America after the French war
    *   the British had wanted the Americans to pay for their own defence/the Quartering Act meant they had to billet British soldiers
    *   Grenville had introduced measures after the war to raise revenue eg the Sugar Act and the Stamp Duty Act
    *   Britain was taxing the colonists without giving them representation
    *   the British had attempted to prevent the Americans moving west
    *   Britain had wanted to control her Empire more firmly
    *   George III was a tyrant (with expansion) eg ruling from 3,000 miles away, who did not understand the colonists etc.

2. The candidate evaluates the usefulness of the source by referring to evidence such as:
    *   primary source from the time when the colonial troops fought the British
    *   author was a surgeon in Washington's army who would know the condition of the troops
    *   to highlight the suffering of the army
    *   they suffered poor food and vomiting, starving and freezing.
    Maximum of one mark for commenting on content omission such as:
    *   generally served only a few months
    *   Washington still turned them into an effective fighting force.

3. The candidate explains the reasons why the British lost the war with the American colonists by referring to evidence such as:
    from the source
    *   Britain had no clear military strategy
    *   they had supply and communication problems
    *   Washington held his army together and maintained morale
    *   British Parliament was not united behind the war
    from recall
    *   the French alliance strengthened the colonists
    *   the involvement of Spain and Holland in 1779
    *   Britain lost control of the Atlantic
    *   British troops were not used to fighting in woods and mountains
    *   poor quality of British generals.

Context 6: "This Accursed Trade": The British Slave Trade and its Abolition, 1770–1807

1. The candidate evaluates the usefulness of the source by referring to evidence such as:
    *   primary source from the time of the slave trade
    *   author was an explorer and therefore an eyewitness, unlikely to be biased
    *   to show the cruelty toward captured Africans
    *   describes slaves being chained together.
    Maximum of one mark for commenting on content omission such as:
    *   kidnapped from their homelands.

2. The candidate describes what happened to slaves at the end of the Middle Passage by referring to evidence such as:
    *   slaves were made to look as healthy as they could
    *   they were fed well for a number of days before
    *   slaves were shaved
    *   older slaves had their grey hair dyed
    *   they were washed in fresh water
    *   their skin was rubbed with palm oil or beeswax to make it shine
    *   older slaves or sick ones were often left aside, 'refuse' slaves, to die
    *   slaves were auctioned off to plantation owners.

3. The candidate explains the reasons why the slave trade was abolished in 1807 by referring to evidence such as:
    from the source
    *   Quakers launched a public campaign
    *   Methodists and Baptists supported the campaign
    *   slavery seemed offensive after the French Revolution when more people talked of liberty
    *   British manufacturers promoted the idea of free labour
    from recall
    *   the nation was bombarded with tracts and pamphlets about the cruelty of the trade
    *   movement was helped by the increase in those who could read and write
    *   petitions signed by millions, mostly carried out in churches and chapels

- perfected the modern tactics of lobbying Parliament and pressurising MPs
- enthusiasm of individuals – Sharp, Clarkson and Wilberforce
- opposition of West Indian planter now a spent political force.

Context 7: Citizens! The French Revolution, 1789-1794

1. The candidate explains why new ideas encouraged people to question the way France was ruled in 1789 by referring to evidence such as:

from the source
- Diderot said government should not simply be the will of the king
- Montesquieu said the king should share power with parliament
- Montesquieu said parliament should make laws and raise taxes
- Rousseau attacked the idea that the king and nobles were born to rule over others

from recall
- there was a challenge to the 'Divine Right of Kings'
- philosophers stressed the idea that the people had rights
- there was the idea that power came from the people
- governments should carry out the wishes of the people, not the king.

2. The candidate describes the events leading up to the storming of the Bastille by referring to evidence such as:
- Necker, popular as a reformer, was sacked which led to riots
- bread prices in Paris rose to an all time high which led to further riots
- the French Guard deserted the king and joined the Paris mob
- Government weapons' stores were attacked by the mob
- the Bastille garrison was loyal to the king and trained its cannon on working class areas of Paris
- the mob decided to capture the Bastille to take weapons stored there and release the prisoners.

3. The candidate evaluates the usefulness of the source by referring to evidence such as:
- primary source from the actual execution
- author is an eyewitness/first hand knowledge and may be biased as he was responsible for the king's death
- to show that the execution was popular
- source refers to people cheering and dipping their fingers in his blood.

Maximum of one mark for commenting on content omission such as:
- Louis had been sentenced to death by the Convention
- the execution was less popular in other areas of France.

Context 8: Cavour, Garibaldi and the Making of Italy, 1815-1870

1. The candidate evaluates the usefulness of the source by referring to evidence such as:
- primary source written at the time of rising nationalist feeling
- written by a nationalist poet/possible bias
- poem written to remind Italians of their glorious past
- sees the greatness that was Rome/where is that glory now.

Maximum of one mark for commenting on content omission such as:
- no mention of political reasons for nationalist feeling eg reaction against Vienna Settlement
- no mention of economic reasons for nationalist feeling eg breaking down trade barriers.

2. The candidate describes the difficulties faced by the Italian nationalists during the revolutions of 1848-1849 by referring to evidence such as:
- only when Austria was defeated could Italians unite

- Charles Albert had been wrong to think Italy could go it alone (Fara de se)
- Italians would need foreign help to unite their country
- more planning and organisation would be needed
- Pope Pius IX could not be relied upon to support the nationalist movement
- Mazzini's dreams of a democratic republic lost support
- peasants could not be relied upon to support the nationalist movement
- nationalists learned to focus their hopes on Piedmont because it was the only state that held on to its constitution.

3. The candidate explains why Piedmont had become a wealthy and powerful state by 1859 by referring to evidence such as:

from the source
- signed trade agreements with France, Britain and Belgium/imports and exports grew by 300%
- building of 850 km of railway
- electric telegraph linked Turin with Paris
- canal building programme helped the growth of industry

from recall
- reduction in tariffs also encouraged trade
- development of the port of Genoa
- influence of the Church declined/guarantees on individual liberty
- gained influence by joining Britain and France in the Crimean War/Austria lost influence after the Crimean War
- made an alliance with France at Plombieres
- gained Lombardy after the victories at Magenta and Solferino.

Context 9: Iron and Blood? Bismarck and The Creation of the German Empire, 1815-1871

1. The candidate describes the growth of nationalism in the German states by referring to evidence such as:
- German states had united to defeat Napoleon's invasions
- growth of cultural nationalism; eg literature, music, common language encouraged a sense of national identity
- student movement encouraged a united Germany
- developments in transport allowed easy spread of nationalist ideas
- Zollverein increased influence of Prussia
- 1848 revolutions popularised idea of unification.

2. The candidate explains why the 1848 revolutions in Germany failed by referring to evidence such as:

from the source
- wide differences in political aims of the revolutionaries
- liberals wanted a united German Empire with a parliament
- divisions over the size of the new Germany
- many people did not want to abolish the monarchy/wanted to give more power to the people
- they could not agree on the borders

from recall
- King William refused the crown
- Frankfurt Parliament had no strong leader
- spent long time arguing
- old rulers of German states used armies to restore power.

3. The candidate evaluates the usefulness of the source by referring to evidence such as:
- primary source written at time of the Austro-Prussian War
- written by Bismarck, Chancellor of Prussia
- to advise King of Prussia to treat Austria leniently
- explains treating Austria leniently will avoid her becoming bitter and wanting revenge.

Maximum of one mark for commenting on content omission such as:
- unwise to march on Vienna
- Bismarck wanted to prevent Austrian interference in Germany.

Context 10: The Red Flag: Lenin and the Russian Revolution, 1894-1921

1. The candidate explains why the lives of some peasants improved as a result of Stolypin's reforms by referring to evidence such as:

from the source
- peasants could consolidate the size of their holdings
- peasant banks were set up to allow peasants to buy more land
- peasants were able to invest in more modern methods
- they made greater profit/grain production increased.

from recall
- cancellation of debt
- land inherited by the eldest son only
- peasants could buy their way out of the mir
- peasants encouraged to move to find new land.

2. The candidate describes the problems facing the Provisional Government by referring to evidence such as:
- Lenin published the April Theses which encouraged a new revolution
- war was going badly eg failure of June offensive
- soldiers were deserting in large numbers
- peasants were seizing the land
- increasing hardships for industrial workers eg shortages
- activities of the soviets eg Soviet Number 1 undermined government control
- demonstrations against the government in July
- Kornilov revolt showed weakness of the government
- Petrograd and Moscow soviets voted to support Bolsheviks
- Lenin's return to Finland station.

3. The candidate evaluates the usefulness of the source by referring to evidence such as:
- primary source written in February 1918 in the early days of the communist government
- written by foreigner showing bias against the communists/not meant to be read by others, so an honest first-hand account
- written to criticise the way the communists were running the country
- describes problems caused for middle-class people in the new state.

Maximum of one mark for commenting on content omission such as:
- land transferred to the peasants
- industry transferred to the workers.

Context 11: Free at Last? Race Relations in the USA, 1918-1968

1. The candidate describes the effects of the Jim Crow laws on Black Americans by referring to evidence such as:
- enforced segregation between Blacks and Whites – created a segregated society
- some states made marriages between Whites and Blacks illegal
- enforced separate schools for Blacks and Whites
- enforced separate toilets and restrooms
- ensured that transport facilities – trains and buses – were segregated
- Supreme Court decision in 1896 Plessy case enshrined the "separate but equal" idea in law and made Jim Crow laws acceptable
- led to Black Americans feeling humiliated/feeling like second citizens/feeling inferior
- led to anger and demands for change
- prevented Blacks from voting.

2. The candidate explains why the protest in Birmingham in 1963 was an important event in the civil rights' campaign in the USA by referring to evidence such as:

from the source
- Birmingham was the most racist city in the USA
- civil rights protestors would risk their lives by entering Birmingham
- a successful demonstration in Birmingham could spark off changes across the South
- over nine hundred children were arrested on the first day

from recall
- police used massive violence against protestors – use of clubs, dogs, fire hoses
- the march gained huge media coverage and shocked American society
- President Kennedy announced a new civil rights law within weeks
- Connor, the police chief, was a racist.

3. The candidate evaluates the usefulness of the source by referring to evidence such as:
- primary source from 1966 when the Black Power movement was founded
- speech by Stokely Carmichael, a leader of the Black Power movement
- to show that Black Americans were not going to put up with discrimination any more
- Carmichael says the only way is to take over.

Maximum of one mark for commenting on content omission such as:
- Civil Rights Act 1964 and Voting Rights Act 1965 had been gained
- Black Americans should not rely on White people – they should build their own schools, communities.

Context 12: The Road to War, 1933-1939

1. The candidate describes how Hitler increased German military power by referring to evidence such as:
- the introduction of conscription
- the creation of a large German air force
- building up the German navy with the Anglo- German Naval Agreement
- huge amounts of money were spent on rearmament/German industry was geared towards rearmament
- the reoccupation of the Rhineland meant the German army was closer to France
- Anschluss meant that the Austrian army became part of the German army
- gaining the Sudetenland provided men for conscription into the army
- invasion of Czechoslovakia meant seizure of Skoda armaments factory.

2. The candidate evaluates the usefulness of the source by referring to evidence such as:
- primary source from the month that the Anschluss was happening
- author is a British politician who would know how the government felt
- to show that Britain was appeasing Germany over Anschluss
- source refers to foolishness of Versailles treaty.

Maximum of one mark for commenting on content omission such as:
- anti-appeasers such as Churchill were criticising the policy of appeasement.

3. The candidate explains why Germany declared war on Poland in 1939 by referring to evidence such as:

from the source
- the Nazis hated Poland for racial reasons
- Germany had lost land to Poland

- millions of Germans were forced to live under Polish rule
- Danzig was run to suit the Poles

from recall
- the 'Polish Corridor' divided East Prussia from the rest of Germany
- the Nazi-Soviet Pact meant that Russia would not protect Poland
- Hitler did not believe that Britain would help Poland in the event of war.

Context 13: In the Shadow of the Bomb: The Cold War, 1945–1985

1. The candidate evaluates the usefulness of the source by referring to evidence such as:
   - primary source from the period of the crisis over Berlin
   - expressed by the American President who would have developed the policy
   - to play down the threat of war
   - if I'm going to threaten nuclear war it will have to be for more important reasons than that.

   Maximum of one mark for commenting on content omission such as:
   - the wall was built, ending the crisis.

2. The candidate describes the part played by the USA in the Cuban Missile Crisis by referring to evidence such as:
   - America refused to trade with Cuba after Batista's fall
   - the American government backed a rebellion against Castro – 'Bay of Pigs'
   - the Bay of Pigs worsened the situation and pushed Cuba closer to the USSR
   - Khrushchev complained about American missile bases in Turkey
   - American spy planes got pictures of Soviet missile sites in Cuba
   - Kennedy declared a naval blockade of Cuba
   - Americans prepared for a head on clash
   - USSR tried to set up missile bases in Cuba
   - Khrushchev backed down.

3. The candidate explains why the USA lost the war in Vietnam by referring to evidence such as:
   from the source
   - USA failed to win the hearts and minds of the peasants
   - American troops did not cope with the guerrilla tactics
   - communists were backed by China and Russia
   - most American troops just wanted to go home
   from recall
   - the US was trying to supply a war 8,000 miles from America
   - the South Vietnamese regime was weak, brutal and corrupt
   - American troops were inexperienced
   - the war became very unpopular in the USA.

PART 1 THE SHORT ESSAY

Scottish and British

Context 1: Murder in the Cathedral: Crown, Church and People, 1154-1173

1. The candidate explains why knights were important in medieval times by referring to evidence such as:
   - they were an important part of a feudal army
   - they were part of the feudal system and gave part of their land to peasants
   - they were used in local government/member of a jury
   - they protected the weak, young and old in society
   - they fought for the Church against non-Christians eg crusade
   - their behaviour made them role models for the rest of society
   - they performed services such as castle-guard in return for their land.

Context 2: Wallace, Bruce and the Wars of Independence, 1286-1328

2. The candidate explains why John Balliol lost his position as King of Scots in 1296 by referring to evidence such as:
   - John Balliol had accepted Edward I as his overlord
   - John Balliol had been bullied by King Edward (eg orders, legal decisions overturned)
   - John Balliol refused King Edward's order to join him in a war against France
   - John Balliol withdrew his homage to King Edward
   - John Balliol had made an alliance with the King of France against Edward ie treason
   - King Edward defeated John Balliol at Dunbar
   - King Edward forced John Balliol to surrender to him
   - King Edward had stripped John Balliol of his crown and title
   - Robert Bruce had been plotting against John Balliol
   - not all the Scots supported Balliol in his campaign against King Edward.

Context 3: Mary, Queen of Scots and the Scottish Reformation, 1540s-1587

3. The candidate explains why Mary, Queen of Scots, faced difficulties ruling Scotland when she returned in 1561 by referring to evidence such as:
   - Mary was female – many people were suspicious of a female ruler (eg Knox)
   - Mary was young – possibly inexperienced in governing a country
   - nobles were in competition to win her support eg Huntly, Moray
   - there had recently been a revolt in Scotland against her mother, Mary of Guise
   - Mary had come from France but the French were unpopular in Scotland
   - Mary was Roman Catholic and Scotland had recently become Protestant
   - Elizabeth of England was hostile to Mary because she claimed to be Queen of England.

Context 4: The Coming of the Civil War, 1603-1642

4. The candidate explains why there were problems between Crown and Parliament during the reign of James VI and I by referring to evidence such as:
   - James VI and I's belief in the Divine Right of Kings
   - over-confident/naive character of James VI and I
   - extravagant spending/debts of James VI and I eg clothing, banquets, gifts, pensions

- raised taxes without consulting Parliament eg feudal dues, customs duties
- James VI and I's desire for a union between Scotland and England
- gave money and power to favourites at court
- impositions and the "Bates Case" 1606/resentment over extra customs duties
- failure of the "Great Contract" 1610 resulted in James VI and I dismissing Parliament
- failure of "Addled" Parliament 1614
- monopolies caused anger/resentment within Parliament
- war with Spain 1621 caused debates between James and Parliament.

Context 5: "Ane End of Ane Auld Sang": Scotland and the Treaty of Union, 1690s-1715

5. The candidate explains why there was so much opposition to a Union in Scotland before 1707 by referring to evidence such as:
- the Scots felt key members of Parliament had been bribed
- the Scots felt their friendship/trade with France would be affected
- Scots were critical of the joint monarchy and feared the effects of a Parliamentary union
- the Scots blamed England for the failure of their colony at Darien
- the Scots feared that Union would bring economic ruin
- the Scots feared for the position of their Presbyterian church
- Scots feared that their legal system would be changed
- Jacobites opposed the Union
- the Scots were not being offered sufficient compensation
- the Scots were afraid of increased taxes.

Context 6: Immigrants and Exiles: Scotland, 1830s-1930s

6. The candidate explains why Scots emigrants made a valuable contribution in Canada and the United States by referring to evidence such as:
- Scots were comparatively well educated
- had a pioneering spirit
- many Scots had practical farming skills
- others had financial and commercial ability
- Scots often managed to arrive with some capital to invest
- skilled craftsmen contributed their skills
- played an important role in education and politics
- reference to individual Scots whose contribution was valuable.

Context 7 (a): From the Cradle to the Grave? Social Welfare in Britain, 1890s-1951

7. (a) The candidate explains why the Liberal reforms, 1906-14, failed to solve the problems of the poor by referring to evidence such as:
- Liberals had no overall plan – tackled problems one by one
- legislation gave powers to local authorities – some did not introduce free school meals at first
- medical inspections did not provide treatment
- amount of old age pensions was inadequate
- pension age was set too high at 70 for most people to benefit
- health insurance only provided free treatment for worker not family
- unemployment insurance was only for certain industries
- benefit rates were not sufficient to overcome poverty
- Liberals did not tackle poor housing at all.

Context 7 (b): Campaigning for Change: Social Change in Scotland, 1900s-1979

(b) The candidate explains why many industries in Scotland experienced problems in the years between the two world wars by referring to evidence such as:

- the end of the Great War had led to a drop in demand for warships
- the slump of the 1920s had led to a drop in demand for merchant ships
- there was a decline in the old industries producing coal and steel
- British markets had been lost to foreign competition
- industrial unrest undermined the reputation of Scottish industries
- the Great Depression made matters even worse for the heavy industries – shipyards, coal mines closed
- there was little investment in new technology
- the Government did little to help industry in the 1930s
- new industries eg light engineering, cars were mainly located in England.

Context 8: A Time of Troubles: Ireland, 1900-1923

8. The candidate explains why support for Sinn Fein increased after 1916 by referring to evidence such as:
- execution of rebel leaders in the Easter Rising caused resentment against the British
- Sinn Fein opposed the First World War eg organised strikes against conscription
- Sinn Fein was supported by the Catholic Church
- leadership of De Valera and Collins encouraged support
- returning Easter Rising rebels were treated as heroes. Many stood as Sinn Fein candidates in local by-elections
- Sinn Fein were successful in the 1918 General Election encouraging others to support them
- Sinn Fein became the leading Irish Political Party
- Sinn Fein refused to go to London to work in Parliament as a protest
- Sinn Fein set up an illegal Irish Parliament in Dublin i.e. they stood for independence.

European and World

Context 1: The Norman Conquest, 1060-1153

9. The candidate explains why David I introduced feudalism to Scotland by referring to evidence such as:
- influence of David's experiences at the court of King Henry as a young man
- Scotland was difficult for David to control eg different tribes had their own leaders
- feudalism gave the king a means of control over his subjects
- it made administration of the country easier
- encouraged the development of castles across the kingdom
- church received large amounts of land which encouraged its support for the king
- charters were given to encourage the development of burghs
- David was provided with knights for his army.

Context 2: The Cross and the Crescent: The First Crusade, 1096-1125

10. The candidate explains why Pope Urban II called the First Crusade by referring to evidence such as:
- to recapture Jerusalem
- to help the Christians in the east who were being persecuted
- to protect Christian churches and relics which were being destroyed
- to help Emperor Alexius, who had sent ambassadors asking for help
- to reopen the trade/pilgrim routes to the east
- to heal the schism between the western and eastern churches
- to place himself as head of a united church
- to show European rulers eg The Holy Roman Emperor that he could call an army
- to prevent knights in the west from killing each other.

Context 3: War, Death and Revolt in Medieval Europe, 1328-1436

11. The candidate explains why the Hundred Years' War broke out between England and France in 1337 by referring to evidence such as:
    - French kings claimed overlordship of English possessions in France
    - English economic interests in France – wine, wool and grain
    - English reaction to the continuing French alliance with Scotland
    - English kings claimed the throne of France
    - dispute over the succession following the death of Charles IV in 1328
    - French attacks on English and Flemish merchants in the Channel
    - King Philip IV declared Edward III's land in France forfeit
    - King Philip IV's invasion of Gascony.

Context 4: New Worlds: Europe in the Age of Expansion, 1480s-1530s

12. The candidate explains why European countries wanted to search for new lands between the 1480s and the 1530s by referring to evidence such as:
    - religious motives/they wanted to spread Christianity
    - there was rivalry between countries eg Spain and Portugal
    - countries/individuals wanted fame and fortune
    - they wished to find valuable spices
    - they wished to increase trading links with the East
    - the Turks had disrupted the old spice routes
    - there was a desire for increased knowledge about the world
    - improvements in technology made voyages easier ie caravels, quadrants
    - there was a search for new fishing grounds.

Context 5: "Tea and Freedom": The American Revolution, 1763-1783

13. The candidate explains why the colonists won the American War of Independence by referring to evidence such as:
    - the skill of George Washington and his leadership of the Colonial army
    - knowledge of the terrain gave the colonists an advantage
    - poor leadership and tactics by British officers
    - difficult to supply the British army across the Atlantic
    - British surrender at Saratoga in October 1777 was a decisive event
    - French involvement in 1778
    - involvement of Spain and Holland in 1779
    - Britain lost control of the Atlantic
    - defeat at Yorktown persuaded British government to negotiate the end of the war.

Context 6: "This Accursed Trade": The British Slave Trade and its Abolition, 1770–1807

14. The candidate explains why there was increasing support for the campaign against the slave trade by referring to evidence such as:
    - influence of Christian groups who believed slavery was against the ten commandments
    - role of William Wilberforce in taking the campaign to parliament
    - testimony of former slaves
    - awareness of conditions on middle passage
    - awareness of conditions in slave factories
    - awareness of treatment of slaves on plantations
    - public meetings, petitions being used to inform people about trade
    - British economy no longer so reliant on slave trade.

Context 7: Citizens! The French Revolution, 1789-1794

15. The candidate explains why few French people supported Louis XVI in 1789 by referring to evidence such as:
    - the peasants blamed the king for the power of the landlords
    - the peasants blamed the king for having to pay most of the taxes
    - the workers in the cities were suffering from poor wages and conditions
    - Louis XVI was a weak and ineffective king
    - Marie Antoinette was blamed for spending too much money on luxuries
    - there were new political ideas saying that kings must share power
    - the middle class resented the political power of the nobility and the king
    - the peasants and middle class wanted more power for the Estates General
    - the king refused to listen to the demands of the Third Estate.

Context 8: Cavour, Garibaldi and the Making of Italy, 1815-1870

16. The candidate explains why Cavour was important to Italian unification by referring to evidence such as:
    - he adopted a realistic and opportunist approach to situations
    - as PM of Piedmont from 1852 his main aim was expansion of territory and expulsion of Austria from Italy
    - modernised Piedmont's economy eg built railways, roads, modernised port of Genoa
    - made treaties with Britain and France
    - built up military strength of Piedmont
    - following Crimean War, recognised that diplomacy alone would not work
    - met with Napoleon III at Plombieres 1858 to agree to drive Austria out of Italy
    - provoked Austria into war in April 1859
    - following reinstatement in 1860 he signed a deal with France: Piedmont would take 3 duchies of Tuscany, Modena and Parma; France would take Nice and Savoy.

Context 9: Iron and Blood? Bismarck and The Creation of the German Empire, 1815-1871

17. The candidate explains why Bismarck's leadership was important to the unification of the German states by referring to evidence such as:
    - he encouraged the nationalist ambitions of the Liberals in the Prussian Parliament
    - he backed army reforms which strengthened the Prussian army
    - he wanted to unify Germany under Prussian leadership
    - he followed policies of "realpolitik" eg "iron and blood" speech
    - he engineered war between Prussia and Denmark in 1864
    - he outmanoeuvred Austria at the Treaty of Vienna
    - he engineered war with Austria in 1866 to secure dominance of Prussia
    - his leniency in the Treaty of Prague left open possibility of Austria as an ally in future
    - he masterminded the formation of the North German Confederation
    - he edited the Ems telegram to bring about Franco-Prussian War
    - the defeat of France led to the creation of the German Empire in 1871.

Context 10: The Red Flag: Lenin and the Russian Revolution, 1894-1921

18. The candidate explains why the Reds won the Civil War by referring to evidence such as:

- Red army had good supplies of food – mostly taken from the peasants
- Reds controlled the industrial centres of Russia
- Reds had good rail routes/communications
- Whites were divided/did not always act together
- peasants were afraid that they would lose land if the Whites won
- Trotsky moulded his army into a good fighting unit
- Reds controlled main cities
- large proportion of the population supported the Reds.

Context 11: Free at Last? Race Relations in the USA, 1918-1968

19. The candidate explains why black people rioted in many American cities in the 1960s by referring to evidence such as:
    - poverty – 40% of black Americans still lived in poverty
    - nothing had been done about slum housing with overcrowding and high rents
    - blacks were in low paid jobs or had no jobs
    - they had poor quality schools and facilities
    - blacks had poor health and little access to health care
    - ghettos were places of crime, gangs and drugs
    - feeling that Civil Rights Act had not solved problems in northern cities
    - assassination of Martin Luther King
    - riots broke out during summer heatwaves
    - disillusionment with the draft/Vietnam War
    - influence of Radical leaders encouraged action
    - heavy-handed policing/brutality caused anger among blacks.

Context 12: The Road to War, 1933-1939

20. The candidate explains why events after Munich, September 1938, led to the outbreak of war in 1939 by referring to evidence such as:
    - the take-over of the Sudetenland gave Germany dominance in Central Europe
    - Hitler threatened Czechoslovakia despite his promise of no more territorial demands
    - Germany invaded Czechoslovakia in March 1939 and so broke the Munich settlement of 1938
    - Britain realised appeasement had failed
    - Great Britain no longer trusted Hitler and sped up her rearmaments programme/led to conscription
    - Hitler's aggression against Poland and the demand for the return of Danzig increased tension
    - Britain promised to defend Poland if she were attacked
    - August 1939, Germany and Russia signed the Nazi-Soviet Non-Aggression Pact which left Hitler free to attack Poland
    - September, Germany invaded Poland
    - Germany ignored the British ultimatum to stop the attack so Britain declared war on Germany.

Context 13: In the Shadow of the Bomb: The Cold War, 1945-1985

21. The candidate explains why the USA became involved in a crisis over Cuba in 1962 by referring to evidence such as:
    - Cuban leader Castro had formed a close alliance with the Soviet Union
    - Castro had angered American businesses by nationalising key industries
    - evidence of missile bases being constructed in Cuba
    - Cuba lay close to the American mainland
    - American public opinion would not accept the threat posed by Soviet missiles on the island
    - fear in America that their country was falling behind in the Cold War
    - Kennedy was looking for an opportunity to gain revenge after Bay of Pigs fiasco.

PART 2 HISTORICAL STUDY

Scottish and British

Context 1: Murder in the Cathedral: Crown, Church and People, 1154-1173

1. The candidate evaluates the usefulness of the source by referring to evidence such as:
   - primary source written at the time of Henry II's reign
   - author knew Henry/possible bias
   - to describe Henry's character/to flatter the king
   - states that Henry was honest, polite and generous.

   Maximum of 1 mark for commenting on content omission such as:
   - does not mention Henry's famous temper
   - does not mention that Henry was stubborn eg quarrel with Becket.

2. The candidate describes the life of a monk in medieval times by referring to evidence such as:
   - took vows of poverty, obedience and chastity
   - spent much of the day in prayer or attending religious services
   - lived strictly according to the rules of his order
   - had a simple diet eg fruit, bread and water
   - owned no personal possessions
   - prayed for the souls of the dead
   - wrote chronicles, recording events
   - worked in monastic fields eg rearing sheep
   - looked after the sick in the monastery's infirmary.

3. The candidate explains why Henry II and Archbishop Becket quarrelled by referring to evidence such as:

   from the source
   - Becket resigned as Chancellor
   - Becket refused to sign the Constitutions of Clarendon
   - Becket would not reduce the power of the Church
   - Becket fled to France without the king's permission

   from recall
   - Henry wanted all clergymen (criminous clerks) to be tried in the king's court
   - Henry charged Becket with contempt of court and confiscated his lands
   - Becket appealed to the Pope and gained his full support
   - Becket excommunicated the Archbishop of York and sacked the bishops who had crowned Henry's son.

Context 2: Wallace, Bruce and the Wars of Independence, 1286-1328

1. The candidate evaluates the usefulness of the source by referring to evidence such as:
   - primary source/secondary source written some time after the events it describes
   - a chronicle was to record what happened/the author would have to research the events
   - to describe the events of that night
   - it describes the bad weather which contributed to the accident/states that the King's horse stumbled and he was killed.

   Maximum of 1 mark for commenting on content omission such as:
   - King Alexander III fell over a cliff.

2. The candidate describes what happened at the Battle of Stirling Bridge by referring to evidence such as:
   - the Scots and English were on different sides of the bridge
   - the Scots were formed up on the high ground (Abbey Craig)
   - the English were slow in getting organised (slept in and/or a knighting ceremony)

- the English debated whether to use Stirling Bridge or a slightly distant ford
- the English crossed the bridge (which was narrow) slowly
- Wallace ordered the Scots to attack the English when enough had crossed to defeat them
- the Scots cut off the end of the bridge and isolated the English/many were drowned
- the English were defeated and/or Cressingham was killed.

3. The candidate explains why the Scots sent the Declaration of Arbroath to the Pope in 1320 by referring to evidence such as:

from the source
- the Scots wanted Bruce recognised internationally as king
- the raids on northern England had not been successful
- the invasion of Ireland had failed to put pressure on Edward II
- they wanted the Pope to recognise Bruce as King

from recall
- Edward II would not agree that Bruce was King of Scots
- the Pope was a person of international authority
- the Pope could put pressure on Edward II to change his policy
- the Church had excommunicated Bruce and would not accept him as king.

Context 3: Mary, Queen of Scots and the Scottish Reformation, 1540s-1587

1. The candidate explains why Protestantism spread in Scotland in the 1540s and 1550s by referring to evidence such as:

from the source
- some Scots began to question the teachings of the Catholic Church
- English translations of the Bible were distributed
- religious pamphlets were smuggled from abroad
- the Good and Godly Ballads spread Protestant ideas

from recall
- criticism of the wealth of the Church in Scotland and its concerns with money
- criticism of the lack of spirituality among some members of that Church
- criticism of how some Protestant preachers had been treated (eg Wishart)
- resentment of French/Catholic influence over Scotland.

2. The candidate describes the events surrounding the murder of Darnley by referring to evidence such as:
- Darnley was killed in Edinburgh in 1567
- Mary had encouraged Darnley to return to Edinburgh because he was ill
- Darnley had settled in lodgings in Kirk o' Fields
- Mary was supposed to stay with Darnley on his last night in Kirk o' Fields, but she left
- the house was blown up by gunpowder
- Darnley's body was found in the garden behind the house
- Darnley had not died in the explosion, he had been suffocated.

3. The candidate evaluates the usefulness of the source by referring to evidence such as:
- primary source written by Mary while she was in an English prison
- it was a personal letter from Mary to Elizabeth/possible bias against Elizabeth
- to accuse Elizabeth of helping cause trouble in Scotland
- English agents, spies etc encouraged rebellion in Scotland/these agents had been very well rewarded afterwards.

Maximum of 1 mark for commenting on content omission such as:
- Mary was Elizabeth's prisoner/Elizabeth would not let Mary return to Scotland.

Context 4: The Coming of the Civil War, 1603-1642

1. The candidate evaluates the usefulness of the source by referring to evidence such as:
- secondary source written more than 300 years after the religious disagreements developed between the king and the Scots
- the historian is well informed as he will have studied the Scottish records
- written to show that the (ordinary) Scots were opposed to the Prayer Book/to show that women took the lead in the opposition
- it says there was a riot in St Giles when the Prayer Book was first used/that Jenny Geddes egged the women on.

Maximum of 1 mark for commenting on content omission such as:
- Jenny Geddes threw her stool at the Dean
- the Scots objected because they thought the new Prayer Book seemed to be going back to mass (Roman Catholicism).

2. The candidate explains why Charles I became unpopular in England by referring to evidence such as:

from the source
- the King imposed the "Ship Money" tax on inland areas
- he imposed "Ship Money" tax without the consent of Parliament
- anyone who refused to pay the taxes was tried in special courts
- he imposed fines on people who built on common land or in royal forests

from recall
- appointment of Archbishop Laud/introduction of Laudianism unpopular with the Puritans
- Standing Army was unpopular with the people
- Charles raised taxes to pay for own extravagances eg art
- Royal Monopolies were unpopular.

3. The candidate describes the events between 1640 and 1642 which led to the outbreak of the Civil War by referring to evidence such as:
- Long Parliament led by Pym led to "anti-court" consensus
- Strafford impeached by Parliament 1640/executed 1641
- Triennial Act 1641 restricted power of king to call Parliament
- emergence of Hyde/"Constitutional Royalists"
- Ten Propositions 1641 put further restrictions on king's power
- the Grand Remonstrance 1641 divided House of Commons
- formation of "King's Party" in House of Commons
- Five Members Coup January 1642 made Civil War likely
- rebellion in Ireland
- widespread social disorder eg weavers, fens
- Militia Ordinance 1642 issued by Parliament/Commission of Array issued by king
- the Nineteen Propositions June 1642 were rejected by Charles I
- Committee of Public Safety appointed by Parliament
- Charles declares war on Parliament 22 August 1642.

Context 5: "Ane End of Ane Auld Sang": Scotland and the Treaty of Union, 1690s-1715

1. The candidate evaluates the usefulness of the source by referring to evidence such as:
- primary source, published at the time they were recruiting for the expedition
- published by the Directors who were in charge of the expedition

- to recruit people to go to Darien
- it tells that the ships were loaded with everything needed for the expedition/it promises them fifty acres of good ground.

Maximum of 1 mark for commenting on content omission such as:

- the expedition was badly equipped/the ground at Darien was not good.

2. The candidate explains why many Scottish nobles agreed to the Act of Union by referring to evidence such as:

from the source

- they were convinced of the prosperity it would bring to Scotland
- they saw the opportunities of investing in England's colonies
- they saw it would guarantee the Protestant Succession (v. Jacobites)
- they would gain royal approval and its benefits

from recall

- they received money through the Equivalent
- they received bribes
- they received new titles
- they were offered government jobs for their families
- they received back payment of their salaries.

3. The candidate describes how Scotland changed as a result of the Act of Union by referring to evidence such as:
- the Pound Sterling replaced the Pound Scots and coins changed
- English weights and measures replaced Scottish ones
- a Union flag replaced the Scottish flag
- new taxes applied in Scotland (Malt Tax)
- Customs and Excise men appeared in Scotland
- Scottish Parliament and Scottish nobles moved to London
- Scots Law was affected by appeals to the House of Lords
- The Patronage Act (1712) affected the Kirk.

Context 6: Immigrants and Exiles: Scotland, 1830s-1930s

1. The candidate evaluates the usefulness of the source by referring to evidence such as:
- primary source from 1836 when Irish people were coming to Scotland
- authorship: a Catholic priest in Aberdeen would know why the Irish came to the city
- to show the kind of work done by the Irish in Aberdeen
- they came to Scotland as jobs were easy to find and wages were fairly high.

Maximum of 1 mark for commenting on content omission such as:

- Scotland was close to Ireland so a short voyage
- Scotland was cheap to get to.

2. The candidate describes the experience of Irish immigrants in the west of Scotland by referring to evidence such as:
- found work in factories, mines and farms
- lived in poorest housing – overcrowded, little furniture, poor sanitation
- hit by disease such as cholera and typhus
- kept to themselves in their own communities
- welcomed by employers
- disliked by Scots for taking their jobs and keeping wages low
- received support from Catholic Church/used church as centre for social activities
- those from the north of Ireland settled more easily.

3. The candidate explains why many Scots emigrated overseas in the twentieth century by referring to evidence such as:

from the source

- former pupils who had gone to Canada were succeeding
- money and letters sent home encouraged people to go

- Canada had great opportunities for farming
- agents persuaded people by enthusiasm and slides

from recall

- poverty in Scotland encouraged emigration
- unemployment eg in fishing after World War I or during depression
- some countries paid fares
- advertisements persuaded people of benefits.

Context 7 (a): From the Cradle to the Grave? Social Welfare in Britain, 1890s-1951

1. The candidate explains why attitudes towards poverty changed in the early twentieth century by referring to evidence such as:

from the source

- Trade Unions did not feel Liberals and Conservatives did enough for the poor
- Socialists felt a high level of poverty was wrong
- the new Labour Party stood for practical reforms to tackle poverty
- Liberals thought of ways to help the poor because they thought they would lose votes to Labour

from recall

- reports of Booth and Rowntree showed the scale of poverty
- worries about effect of poverty on health and the defence of the country
- concern that industrial output was being held back because of poverty
- countries such as Germany showed poverty could be tackled eg with pensions.

2. The candidate evaluates the usefulness of the source by referring to evidence such as:
- primary source from 1942 when the Beveridge Report issued
- authorship: newspaper reporting events/cartoonist may exaggerate
- to show clearly the problems Beveridge identified
- problems were want, squalor, disease, ignorance and idleness/shows "Giants".

Maximum of 1 mark for commenting on content omission such as:

- Beveridge wanted to introduce a comprehensive national insurance scheme
- Beveridge assumed the existence of eg a National Health Service.

3. The candidate describes the reforms introduced by Labour after 1945 to improve the lives of the British people by referring to evidence such as:
- National Insurance Act 1946 – comprehensive, universal scheme
- National Assistance Act 1948 – to help those not covered by Insurance
- National Health Service set up in 1948
- huge house building programme started
- New Towns were set up throughout the country
- investment in education eg built new schools
- had a policy of full employment/kept unemployment at a very low level
- nationalised industries eg coal.

Context 7 (b): Campaigning for Change: Social Change in Scotland, 1900s-1979

1. The candidate describes the ways sport became more popular in Scotland between 1900 and 1939 by referring to evidence such as:
- introduction of half day on Saturday gave people more time to participate/watch sport
- football and rugby became better organised in leagues

- sports such as football became professionalised
- large stadiums were built for the growing number of fans
- better transport meant nationwide competitions could be organised
- better transport meant people had more access to the countryside for activities such as hill-walking
- local councils built golf courses so golf was available to more people
- local councils built swimming pools that were cheap to use.

2. The candidate explains why women had not gained the right to vote by 1914 by referring to evidence such as:

from the source
- votes for women was not an important issue for the government
- the Prime Minister was opposed to the female franchise
- most men believed that women had no place in politics
- militant actions led to women being accused of irresponsibility

from recall
- suffragette militancy hindered progress towards getting the vote
- actions such as setting fire to buildings were seen as very serious crimes
- the press were mostly opposed to votes for women
- the government refused to be blackmailed/intimidated into granting the vote.

3. The candidate evaluates the usefulness of the source by referring to evidence such as:
- primary source from a Scottish school in the 1930s, photograph is likely to be accurate/could be posed
- to show that pupils are being trained in practical skills
- it shows girls washing clothes/girls are wearing aprons

Maximum of 1 mark for commenting on content omission such as:
- girls were also taught to cook
- boys were taught technical subjects.

Context 8: A Time of Troubles: Ireland, 1900-1923

1. The candidate explains why the Ulster Unionists were against Home Rule by referring to evidence such as:

from the source
- believed it would destroy their way of life
- believed they would be forced into poverty
- feared isolation from the empire
- feared the Protestant Church could be weakened

from recall
- Catholic Church could dominate
- businesses and trade could be harmed
- industries such as ship building could be harmed
- agriculture could become main business
- Ireland was too weak to exist on its own, needed to be in the union
- living conditions in Ireland had improved, these improvements could be compromised.

2. The candidate evaluates the usefulness of the source by referring to evidence such as:
- primary source produced at the time of the First World War
- poster produced by the Irish National Party who supported the First World War
- to encourage Irishmen to join the army/postpone the campaign for Home Rule
- it says their first duty was to take part in ending the war/join an Irish regiment.

Maximum of 1 mark for commenting on content omission such as:
- not all Irish Nationalists supported the First World War
- the Nationalist movement split, Sinn Fein gained more support as a result of this.

3. The candidate describes the Civil War by referring to evidence such as:
- Republicans occupied a number of buildings in Dublin including the Four Courts
- Republicans occupied ex-British and RIC barracks
- Free Staters attacked the Four Courts
- the Republicans were defeated within nine days in Dublin
- the Republicans continued the fight in the countryside
- guerrilla warfare was used by both sides
- Free State General, Henry Wilson MP for North Down was kidnapped and murdered by Republicans
- Michael Collins was assassinated in a Republican ambush
- Republican leader Liam Lynch was murdered
- fighting lasted for a year
- as many as 4000 people are believed to have been killed
- Free State Government had imprisoned 1100 Republicans without trial
- Special Powers Act was issued by the Dail offering amnesty for Republicans until October 1922
- 77 Republicans were executed by the Irish Free State government after October 1922
- De Valera conceded defeat/men were ordered to lay down their arms.

PART 3   HISTORICAL STUDY

European and World

Context 1: The Norman Conquest, 1060-1153

1. The candidate makes an accurate comparison of the sources by referring to evidence such as:

The sources disagree completely

Source A	Source B
• Edward had nominated Harold as his rightful successor.	• Harold broke his oath to support William's rightful claim.
• Harold was chosen as King by all the powerful lords of England.	• Harold did not wait for public support/with the help of a few of his supporters.
• Harold was crowned legitimately by Aldred.	• He was illegally crowned by Stigund who had been excommunicated.

2. The candidate describes the methods used by William to increase his royal authority by referring to evidence such as:
- built castles throughout England eg Tower of London
- Norman barons were given land
- established feudal ties based on homage
- ruthless destruction of challengers eg Harrying of the North
- used knights as basis for the royal army
- heavy taxation was ruthlessly enforced
- the church was controlled by Norman bishops
- produced Domesday Book to show who held land from him.

3. The candidate explains why there was an increase in the number of abbeys and monasteries during the reign of David I by referring to evidence such as:

from the source
- David was very religious
- David poured wealth from his burghs into building abbeys and monasteries
- David encouraged his nobles to leave land to the church
- master craftsmen were brought from England and France

from recall
- David gave charters providing land for the church

- David's link with Europe encouraged monks to come to Scotland from abroad
- churchmen had important position in David's government
- the support of the church helped strengthen royal control.

Context 2: The Cross and the Crescent: The First Crusade, 1096–1125

1. The candidate explains why the People's Crusade failed by referring to evidence such as:

from the source

- many of the people's army had been killed
- the Crusaders ignored the Emperor Alexius' advice not to attack without the knights
- the Crusaders argued amongst themselves
- Peter the Hermit left the Crusade

from recall

- the Crusaders were not trained soldiers/they were disorganised
- Peter the Hermit was not a good military leader
- the Crusaders had split up and were easy to attack
- the Crusaders had lost their money and supplies
- their poor reputation meant people were unwilling to help the Crusaders.

2. The candidate describes the capture of Nicaea by the First Crusade by referring to evidence such as:
   - the Crusaders failed to starve the Muslims inside Nicaea into surrendering
   - the governor of Nicaea, Kilij Arslan was away fighting his Muslim neighbours, he did not return to protect the city
   - the Crusaders asked Emperor Alexius for boats to blockade the city
   - the city was surrounded and the Muslims inside had their supplies cut off
   - Emperor Alexius agreed to let the Muslims go free in return for the city
   - without the knowledge of the Crusaders the city was returned to Emperor Alexius in the middle of the night
   - the Crusaders were denied their plunder of the city
   - the relationship between Emperor Alexius and the Crusaders was damaged.

3. The candidate makes an accurate comparison of the sources by referring to evidence such as:

The sources disagree

Source B	Source C
• Attacked the minute they left the city.	• Did not attack when they left the city.
• Bohemond organised the knights.	• Bohemond could not organise the knights.
• Muslims were forced to flee the battlefield.	• Muslims refused to fight, fled the battlefield.
• Muslims were brave.	• Muslims were cowardly.

Context 3: War, Death and Revolt in Medieval Europe, 1328–1436

1. The candidate explains the spread of the Black Death in the fourteenth century by referring to evidence such as:

from the source

- fleas carried the disease to humans
- people lived in close proximity to rats
- plague infected rats from trading ships spread the disease to ports of call
- diseased rats got on to merchants' wagons and were carried across the country

from recall

- insanitary conditions in towns encouraged large populations of rats
- people escaped plague affected towns often carrying the fleas with them
- people did not understand what caused the Black Death
- other theories eg Black Death was an ebola viral infection.

2. The candidate makes an accurate comparison of the sources by referring to evidence such as:

The sources mainly disagree

Source B	Source C
• He believed strongly in his right to the French throne.	• Henry had no right to the crown of France.
• Henry inspired victory.	• Henry's success in the war with France was due to gambler's luck.
But • he could be cruel towards defeated enemies.	But • Henry massacred prisoners after Agincourt in defiance of the conventions of war.

3. The candidate describes the part played by Joan of Arc in reawakening French national pride by referring to evidence such as:
   - she inspired the Dauphin to restart the war against England
   - led the Dauphin's army to lift the siege of Orleans
   - showed defiance towards the English eg sent messages
   - showed bold military leadership
   - restored the pride of the French soldiers
   - claimed that God had called her to drive the English out of France
   - helped to bring about the coronation of the Dauphin at Reims
   - defeated English forces at Patay.

Context 4: New Worlds: Europe in the Age of Expansion, 1480s–1530s

1. The candidate explains why developments in shipbuilding and navigation made voyages of exploration easier between the 1480s and 1530s by referring to evidence such as:

from the source

- lateen sails made ships more manoeuvrable and faster
- longer voyages were now possible
- astrolabes helped sailors identify location at sea
- loglines were used to calculate speed and longitude

from recall

- caravels also used lateen sails
- bigger ships could carry more men
- better compasses/cross-staff improved navigation
- quadrants helped sailors calculate position/direction.

2. The candidate makes an accurate comparison of the sources by referring to evidence such as:

The sources agree fully

Source B	Source C
• The local people came to watch them.	• Watched by silent, naked natives.
• Took possession of the said island for the King and Queen.	• Took control of the island in the name of the King and Queen of Spain.
• He presented the natives with red caps and strings of beads.	• Gifts were exchanged with the natives.

3. The candidate describes the exploration of North America up to 1540 by referring to evidence such as:
   - exploration of Canada by Cabot 1497
   - Cabot mapped North American coast from Nova Scotia to Newfoundland
   - Ponce de Leon explored south and west coasts of Florida in 1513
   - De Vaca explored Gulf coast to Rockies 1528-36 eg Texas, New Mexico, Arizona
   - Jacques Cartier explored the Gulf of the St Lawrence in 1534
   - Cartier sailed past Newfoundland looking for a north west passage to China in 1535-36
   - Cartier discovered the area which became known as Montreal
   - Spanish exploration of Florida, North and South Carolinas by de Soto.

Context 5: "Tea and Freedom": The American Revolution, 1763-1783

1. The candidate explains why colonists were unhappy with British rule by referring to evidence such as:

   from the source
   - colonists blamed the British government for trade being poor
   - Granville's tough trade policies made the economic situation more difficult
   - British officials were seen as greedy
   - the British government was seen as distant and unsympathetic

   from recall
   - anger at unfair taxation – Stamp Act, Sugar Act etc
   - lack of representation in British Parliament
   - George III was viewed as a tyrant
   - acts of violence by British, eg Boston massacre
   - anger at continuing presence of British soldiers in colonies.

2. The candidate makes an accurate comparison of the sources by referring to evidence such as:

   The sources agree fully

Source B	Source C
• Poor leadership – American forces were often led by inefficient, incompetent commanders.	• Poor leadership – many American officers lacked training in the different types of warfare.
• They were badly armed and lacked supplies.	• Were short of artillery, cavalry and almost all sorts of supplies; many did not have a uniform.
• Most men were part-time soldiers.	• Many militia men met and trained in their spare time; part-time soldiers within each state.

3. The candidate describes the events leading up to the British surrender at Saratoga by referring to evidence such as:
   - capture of 1000 British on 26/12 1776 at Trenton
   - General Howe sends Cornwallis with 5000 men to take revenge
   - Cornwallis postpones attack and allows Washington's army to escape
   - poor leadership/tactics of British forces during 1777
   - lack of communication between the British armies
   - overconfidence of General Burgoyne
   - native Americans desert the British
   - defeat of Burgoyne's forces at Saratoga
   - surrender of 6000 men and 30 cannon.

Context 6: "This Accursed Trade": The British Slave Trade and its Abolition, 1770–1807

1. The candidate describes conditions for slaves during the Middle Passage by referring to evidence such as:
   - slaves were held in chains below deck
   - description of different methods of packing slaves – loose pack/tight pack
   - violence against slaves was common
   - illness and disease were common
   - dead slaves were thrown overboard
   - occasional exercise on deck was forced on the slaves
   - slaves were fed unfamiliar food which made them ill
   - there was a lack of sanitation
   - abuse of female slaves was common.

2. The candidate makes an accurate comparison of the sources by referring to evidence such as:

   The sources mainly agree

Source A	Source B
• Slaves were treated like animals (cattle).	• Examined like they were animals (horses).
• Slaves sold to highest bidder.	• Sold to man who offered most money.
• Wives sold to different owners than their husbands/owner wouldn't buy the baby.	• Son sold on his own.

3. The candidate explains why some people were in favour of the slave trade by referring to evidence such as:

   from the source
   - businessmen made large profits – 30% from a single voyage
   - Triangular Trade contributed to Britain's industrial development
   - helped growth of manufacturing in Manchester
   - provided jobs at the port of Liverpool

   from recall
   - slave trade was supported by powerful people (many MPs, King George III)
   - slave trade created wealth for powerful individuals and for Britain
   - British cities such as Bristol, Glasgow benefited from the trade and the raw material produced
   - steady supply of slaves were needed to work on plantations
   - end of slave trade might threaten the position of the British Empire.

Context 7: Citizens! The French Revolution, 1789-1794

1. The candidate describes the changes introduced by the Legislative Assembly in 1791 by referring to evidence such as:
   - the king no longer "owned" France
   - the king could not suggest nor delay laws/king lost a great deal of authority
   - only Active Citizens were to be given the vote
   - Active Citizens elected "Electors" to represent them
   - only the Assembly had the right to pass laws
   - the Assembly recognised local government
   - France was divided into departments
   - Courts were reorganised and judges were elected.

2. The candidate explains why there was a growing dislike of the monarchy in France in 1792 by referring to evidence such as:

   from the source:
   - king disliked sharing power with the assembly
   - wanted French army to be defeated to restore his power

- Louis refused to implement the constitution
- many suspected that he supported counter-revolution

from recall

- the royal family had attempted to escape from Paris
- Marie Antoinette was held responsible for France being attacked
- the Brunswick Manifesto was seen as a threat against the people of Paris
- the king's dealings with foreign counter-revolutionaries had been discovered.

3. The candidate makes an accurate comparison of the sources by referring to evidence such as:

The sources mainly agree

Source B	Source C
• Danton encouraged the Paris mobs to rise up.	• Working class people rioted to defend the revolution.
• One and a half thousand people were killed.	• At least fifteen hundred women, priests and soldiers were brutally murdered.
• Danton encouraged the mob to rise up.	• Danton must take the blame for having stirred up the sans-culottes.

Context 8: Cavour, Garibaldi and the Making of Italy, 1815-1870

1. The candidate describes the growth of nationalism in Italy between 1815 and 1847 by referring to evidence such as:
   - impact of French Revolution encouraged Italian intellectuals
   - invasions of Napoleon brought Italian states closer in terms of transport links
   - resentment of Austrian domination of Lombardy and Venetia
   - emergence of secret societies eg Carbonari inspired Italians to join struggle for change
   - Romantic Movement eg novelists, poets, composers, philosophers, spread nationalist ideas
   - business classes wanted greater economic integration
   - Mazzini formed Young Italy and inspired young Italians to dedicate energies to campaigning for a united Italy
   - 1831 King Charles Albert of Piedmont wanted to drive Austrians from Italy/allowed publication of liberal newspapers
   - Pope Pius IX 1846 gave amnesty to political opponents/encouraged nationalist feeling.

2. The candidate makes an accurate comparison of the sources by referring to evidence such as:

The sources mainly agree

Source A	Source B
• Small-scale fights broke out.	• There were clashes between the people and troops.
• Followed by larger riots and eventually a full scale revolution.	• Protests grew as peasants from outside the city arrived to join the rising.
• The revolutionaries set up a provisional government.	• Middle and upper class nationalists set up a provisional government.

3. The candidate explains why Garibaldi was important to the unification of Italy in 1861 by referring to evidence such as:

from the source

- brilliant commander/excellent at sizing up the situation
- inspired great enthusiasm and devotion in his men
- conquest of the south was a remarkable achievement
- he was totally devoted to the idea of national unity

from recall

- helped Mazzini defend the Roman Republic, 1849
- Garibaldi and the Thousand sailed to Sicily in 1860/defeated forces of King Ferdinand II
- he had a military success on River Volturno near Naples in October
- won over mass support from the peasants
- handed over South to King Victor Emmanuel at Teano in 1860.

Context 9: Iron and Blood? Bismarck and The Creation of the German Empire, 1815-1871

1. The candidate makes an accurate comparison of the sources by referring to evidence such as:

The sources agree fully

Source A	Source B
• The Austrian government was determined to prevent further incidents.	• Metternich and the Austrian government were determined to stop the nationalist feeling in the universities.
• At the Confederation at Carlsbad student organisations were outlawed.	• At the Confederation of Carlsbad in 1819 decrees were passed which suppressed the student societies.
• The effects of the decrees was the dismissal of a number of professors.	• Many university teachers were dismissed.

2. The candidate explains why there was a growth in nationalism in the German states between 1815 and 1850 by referring to evidence such as:

from the source

- Grimm folk tales celebrated Germany's past and looked to a day when it would be one nation
- many felt that their common language could lead to being united by the same government
- the Zollverein brought 25 German states together by 1836
- the development of railways pushed German states into greater cooperation

from recall

- growing middle class were won over to nationalism because of economic reasons
- the Zollverein set up an economic free trade area
- student movements promoted idea of national unity
- other cultural developments eg music, (Beethoven); German authors (Hegel, Goethe) encouraged unity
- 1848 revolutions/Frankfurt Parliament gave German states first taste of political unity.

3. The candidate describes the events leading to Prussia's war with Austria in 1866 by referring to evidence such as:
   - the war lasted 7 weeks
   - decisive battle at Konnigtratz/Sadowa 3 July 1866
   - Prussians used railway network to mobilise armies and supplies
   - superior Prussian tactics and weapons/Austrians had old-fashioned weapons
   - Prussian generals used the telegraph system to communicate with Berlin

- Austria was forced to fight a war on two fronts with Italy
- Austrians lost 240,000; 13,000 taken prisoner.

Context 10: The Red Flag: Lenin and the Russian Revolution, 1894-1921

1. The candidate explains why there was a revolution in Russia in 1905 by referring to evidence such as:

from the source
- repression in Russia by the Tsar and his government
- there was a great deal of poverty in the cities and countryside
- defeat by Japan strengthened the revolutionary movement
- revolutionary groups became more organised eg formation of St Petersburg soviet

from recall
- impact of Bloody Sunday which angered people
- shortages of food and fuel made people desperate
- high unemployment caused distress
- discontent in the armed forces was increasing.

2. The candidate describes the effects of the First World War on the Russian people by referring to evidence such as:
- outbreak of war led to patriotic demonstrations
- increasing economic hardship was caused by shortages of fuel and food
- there was increasing bereavement due to heavy losses in battles
- the increase in conscription left fewer people to work the land
- rising inflation meant prices rose ahead of wages
- people lost faith in their leaders
- anti-German feeling led to distrust of the Tsarina
- there was a growing desire for peace by 1917.

3. The candidate makes an accurate comparison of the sources by referring to evidence such as:

The sources disagree completely

Source B	Source C
• The party is ready and can seize power.	• An uprising now would put the party and revolution at risk.
• Our supporters in Petrograd and Moscow are strong.	• Our supporters among workers and soldiers are not ready to take to the streets now.
• By seizing power in Moscow and Petrograd we shall be successful.	• An uprising war will destroy what we have achieved/it will ruin us.

Context 11: Free at Last? Race Relations in the USA, 1918-1968

1. The candidate describes the problems that faced black Americans who moved north in the 1920s and 1930s by referring to evidence such as:
- skin colour identified them as "different" and marked them out for discrimination
- Whites felt they were superior to black migrants
- seen as uneducated and unskilled so poorly paid jobs
- White unskilled workers saw them as a threat to their jobs
- there was competition for jobs with immigrants to USA
- there were riots between Blacks and Whites in north
- they were separated into ghetto communities in northern cities
- housing conditions were very poor.

2. The candidate explains why black Americans felt that progress towards civil rights had been made between 1945 and 1959 by referring to evidence such as:

from the source
- NAACP were the moving force behind Supreme Court decisions
- the Supreme Court declared segregated schools unconstitutional
- black pressure forced Eisenhower to propose a Civil Rights Act
- Civil Rights Movement was gaining heroes such as Rosa Parks

from recall
- mass action such as Montgomery Bus Boycott was successful
- protest at Little Rock saw black students admitted to a white school
- details of Brown v Topeka Board of Education decision
- rise of new civil rights' leaders such as Martin Luther King and SCLC.

3. The candidate makes an accurate comparison of the sources by referring to evidence such as:

The sources agree fully

Source B	Source C
• Sit-ins showed students/young people could take action themselves.	• Students believed they could make a difference. • Sit-ins gave students/young people a sense of their own worth.
• Could make a difference by winning support of both blacks and whites.	• Actions encouraged black community support and won the respect of whites.
• Only limited success in some towns and cities.	• Only enjoyed success in a few Southern states. Refusal to desegregate in Deep South.

Context 12: The Road to War, 1933-1939

1. The candidate explains why Britain followed a policy of Appeasement in the 1930s by referring to evidence such as:

from the source
- the Great Depression meant there was no money for rearmament
- the British people were opposed to war
- Chamberlain believed that he could negotiate directly with Hitler
- communist Russia was the real threat to peace

from recall
- British opinion felt that the Treaty of Versailles had been too harsh
- there was the fear of bombing from the air
- Chiefs of Staff warned the government that British forces were unprepared
- Britain had no reliable allies – Empire unwilling, France was not trusted and USA was neutral.

2. The candidate describes the aims of Hitler's foreign policy between 1933 and 1936 by referring to evidence such as:
- he wanted to destroy the Treaty of Versailles
- he wanted to regain the territory that Germany had lost
- he wanted to remilitarise the Rhineland
- he wanted to increase Germany's power in Europe
- he wanted to create a Greater Germany for all Germans
- he wanted to gain *Lebensraum* for the German people
- he wanted to achieve Anschluss with Austria
- he wanted to isolate France.

3. The candidate makes an accurate comparison of the sources by referring to evidence such as:

The sources disagree completely

Source B	Source C
• Anschluss is popular among the Austrian people.	• The population has no love for Nazism.
• Versailles had been wrong to keep Germany and Austria apart.	• The decision of 1919 to forbid Anschluss had been sensible.
• Europe will benefit from a period of peace and prosperity.	• A powerful Germany is a threat to the peace and stability of Europe.

Context 13: In the Shadow of the Bomb: The Cold War, 1945-1985

1. The candidate explains why the Soviet Union built the Berlin Wall in 1961 by referring to evidence such as:

from the source
- record numbers of East Germans were escaping to the West
- those who left East Berlin were young and well educated
- enemy agents (spies) were stationed in East Berlin
- agents were using West Berlin as a centre of operations against East Germany and the Soviet Union

from recall
- West Berlin was in the middle of communist East Germany
- future of Berlin had been in dispute since the end of World War II
- West Berlin was a shining example of capitalism
- Khrushchev needed a foreign policy success to divert attention from domestic problems.

2. The candidate evaluates the sources by referring to evidence such as:

The sources mainly disagree

Source B	Source C
• The Vietcong generally avoided large scale attacks.	• Thousands of Vietcong launched wave after wave of attacks on our camp.
• The Vietcong travelled light carrying few supplies and basic weapons.	• They had all kinds of weapons such as Chinese flamethrowers, Russian rocket launchers.
• The Vietcong caused heavy American casualties.	• Americans only lost 7 guys/Vietcong body count was reported to have been 800.

3. The candidate describes steps taken to reduce tensions between the USA and USSR during the 1960s and 1970s by referring to evidence such as:
- they set up a "hot line" post Cuba
- non-proliferation treaty was signed in the 1960s
- SALT talks agreed to limit testing of nuclear weapons
- USA begins to sell the USSR wheat in 1970s
- the end of the Vietnam War eased tension
- USA and USSR signed Helsinki agreement in 1975
- changing personalities among the leadership of the USA and USSR
- joint space mission between USA and USSR in 1975.

HISTORY INTERMEDIATE 2 2010

PART 1 THE SHORT ESSAY

Scottish and British

Context 1: Murder in the Cathedral: Crown, Church and People, 1154-1173

1. The candidate explains why Henry II faced difficulties on becoming king in 1154 by referring to evidence such as:
   - Henry's empire was vast with no common language or traditions
   - barons had built illegal castles
   - barons hired mercenaries/had illegal private armies to protect their land
   - some barons openly challenged Henry eg Earl of York, Scarborough Castle
   - barons were stealing land from their weaker neighbours
   - sheriffs were corrupt and were keeping fines and possessions which should have gone to the king
   - there was no uniform law in the kingdom/sheriffs decided the law in their local area
   - the Church had increased its authority eg Criminous Clerks/Canon Law.

Context 2: Wallace, Bruce and the Wars of Independence, 1286-1328

2. The candidate explains why the Scots won the battle at Bannockburn by referring to evidence such as:
   - Robert Bruce's leadership was a key factor
   - Robert Bruce had trained his men to fight as mobile schiltrons
   - Robert Bruce fought the battle on ground which suited his men/tactics
   - the English did not expect Bruce to attack them (they expected to attack)
   - the English had moved onto ground which was too marshy for them to manoeuvre
   - the English were trapped in an area which was too small for their army to manoeuvre
   - the English were arguing with each other before the battle
   - the English did not have confidence in King Edward II
   - the English were disheartened after the death of de Bohun etc
   - English bowmen were defeated by the Scottish cavalry
   - the English panicked when the "small folk" charged towards the battle.

Context 3: Mary, Queen of Scots and the Scottish Reformation, 1540s-1587

3. The candidate explains why Riccio became unpopular with Darnley and the Scottish nobles by referring to evidence such as:
   - Darnley thought he had persuaded Mary not to give him the crown matrimonial
   - Scottish nobles persuaded Darnley that Riccio was too friendly with his Mary
   - Riccio was behaving like a noble although he was below them in status
   - Riccio was dressing like a nobleman
   - Riccio was humiliating the Scottish nobles by making them ask him to see Queen Mary
   - Riccio was boasting about his influence over Queen Mary
   - Riccio was foreign (Italian)
   - some thought that Riccio was really a spy sent by the Pope
   - some Scottish nobles wanted to create trouble between Queen Mary and Darnley.

Context 4: The Coming of the Civil War, 1603-1642

4. The candidate explains why Charles I was an unpopular monarch in England by 1640 by referring to evidence such as:
   - he believed in the Divine Right of Kings which undermined Parliament
   - his religious policies angered the Puritans and Parliament
   - he used 'forced loans' to raise money for war against Spain
   - he imposed the 'Ship Money' tax without Parliament's consent
   - failures in foreign policy led to unpopularity eg the United Provinces
   - policy of impressments was unpopular
   - he collected 'tonnage and poundage' without Parliament's consent
   - he introduced fines for people who had built on common land or in royal forests
   - during the Period of Personal Rule (1629-1640) Charles ruled without consulting Parliament
   - he was seen as a tyrant.

Context 5: "Ane End of Ane Auld Sang": Scotland and the Treaty of Union, 1690s-1715

5. The candidate explains why many Scots were disappointed by the Act of Union by 1715 by referring to evidence such as:
   - Scotland had not become richer
   - there was fear that English imports were ruining Scottish businesses
   - there were new Customs and Excise taxes (eg Malt Tax)
   - they disliked the changes in Scotland's weights, measures, money etc
   - nobles and important politicians had left Edinburgh for London
   - the House of Lords had allowed "patronage" in the Church of Scotland (Patronage Act)
   - Episcopalians were allowed in Scotland (Toleration Act)
   - they were now ruled by George of Hanover (rather than a Stuart)
   - the Equivalent had not been paid.

Context 6: Immigrants and Exiles: Scotland, 1830s-1930s

6. The candidate explains why Irish immigrants were attracted to Scotland between 1830 and 1930 by referring to evidence such as:
   - Scotland was close to Ireland
   - travel was cheap
   - there was work to be found in cotton/textile factories
   - there was work in the coal mines
   - many found work as navigators of the canals and railways
   - there was work to be found on farms at harvest time
   - the whole family could find employment
   - work was more constant
   - many Irish had already settled in Scotland which encouraged more to come
   - Protestant Irish found it easy to settle into Scottish society.

Context 7: From the Cradle to the Grave? Social Welfare in Britain, 1890s-1951

7. The candidate explains why the Liberal government passed social welfare reforms between 1906 and 1914 by referring to evidence such as:
   - changing attitudes towards the reasons for poverty
   - inadequate provision by the Poor Law system and charitable organisations
   - surveys of Booth and Rowntree showed the extent of poverty
   - poor physical condition of recruits for the Boer War raised concerns about national security
   - concerns about Britain's industrial strength/health of the workforce
   - growth of the Labour Movement/spread of socialist ideas
   - changing political ideology/emergence of 'New Liberalism'
   - welfare reform had begun in other countries eg Germany.

Context 8: Campaigning for Change: Social Change in Scotland, 1900s-1979

8. The candidate explains why there was still a need to improve many women's lives after 1918 by referring to evidence such as:
   - only women over 30 had the vote until 1928, so no political voice
   - fewer than 20 women MP's by 1939
   - many woman were forced to give up their jobs to returning soldiers, even when they were the family breadwinner
   - a woman's place was still seen as being in the home eg women's magazines concentrated on recipes, knitting etc
   - women were still excluded from top jobs eg in the Civil Service
   - many employers, such as local authorities, imposed a marriage bar
   - women's wages were still much less than men's – up to 50% lower for working class women
   - Trades Unions still opposed employing women in many workplaces – argued they deprived men of jobs
   - many women were widowed or remained unmarried as fiancés and husbands were killed in the war and there was a subsequent shortage of men
   - many working class women could not afford the new labour saving devices which were being developed.

Context 9: A Time of Troubles: Ireland, 1900-1923

9. The candidate explains why the Anglo-Irish War broke out in 1919 by referring to evidence such as:
   - Republicans refused to accept Home Rule
   - Republicans would only agree to full independence
   - 73 Sinn Fein MPs refused to go to Westminster to take their seats
   - Irish independence declared/Republican government formed
   - Dail established in Dublin
   - Sinn Fein challenged the authority of the British/established legal, financial and local government infrastructure
   - Sinn Fein organised, trained and armed Irish Volunteers Force
   - British used armed forces to try and stop the Irish taking control
   - Irish Volunteers killed two members of the Royal Irish Constabulary, sparking violence.

European and World

Context 1: The Norman Conquest, 1060-1153

10. The candidate explains why knights were important in medieval society by referring to evidence such as:
    - provided protection for other social groups eg churchmen
    - maintained the control of Norman lords over their Saxon subjects
    - knights were key figures in 11th century warfare
    - made up King's chief fighting force in war
    - highly trained warriors
    - carried out duties such as castle-guard
    - maintained order on their own land
    - managed the economy of the land.

Context 2: The Cross and the Crescent: The First Crusade, 1096-1125

11. The candidate explains the reasons why the Crusaders were able to keep control of the Holy Land after 1097 by referring to evidence such as:

- the Crusaders appointed a king (Godfrey and later Baldwin) in Jerusalem ensuring law and order was maintained
- Hospitallers and Templars arrived from Europe specifically to protect Jerusalem
- the Crusaders traded with the Italian city states providing supplies for those in the east
- the Crusaders cooperated with Muslims in order to get them to tend the fields and grow crops
- the Crusaders built castles to protect the territory they had taken
- extra settlers from the east arrived, having been offered incentives to stay in Holy Land
- the feudal system was established in the east, organising the Crusaders.

Context 3: War, Death and Revolt in Medieval Europe, 1328-1436

12. The candidate explains why France was unsuccessful in the war against England between 1415 and 1422 by referring to evidence such as:
- French weakness due to the insanity of their King
- Dauphin was weak and mentally immature
- civil war between the Houses of Armagnac and Burgundy
- English alliance with the House of Burgundy
- effective leadership of Henry V eg tactics at Agincourt
- effectiveness of the English longbow
- disorganisation of the French armies eg divisions over tactics at Agincourt
- ruthlessness of Henry's tactics after Agincourt eg naval blockade, murder of captives, sieges of Rouen and Meaux.

Context 4: New Worlds: Europe in the Age of Expansion, 1480s-1530s

13. The candidate explains the reasons why the Spaniards were able to defeat **either** the Aztecs **or** the Incas by referring to evidence such as:
- they were deceitful in their dealing with the kings
- the religious beliefs of both Aztecs and Incas weakened them
- Spanish had horses and knew how to use them in battle
- Spanish had better weapons than the Aztecs or Incas
- Spanish had better (metal) armour
- Spanish captured the rulers of these states
- rulers underestimated Spanish greed/underestimated Spanish intentions
- both Aztecs and Incas had dominated/made enemies of their local neighbours
- Spanish made alliances with enemies of Aztecs/Inca Empire divided over succession
- Aztecs and Incas both unable to put up effective resistance (no steel, cannons).

Context 5: "Tea and Freedom": The American Revolution, 1763-1783

14. The candidate explains the reasons why the American War of Independence broke out in 1775 by referring to evidence such as:
- growing divide between the colonists and Britain
- colonists were angry at the continuing presence of British troops following the defeat of the French in 1763
- colonists were angry at George III's desire to exert greater control over colonies
- frustration over Britain's refusal to allow the colonies to expand westward
- growing anger over continuing taxation of colonies without direct representation in British parliament
- anger over the imposition of Sugar Act/Stamp Act/the Tea Act/Quartering Acts/Intolerable Acts

- events such as the Boston Massacre
- formation of the Continental Congress in 1774
- fighting at Lexington and Concord in April 1775 led to formation of Continental Army under leadership of George Washington in June 1775.

Context 6: "This Accursed Trade": The British Slave Trade and its Abolition, 1770–1807

15. The candidate explains the reasons why it took so long for Britain to abolish the slave trade by referring to evidence such as:
- there was a great deal of support for the slave trade from powerful people in business and parliament
- bribery used to ensure the continued support for the trade among some MPs
- many accepted the argument that the success of the British economy relied on the continuation of slavery
- fear of job losses in industries dependent on the slave trade
- fear of loss of tax revenue
- King George III supported the slave trade
- many towns such as Liverpool and Bristol benefited directly from the trade
- profits from the trade were essential to fund the war with France
- people believed the slave trade was a training ground for the British navy.

Context 7: Citizens! The French Revolution, 1789-1794

16. The candidate explains the reasons why the French people were unhappy with their government by 1789 by referring to evidence such as:
- Louis XVI was determined to rule the country alone/claimed 'Divine right of kings'
- people were listening to new political ideas saying that the people had a right to share power
- the middle class resented the political power of the nobility
- the Estates General had not been called for over a century
- the peasants resented the feudal power of the nobility to rule over them
- the French government was bankrupt and inefficient
- the peasants resented having to pay most of the taxes to the government
- the taxation system was seen as corrupt and wasteful
- the workers in the cities were suffering from poor wages and high food prices but the government did nothing to help them.

Context 8: Cavour, Garibaldi and the Making of Italy, 1815-1870

17. The candidate explains the reasons why Garibaldi's leadership was important to the unification of Italy by referring to evidence such as:
- brilliant military leader and commander
- initially supported aims of Mazzini's 'Young Italy' to unite states in a democratic republic
- defended Rome against the French in 1849 – respected by other nationalists
- reputation grew because he won victories over the Austrians eg Verese, Como
- was a member of the nationalist society from 1857
- popular with foreign powers eg Britain
- was hugely popular with the peasants
- used the peasant disturbances in Sicily to unite north and south
- led 'The Thousand' and sailed to Sicily in 1860
- conceded his conquests to Victor Emmanuel at Teano in 1860
- good oratorical skills.

Context 9: Iron and Blood? Bismarck and The Creation of the German Empire, 1815-1871

18. The candidate explains the reasons why the nationalist movement had failed to unite the German states by 1850 by referring to evidence such as:
    - liberalism/nationalism only affected the middle and upper classes
    - power/influence of Metternich/Austria eg German Confederation
    - desire for individual rulers to retain power/used armies to crush revolutionaries
    - lack of support for a united Germany from foreign powers eg Britain, Russia
    - student nationalist movements crushed eg Carlsbad Decrees 1819
    - failure of the 1848 revolutions
    - nationalists divided/'Kleindeutschland' or 'Grossdeutschland'
    - failure of the Frankfurt Parliament
    - Frederick William IV of Prussia refused crown of a united Germany
    - failure of the Erfurt Union.

Context 10: The Red Flag: Lenin and the Russian Revolution, 1894-1921

19. The candidate explains the reasons why the Tsar was able to remain in power following the 1905 revolution by referring to evidence such as:
    - the Tsar announced his October Manifesto, accepting cabinet government, free speech and a constitution for Russia, splitting his opposition
    - political parties became legal
    - a limited vote was extended to the peasants and industrial workers
    - many Liberals accepted these terms and ceased opposing the Tsar
    - right wing supporters of the Tsar began a wave of attacks on Jews and liberal intellectuals who continued their opposition
    - Witte was appointed Chairman of the Council of Ministers and arrested the entire St Petersburg soviet
    - the troops stayed loyal to the Tsar and crushed opposition in Moscow
    - the general strike came to an end as the middle classes withdrew their support
    - the government announced the end of redemption dues to placate the peasants
    - the Russo-Japanese War ended.

Context 11: Free at Last? Race Relations in the USA, 1918-1968

20. The candidate explains why the demand for civil rights continued to grow after 1945 by referring to evidence such as:
    - impact of the Second World War eg USA fighting against a violent racist regime abroad while violent racism flourished in the southern states
    - experience of black soldiers from the south who witnessed integration abroad
    - actions of early campaigners eg Phillip Randolph, Core (1942)
    - the existence of Jim Crow laws in the southern states
    - effects of segregation – eg schools, transport, restaurants
    - concern at other inequalities faced by Black Americans eg low wages, poor housing
    - refusal of State governments to desegregate following Brown v Topeka judgement
    - continuance of lynching
    - North/South divide became more obvious after 1945.

Context 12: The Road to War, 1933-1939

21. The candidate explains the reasons why Hitler's actions created problems in Europe between 1933 and 1939 by referring to evidence such as:
    - withdrawal from the Disarmament Conference/League of Nations was seen as a threat to rearm
    - Germany rebuilt her army, navy and airforce
    - Hitler declared that he wanted to regain territory lost at Versailles
    - Hitler wanted to take over Austria, an independent country
    - the policy of a greater Germany was a threat to countries with German minorities, especially Poland and Czechoslovakia
    - the policy of Lebensraum was a threat to countries in eastern Europe
    - the reoccupation of the Rhineland threatened the security of France and Belgium
    - Hitler was willing to break voluntary treaties eg the Locarno Pact, the Munich Settlement
    - Germany's involvement in the Spanish Civil War and the spread of Fascism.

Context 13: In the Shadow of the Bomb: The Cold War, 1945-1985

22. The candidate explains the reasons why America lost the war in Vietnam by referring to evidence such as:
    - American soldiers were poorly trained and equipped for jungle warfare
    - the draft system meant that there was a lack of experience among American forces
    - American soldiers had low morale and lacked respect for their officers – incidents of fragging
    - America was propping up South Vietnamese government that did not enjoy popular support among the South Vietnamese people
    - Vietcong benefited from experience of fighting the French
    - Vietcong were expert in conducting guerrilla warfare
    - failure of American tactics – strategic hamlets, carpet bombing, use of defoliants (Agent Orange)
    - American tactics alienated the civilian population of Vietnam and generated negative publicity at home
    - anti-war protests and lack of international support helped persuade American government to withdraw from Vietnam.

PART 2 HISTORICAL STUDY

Scottish and British

Context 1: Murder in the Cathedral: Crown, Church and People, 1154-1173

1. The candidate explains why castles were important in the twelfth century by referring to evidence such as:

   from the source:
   - castles were the key symbol of power
   - administrative centres of each town
   - base for local garrison
   - stored food, drink and other supplies.

   from recall:
   - used as a law court
   - used as a place of protection/to defend the Lord's land
   - used as a home
   - centre of entertainment eg feasts and banquets.

2. The candidate compares the sources by referring to evidence such as:

The sources agree completely

Source B	Source C
• 2 o'clock – monks woken for service	• service began in the middle of the night
• expected to pray at least 8 times a day	• expected to pray several times a day
• breakfast eaten in silence	• meal times, talking strictly forbidden

3. The candidate describes the murder of Archbishop Becket by referring to evidence such as:
   • four knights arrived at Canterbury and asked to see Becket
   • Becket refused to run away or hide/the knights were let into the cathedral
   • the knights attempted to arrest Becket/Becket refused to go with them
   • Becket stated he was willing to die a martyr for God
   • Edward Grim had his arm sliced during the ensuing struggle
   • the knights hit Becket on the head four times
   • one knight struck Becket with such force his sword was broken against his head and the paving stone
   • the crown of Becket's head was sliced off/his brains were extracted
   • the knights ran away.

Context 2: Wallace, Bruce and the Wars of Independence, 1286-1328

1. The candidate describes the events between 1286 and 1292 that led to Edward I becoming overlord of Scotland by referring to evidence such as:
   • death of Alexander III without sons
   • death of the Maid
   • rivalry between Bruce and Balliol/fear of a civil war in Scotland
   • Guardians asked Edward to decide who would be king
   • Edward asked the Guardians to agree he was overlord
   • Edward demanded that the (thirteen) Competitors recognise him as overlord
   • Competitors accepted Edward's demands
   • the Award of Berwick
   • Edward had an army with him
   • John Balliol did homage to King Edward.

2. The candidate explains why the leadership of William Wallace was important during the Wars of Independence by referring to evidence such as:

   from the source:
   • he united people under his leadership as Guardian
   • he organised the army of Scotland
   • he sent Lamberton to Rome and Paris to plead Scotland's case there
   • he obtained iron from Germany for his army.

   from recall:
   • he defeated the English at Stirling Bridge
   • he developed the idea of fighting in schiltrons
   • he made sure that Edward did not select the new Bishop of St. Andrews
   • he continued to resist Edward till he was executed.

3. The candidate compares the sources by referring to evidence such as:

The sources disagree

Source B	Source C
• all the Scots supported Bruce	• some Scots plotting against him
• had royal blood	• other nobles claimed to be more closely related to royalty
• his deeds had won him the support of the Scottish people	• he was a ruthless thug

Context 3: Mary, Queen of Scots and the Scottish Reformation, 1540s-1587

1. The candidate explains why Henry VIII of England ordered the invasions of Scotland after 1544 by referring to evidence such as:

   from the source:
   • Henry wanted to break the Auld Alliance between Scotland and France
   • the Scots had agreed to marry Mary to Henry's son, Edward in the Treaty of Greenwich
   • the Scots resisted the demands of Henry VIII (encouraged by the French)
   • the Scots announced that the treaty was broken.

   from recall:
   • the government of Scotland was moving towards favouring France eg Guise, Beaton
   • Henry disagreed that the Treaty of Greenwich was void because he failed to ratify it in time
   • the French had bribed Arran to change his mind about supporting the marriage
   • Henry intended to force the Scots into changing their mind.

2. The candidate describes the events leading up to the signing of the Treaty of Edinburgh in 1560 by referring to evidence such as:
   • Protestantism had spread within Scotland (encouraged by England)
   • Mary of Guise began to stamp down on Protestants eg executions
   • the Lords of the Congregation began to protest about this
   • Mary of Guise used French soldiers to help crush this rebellion
   • English help was sent to support the Protestants
   • while soldiers from the two nations faced each other Mary of Guise died
   • both sides agreed to withdraw their soldiers and leave the Scots to settle their own affairs.

3. The candidate compares the sources by referring to evidence such as:

The sources disagree

Source B	Source C
• she neglected its government	• she had been a successful ruler/established a successful government
• she left the running of the country to a group of nobles	• she defeated nobles who challenged her authority
• did not care about religion	• her religious policy was tolerant and ahead of its time

Context 4: The Coming of the Civil War, 1603-1642

1. The candidate compares the sources by referring to evidence such as:

The sources agree

Source A	Source B
• James VI and I was well educated and clever	• James VI and I was highly intelligent
• he thought kings were appointed by God and could do as they wished	• he believed in the Divine Right of Kings
• lost people's respect by giving money and power to favourites at court	• he gave gifts and pensions to courtiers

2. The candidate describes the methods used by James VI and I to raise money during his reign by referring to evidence such as:
   - he used forced loans
   - he raised customs duties/impositions
   - he used feudal dues
   - continued to use rights of wardship
   - crown lands were sold
   - he sold titles of honour/knighthoods, baronies, earldoms
   - patents of monopoly given
   - used purveyance to buy discounted goods for royal household
   - employed officials eg Cranfield to raise money for the Crown.

3. The candidate explains why Charles I faced opposition to his rule in Scotland by referring to evidence such as:

   from the source:
   - he tried to enforce his religious views
   - many Scots were Presbyterians and disliked change
   - Scots resented Charles because he was an absentee king/visited Scotland only once
   - Scotland was a poor country/many thought Charles did not care.

   from recall:
   - he introduced the Common Prayer Book in 1637
   - anger over the Prayer Book led to St Giles Riot
   - he tried to raise taxes from the Scots
   - King sent an army to the borders of Scotland/Bishops Wars began.

Context 5: "Ane End of Ane Auld Sang": Scotland and the Treaty of Union, 1690s-1715

1. The candidate describes what happened during the Worcester affair by referring to evidence such as:
   - the Company of Scotland's last ship "Speedy Return" had been lost
   - some of the crew of the Worcester hinted that they were responsible for its loss (pirates)
   - Captain Green and two of his crew were arrested and put on trial
   - Captain Green and two others were found guilty and sentenced to death
   - Queen Anne's government in England wanted her to pardon them
   - Queen Anne wanted her Scottish Government to pardon them
   - the Edinburgh mob ensured that the Scottish Government did not pardon them
   - Captain Green and the two crewmen were hanged.

2. The candidate explains why Queen Anne wanted a Treaty of Union between England and Scotland by referring to evidence such as:

   from the source:
   - the Scottish Parliament was difficult to control
   - the Scottish Parliament complained her policies were harming Scotland
   - the Scottish Parliament was threatening to break the Union of the Crowns
   - the problems with Scotland made it difficult to fight the war against France.

   from recall:
   - she wanted Scotland and England to have the same ruler
   - she wanted to ensure a Protestant succession
   - she was worried about the Jacobites trying to become rulers in Scotland
   - she was worried about French influence in Scotland.

3. The candidate compares the sources by referring to evidence such as:

The sources disagree

Source B	Source C
• the Equivalent was money to help recover from Darien	• money paid to Scotland was to bribe rich and powerful men
• Scots thought they would have influence in a new powerful kingdom	• Scots feared they would have little influence over government decisions
• traders would benefit from access to English colonies	• business would suffer from competition from English imports.

Context 6: Immigrants and Exiles: Scotland, 1830s-1930s

1. The candidate compares the sources by referring to evidence such as:

The sources agree

Source A	Source B
• disliked by native scots	• great deal of resentment against the immigrants
• Irish determination to keep their own culture was looked upon suspiciously	• Irish immigrants criticised for keeping their own language and religion
• Irish did not receive much credit for their contribution to the Scottish economy	• reluctance to admit that Irish labour was essential

2. The candidate explains why many poor Scots were able to emigrate during the nineteenth century by referring to evidence such as:

   from the source:
   - landlords paid travelling costs
   - rent arrears written off so that emigrants had money
   - buying cattle meant emigrants had capital
   - Edinburgh and Glasgow made a contribution towards their expenses in emigrating.

   from recall:
   - Highlands and Islands Emigration Society (HIES) gave assistance
   - charities eg Barnardos, helped orphans/young women to emigrate
   - countries such as Australia and Canada sent agents to advise on emigration

- family members living abroad gave encouragement and sent money for travel.

3. The candidate describes the ways Scots helped to improve the lands to which they emigrated by referring to evidence such as:
    - Scots brought farming skills to Canada
    - Scots developed sheep farming in Australia
    - tradesmen such as stone masons helped the building industry in USA
    - developed businesses, banks and trading companies
    - examples of contributions to economy and other aspects such as Andrew Carnegie (steel); Donald Mackay (Boston shipyards); Alan Pinkerton (detective agency); John Muir (national parks); example such as paper-making in New Zealand
    - Scots established education system eg Canada
    - Scots brought a tradition of hard work.

Context 7: From the Cradle to the Grave? Social Welfare in Britain, 1890s-1951

1. The candidate compares the sources by referring to evidence such as:

    The sources agree

Source A	Source B
• a pensioner with a yearly income of up to £21 received the full 25p a week	• it entitled people with an annual income of £21 to 25p a week
• pensions available to those who had been out of prison for ten years	• entitled to the pension provided they had avoided imprisonment in the previous ten years
• it was not a generous amount	• these payments were not meant to be a complete solution to the problem of poverty

2. The candidate describes the ways the Beveridge Report of 1942 suggested tackling the social problems facing Britain by referring to evidence such as:
    - recommended a welfare system which would look after people from 'the cradle to the grave'
    - recommended the setting up of a National Health Service to tackle disease
    - recommended the introduction of family allowances to tackle want
    - National Insurance contributions to be made by workers
    - benefits for the unemployed to be available for an indefinite period
    - advised the government to adopt a policy of full employment
    - recommended a comprehensive system of benefits including old age pensions, widow's pensions and maternity grants
    - advised benefits to be available without a means test.

3. The candidate explains why some people were disappointed with the Labour welfare reforms by 1951 by referring to evidence such as:

    from the source:
    - poor housing and homelessness were still serious problems
    - little done to enhance the educational opportunities for working class children/most left school at fifteen with no paper qualifications
    - still a shortage of hospitals and health centres
    - problems of poverty and deprivation not adequately solved.

    from recall:
    - not everyone covered by the National Insurance Act/safety net did not cover all
    - charges introduced in NHS eg prescriptions

- school building programme inadequate
- many new houses were only temporary eg prefabs.

Context 8: Campaigning for Change: Social Change in Scotland, 1900s-1979

1. The sources completely agree

Source A	Source B
• number of public houses decreased	• number of pubs fell if people voted for it
• tax on alcohol increased	• alcohol became more expensive when tax was raised by 34%
• people chose to spend money on goods and leisure activities	• there was a greater choice of things to do

2. The candidate describes the unrest on Red Clydeside between 1915 and 1919 by referring to evidence such as:
    - skilled engineers went on strike for more pay – 'tuppence an hour'
    - anger over importation of English and American workers, paid more than Scots workers
    - rent strikes when landlords raised rents and evicted female tenants whose husbands were away fighting
    - Clyde Workers Committee set up to protect munitions workers from compulsory long hours at low rates of pay under Munitions Act
    - Strike at Beardmore's Parkhead Steel Works over 'dilution' by unskilled labour
    - Clyde Workers' Committee organised strike demanding 40 hour week
    - 60,000 strikers gathered in George Square and raised Red Flag
    - police attacked crowd with truncheons and activists were arrested
    - English soldiers and tanks sent to Glasgow in case of further unrest.

3. The candidate explains why the development of North Sea Oil was so important for the economy of the north of Scotland by referring to evidence such as:

    from the source:
    - Aberdeen became oil capital of Europe/boom spread to north east towns
    - oil rig construction yards set up in Nigg and Ardersier
    - 3000 new jobs created in Shetland
    - many companies moved north to provide support and services.

    from recall:
    - construction yards also set up on west coast at Kishorn and at Arnish in Lewis
    - wide range of new, skilled jobs offered much higher wages
    - standard of living also raised by full employment eg good restaurants opened
    - increased demand for housing raised value of property, spreading prosperity.

Context 9: A Time of Troubles: Ireland, 1900-1923

1. The candidate compares the sources by referring to evidence such as:

    The sources completely disagree

Source A	Source B
• Irish people have benefited from the Union	• we have been the losers in the Union with Britain
• better wages for our work	• poor wages have made people desperate
• freedom and rights protected	• until Ireland has rights we still have no freedom

2. The candidate describes the actions taken by the Unionists against the Home Rule Bill by referring to evidence such as:
    - Unionists began to organise an effective campaign against Home Rule
    - organised meetings and rallies
    - gained support from important politicians
    - signed Ulster Covenant
    - Ulster Volunteers Force set up
    - UVF trained, organised and drilled like a real army
    - German rifles/ammunition brought in illegally to Ireland
    - gained support of British army eg "Curragh Mutiny".

3. The candidate explains why De Valera opposed the 1921 Treaty by referring to evidence such as:

    from the source:
    - De Valera had not been consulted about the terms of the Treaty
    - he refused to accept the six counties of Northern Ireland
    - he refused to take an oath of allegiance to the British King
    - he argued only full independence could bring peace.

    from recall:
    - De Valera would not agree to a boundary commission
    - De Valera refused to accept the British King being represented by a Governor-General in Ireland
    - De Valera insisted that Ireland should have full legal rights/would not accept the Irish Free State
    - De Valera wanted full control of Ireland's coasts
    - De Valera did not want the Royal Navy to use Ireland's ports.

PART 3 HISTORICAL STUDY

European and World

Context 1: The Norman Conquest, 1060-1153

1. The candidate explains why Harold lost the battle of Hastings by referring to evidence such as:

    from the source:
    - Normans had a large army including many horsemen and archers
    - Harold forced his exhausted army to march south immediately
    - Harold had lost many brave men in two previous battles
    - some of his soldiers deserted before the battle began.

    from recall:
    - Saxons had already had to fight a long and bloody battle at Stamford Bridge
    - Saxon army fought on foot
    - Saxons were tricked by William's feigned retreat
    - Harold was killed in the fighting.

2. The candidate evaluates **Source B** as evidence about William's attempts to control England after 1066 by referring to evidence such as:
    - primary source written while William was attempting to bring England under his control
    - written by William's priest so biased in favour of William
    - written to claim that William was fair to his enemies
    - says that he rewarded those who had fought for him by granting fiefs.

    Maximum 1 mark for indicating content omission such as:
    - no mention of William's cruelty/military campaigns against the Saxons
    - no mention of the Harrying of the North.

3. The candidate describes the ways in which Scotland changed during the reign of David I by referring to evidence such as:
    - arrival of the Normans in Scotland
    - introduction of Feudalism on the Anglo-Norman model
    - appointment of King's sheriffs
    - increase in power of the king
    - development of castles across Scotland
    - creation and growth of burghs
    - expansion of monasticism
    - government by English style royal council.

Context 2: The Cross and the Crescent: The First Crusade, 1096-1125

1. The candidate explains why Pope Urban II called the First Crusade by referring to evidence such as:

    from the source:
    - Emperor Alexius asked for help
    - Turks were a threat to Christianity
    - wanted to stop western knights fighting among themselves
    - wanted to recapture Jerusalem.

    from recall:
    - wanted to help Christians in the East
    - wanted to reopen trade and pilgrim routes
    - wanted to protect Christian churches/shrines
    - wanted to show kings/emperors of Europe that he could raise an army
    - wanted to heal the schism (split in the church) and unite the Eastern and Western churches
    - wanted to place himself as overall ruler of a united church.

2. The candidate describes the siege and capture of Antioch by the First Crusade by referring to evidence such as:
    - Bohemond bribed a Muslim guard (Firouz) to let him into the city
    - the Crusaders used ladders and ropes to scale the wall
    - the Crusaders captured the three towers commanded by Firouz
    - once inside they opened the gate and let the rest of the army into the city
    - the inhabitants of the city were slaughtered
    - the Crusaders were then surrounded by a Muslim army (Kerbogha's)
    - the Holy Lance inspired the Crusaders to attack the Muslims
    - the Crusaders defeated the Muslim army/Kerbogha's men ran away.

3. The candidate evaluates the usefulness of **Source B** as evidence of the Crusaders' behaviour in the Holy Land by referring to evidence such as:
    - primary source written during the Crusades
    - author was an eyewitness/actually saw the events at Marrat au Numan
    - written to show his disgust at the Crusaders behaviour
    - says they cut their flesh into slices, cooked and ate them.

    Maximum 1 mark for indicating content omission such as:
    - Crusaders slaughtered the inhabitants of Marrat au Numan
    - Crusaders spit roasted babies.

Context 3: War, Death and Revolt in Medieval Europe, 1328-1436

1. The candidate describes the succession problem to the French throne after 1328 by referring to evidence such as:
    - Charles IV died without a direct heir
    - Phillip of Valois seized the throne
    - Phillip claimed that he was the chosen heir of Charles IV
    - the English queen, Isabel claimed the throne of France as she was sister of Charles IV
    - English kings held lands in France
    - Edward claimed that he had a better claim to the throne than Phillip
    - Edward was willing to use his claim to the throne as a pretext for an attack on France.

2. The candidate evaluates the usefulness of **Source A** as evidence of the effects of the Battle of Poitiers on France by referring to evidence such as:
   * primary source written during this phase of the war/ secondary source recorded some years after the battle
   * written by Froissart an important and respected French chronicler
   * written to explain the impact of defeat on France
   * says that France was badly affected by the loss of so many fighting men.

Maximum 1 mark for indicating content omission such as:

   * does not mention the capture and holding to ransom of King John and his son.

3. The candidate explains why the King was able to crush the Peasants' Revolt by referring to evidence such as:

   from the source:
   * the King ordered the capture of the leaders of the revolt
   * gallows set up to put people off
   * many leaders of the revolt were hanged
   * pardons were granted on condition that there would be no future rising.

   from recall:
   * murder of the leader of the revolt, Watt Tyler
   * imprisonment and brutal execution of important figures eg John Ball and Jack Straw
   * King pacified the peasants in London by promising concessions.

Context 4: New Worlds: Europe in the Age of Expansion, 1480s-1530s

1. The candidate evaluates the usefulness of **Source A** as evidence of reasons for European exploration between 1480 and 1530 by referring to evidence such as:
   * primary source written at the time of European exploration and expansion
   * author an experienced sailor/a successful explorer
   * written to highlight his achievements – possible bias, one sided account praising his own actions – dismissive of native culture
   * says that his aim was to conquer the people/bring the land under Spain's rule/make Spain rich.

Maximum 1 mark for indicating content omission such as:

   * need to find new trade routes/desire to convert non-Christians.

2. The candidate describes the benefits Vasco da Gama's voyage brought to Europe by referring to evidence such as:
   * broke Venetian/Arab trade monopoly
   * established new trade route to India
   * established trading colonies at Goa and Ormuz
   * new sources of supply for spice trade found
   * cost of spices brought down
   * allowed Christianity/European influence to spread
   * encouraged further European expansion
   * enabled Empires to be built up
   * more immediate economic impact than New World discoveries.

3. The candidate explains why Magellan faced difficulties during his voyage round the world by referring to evidence such as:

   from the source:
   * he was a Portuguese commanding Spaniards so they did not like him
   * he kept the destination secret from his crew so they did not trust him

   * other captains plotted a mutiny against him
   * lost two ships in straits.

   from recall:
   * voyage took longer than planned – over two years
   * ran out of supplies leading to lowering of morale
   * disease broke out due to lack of supplies leading to death of crew
   * poor decision making – Magellan became involved in a local war in Philippines
   * lack of accurate charts/maps.

Context 5: "Tea and Freedom": The American Revolution, 1763-1783

1. The candidate describes the Boston Tea Party and the British government's response to it by referring to evidence such as:
   * colonists were angered by the passing of the Tea Act in 1773 which allowed the East India Company to undercut the colonial merchants and smugglers
   * Bostonians disguised themselves as Mohawk Indians and boarded the three tea ships
   * tea was emptied into the water of Boston harbour
   * some of the tea was stolen
   * King George III and Parliament were outraged when they heard of these events
   * Lord North rejected the offer of compensation from some of the colonial merchants
   * led to the passing of the 'Intolerable Acts'
   * Port of Boston closed/Massachusetts Act/Administration of Justice Act/Quartering Act/ Quebec Act.

2. The candidate evaluates the usefulness of **Source A** as evidence about what happened at Lexington and Concord in April 1775 by referring to evidence such as:
   * primary source written only a month after events at Lexington and Concord/written at the start of the year
   * author the leaders of the colonies, who would have detailed/first hand knowledge of what had taken place/possible bias
   * written to condemn/criticise the actions of the British army
   * describe attack as unprovoked/murdered colonists/cruelly slaughtered.

Maximum 1 mark for indicating content omission such as:

   * militia in Massachusetts had been training/ preparing for war
   * spies had warned of the British army's movements and counter-attack was launched at Concord.

3. The candidate explains why involvement of foreign countries caused difficulties for Britain in the War of Independence by referring to evidence such as:

   from the source:
   * the French attacked British colonies in the Caribbean and elsewhere which undermined Britain's control
   * the French harassed British shipping in the Atlantic interfering with trade
   * Britain lost control of the seas for the first time that century
   * Britain found it more difficult to reinforce and supply its forces in America.

   from recall:
   * France provided the colonies with finance
   * France provided the colonies with military assistance – soldiers, gunpowder
   * Spain distracted Britain by attacking Gibraltar
   * a Franco-Spanish force threatened Britain with invasion in 1779.

Context 6: "This Accursed Trade": The British Slave Trade and its Abolition, 1770–1807

1. The candidate describes the different stages of the triangular trade by referring to evidence such as:
   - ships sailed from Europe to Africa carrying manufactured goods
   - goods such as guns, alcohol, pots and pans were exchanged for slaves
   - slaves were held in slave factories on the west coast of Africa
   - slave ships left west Africa carrying slaves to the West Indies and the Americas
   - duration of the voyage was very long
   - slaves were usually sold by auction upon arrival in West Indies/America
   - ships carrying tobacco, sugar, molasses, cotton would sail back across the Atlantic
   - ships often departed from/arrived at British ports such as Bristol, Liverpool, Glasgow.

2. The candidate evaluates the usefulness of **Source A** as evidence of slave resistance in the West Indies by referring to evidence such as:
   - secondary source written years after the end of the slave trade
   - author a historian who is likely to have expertise on the subject/has carried out research
   - written to show that slave revolts were a big problem in the West Indies colonies
   - says that there were problems on a number of different islands/damage to property/problem was worse in Jamaica than in other colonies.

Maximum 1 mark for indicating content omission such as:

   - evidence of slave resistance eg dumb insolence, sabotage, running away.

3. The candidate explains why the slave trade was abolished by Britain in 1807 by referring to evidence such as:

   from the source:
   - people had begun to think of Africans as fellow human beings/regarded trade as unacceptable
   - trade with the West Indies was becoming less important to Britain
   - many merchants supported free trade
   - slavery began to be regarded as an inefficient way to produce goods.

   from recall:
   - influence of religious groups/the churches
   - national anti-slavery campaigns involving meetings, petitions, leaflets
   - growing support in parliament for abolition of slavery
   - first-hand accounts from former slaves such as Equiano influenced people
   - contribution of anti-slavery campaigners such as William Wilberforce, Thomas Clarkson.

Context 7: Citizens! The French Revolution, 1789-1794

1. The candidate evaluates the usefulness of **Source A** as evidence of the relationship between the Third Estate and the King in June 1789 by referring to evidence such as:
   - primary source from the period when the Third Estate was not allowed to meet at Versailles
   - part of the oath taken by members of the Third Estate
   - written to show that the Third Estate were determined to be the National Assembly
   - says that no one has the right to stop them from meeting where or when they want to.

Maximum 1 mark for indicating content omission such as:

   - Third Estate wanted to limit the power of the King.

2. The candidate explains why war broke out between France and her neighbours after 1791 by referring to evidence such as:

   from the source:
   - Austria and Prussia objected to the treatment of Marie Antoinette
   - Louis hoped that defeat would destroy the Revolution
   - the revolutionaries wanted to spread the Revolution
   - Britain joined to stop the French interfering in other countries.

   from recall:
   - Austria and Prussia wanted to stop the spread of the Revolution
   - Louis encouraged the Austrians to help him against the Revolution
   - Louis thought that the war would make him more popular
   - Britain feared that the French might interfere in Ireland.

3. The candidate describes the Reign of Terror by referring to evidence such as:
   - Robespierre became the head of the Committee for Public Safety
   - anyone disagreeing with the views of the Jacobins were labelled traitors
   - Committee of Public Safety could issue warrants of search and arrest
   - evidence often came only from informers
   - accusation was counted as evidence
   - Revolutionary Tribunals could order executions
   - death sentence was the only punishment available
   - up to 40,000 people were guillotined during this period
   - the Terror ended with the execution of Robespierre.

Context 8: Cavour, Garibaldi and the Making of Italy, 1815-1870

1. The candidate explains why the revolutions of 1848-1849 failed to unite Italy by referring to evidence such as:

   from the source:
   - nationalists failed to work together eg revolutionaries in Sicily and Naples
   - revolutionaries did not encourage mass participation
   - middle classes feared that democratic government would give power to the lower classes
   - revolutions were not supported by autocratic leaders eg Ferdinand of Sicily.

   from recall:
   - failure of 'Young Italy' to achieve aims
   - revolutionaries were easily suppressed by the Austrian army
   - lack of foreign support eg French sent soldiers to crush the Roman Republic
   - lack of enthusiasm of the peasantry.

2. The candidate describes the steps taken by Piedmont to bring about Italian unification up to 1860 by referring to evidence such as:
   - Piedmont's army sent to fight alongside Britain and France against Russia in the Crimean War (1854)
   - agreement reached between Cavour and Napoleon III at Plombières (1858)
   - if Austria attacked Piedmont, France would assist Piedmont
   - promised France Savoy
   - Piedmont provoked Austria into declaring war on 19 April 1859 following mobilisation of Piedmont's army
   - Piedmont's alliance with France allowed success at Magenta and Solferino

- Piedmont encouraged French influence to inspire Parma, Tuscany and Romagna to demand unification with Piedmont
- Napoleon signed truce of Villafranca with Austria July 1859 ending war with Austria.

3. The candidate evaluates the usefulness of **Source B** as evidence of the skills of Cavour as a leader by referring to evidence such as:
   - primary source from the time of the unification of Italy/time Cavour was Prime Minister
   - author is a politician from Piedmont and may be biased in favour of Cavour/would know about Cavour's leadership style
   - written to highlight Cavour's talents as a leader
   - says Cavour has the talent to assess a situation/manipulate events.

Maximum 1 mark for indicating content omission such as:

- specific actions by Cavour as Prime Minister eg meeting with Napoleon at Plombieres provoking Austria into war in 1859.

Context 9: Iron and Blood? Bismarck and The Creation of the German Empire, 1815-1871

1. The candidate explains why Prussia was able to take the lead in German unification by 1862 by referring to evidence such as:

   from the source:
   - Prussia controlled the great rivers Rhine and Elbe – vital for communication and trade
   - other states hoped to benefit from industrial development in Prussia
   - Prussia took the lead in improving roads and railways
   - Frederick William IV of Prussia promised to work for a united Germany.

   from recall:
   - the Zollverein established Prussia as economic leader of the German states
   - Bismarck became Minister-President of Prussia in November 1862
   - his aim was to unite the German states by 'iron and blood'
   - military strength of Prussia.

2. The candidate evaluates the usefulness of **Source B** as evidence of the methods used by Bismarck to bring about the unification of the German states in 1871 by referring to evidence such as:
   - primary source from Bismarck's memoirs
   - written by Bismarck describing his own thoughts
   - to describe how he wanted to unify the German states
   - says he did not doubt a Franco-Prussian War must take place before a united Germany could be realised.

Maximum 1 mark for indicating content omission such as:

- details of methods used to provoke war eg Ems telegram.

3. The candidate describes the events that led to war between France and Prussia in 1870 by referring to evidence such as:
   - Prussia provoked France over Spanish succession issue
   - Hohenzollern candidate Prince Leopold, put forward by Prussia/relative of Prussian royal family
   - French felt threatened/sent Ambassador to Prussia to meet Prussian King
   - Prussian King agreed to withdraw Leopold as candidate but made no promises never to renew candidature
   - Bismarck edited the tone of the Ems Telegram to provoke the French
   - edited version of telegram released to French and German newspapers
   - French politicians were outranged by telegram
   - French reacted by declaring war on 19 July 1870.

Context 10: The Red Flag: Lenin and the Russian Revolution, 1894-1921

1. The candidate explains why national minorities disliked the policy of Russification by referring to evidence such as:

   from the source:
   - Non-Russians had to use the Russian language
   - Russian clothing and customs were to be used
   - Russian officials were put in to run regional governments
   - Poles were told to change and become Russian citizens.

   from recall:
   - Russians were the minority – only 44% of population
   - Catholic Poles and Asiatic Muslims were pressurised to convert to Russian Orthodoxy
   - Jews were persecuted for being 'anti-Russian'
   - Russian was used in schools and law courts.

2. The candidate evaluates the usefulness of **Source B** as evidence of the problems facing the Provisional Government by referring to evidence such as:
   - primary source from personal letter from period of great unrest/time when the Provisional Government was failing – so likely to be his real feelings about the situation
   - author the leader of the Provisional Government who knew well the extent of the problems in July 1917
   - written to warn the problems in Russia were getting worse/express his feelings about the level of unrest in Russia
   - says there will be chaos/famine/defeat at the front.

Maximum 1 mark for indicating content omission such as:

- failure of Brusilov offensive.

3. The candidate describes the ways the Civil War affected the Russian people by referring to evidence such as:
   - most of the Russian economy taken over by the state to supply Reds
   - foodstuffs were forcibly requisitioned from peasants by requisition squads
   - peasants were imprisoned or shot for hoarding grain
   - peasants ceased to produce surplus food in retaliation
   - famine resulted and millions died
   - cholera and typhus broke out killing thousands more
   - both Reds and Whites terrorised the peasants
   - food and fuel were rationed in the cities as supplies were inadequate/black market and bartering began
   - large enterprises were nationalized and strikes made illegal.

Context 11: Free at Last? Race Relations in the USA, 1918-1968

1. The candidate describes the problems facing European immigrants to the USA in the 1920s by referring to evidence such as:
   - often arrived with little wealth or possessions
   - faced discrimination on the grounds of culture/race/religion
   - faced discrimination in most areas of life and work simply because they were immigrants
   - did the poorest jobs with lowest pay
   - poor housing often in unsanitary slums
   - faced abuse from local politicians/lacked rights and representation
   - became stereotyped by public and media as a threat eg blamed for crime became stereotyped by public and media as a burden eg worsened housing shortages
   - blamed for political extremism eg Red Scare.

2. The candidate evaluates the usefulness of **Source A** as evidence of attitudes towards Black Americans in the southern states at the time of the Civil Rights movement by referring to evidence such as:

- primary source written at a time when the Civil Rights movement was beginning to become more active
- author is a Klan leader with extreme racist views and therefore biased
- speech made to warn them against northern influences/show the Klan in a positive light
- says that black people have nothing to fear from KKK provided they accept an inferior social position.

Maximum 1 mark for indicating content omission such as:

- Klan used violence against Black Americans

3. The candidate explains why Martin Luther King planned a Civil Rights protest in Selma, Alabama in 1965 by referring to evidence such as:

from the source:
- King wanted to put pressure on President Johnson to support new Civil Rights legislation
- Sheriff Clark of Selma was a crude, violent racist
- King thought he could stir up feeling against Clark in the same way as he had against Bull Connor
- there was a march as part of the protest to Governor Wallace about police brutality and racism.

from recall:
- King wanted to win support for a new voting rights act
- Black Americans were being prevented from registering to vote in Selma
- very few Black Americans had succeeded in registering to vote in Selma
- local Civil Rights campaigners had already begun organising protests in Selma
- protests in Selma had been met with extreme violence from police/TV coverage.

Context 12: The Road to War, 1933-1939

1. The candidate describes the ways Britain appeased Germany between 1933 and 1936 by referring to evidence such as:
- allowed Germany to break the Treaty of Versailles
- allowed Germany to break the Locarno Treaty
- British government and public opinion had revised their attitude to the Treaty of Versailles and agreed it was too harsh
- Britain did not protest about the reintroduction of conscription
- Britain took no action over the creation of a German air-force
- the Anglo-German Naval Agreement allowed Germany to build a navy
- the Anglo-German Naval Treaty allowed Germany to break Versailles
- Britain accepted the reoccupation of the Rhineland/Lord Lothian 'Germany is only going into its own backyard'.

2. The candidate explains why Germany wanted Anschluss in 1938 by referring to evidence such as:

from the source:
- Austria was the key to south eastern Europe
- Germany wanted Hungary as an ally
- Anschluss would help to contain Czechoslovakia
- political union with Austria was the next step.

from recall:
- the Austrians were fellow Germans/German speaking
- Hitler was Austrian
- Germany would take over the Austrian army
- Germany would take over Austria's industry.

3. The candidate evaluates the usefulness of **Source B** as evidence of Britain's attitude to Czechoslovakia in 1938 by referring to evidence such as:
- primary source from the period when the Czech/Sudeten crisis was developing
- author was the British ambassador and reflects attitude of the government
- written to show that the Czechs were to blame for the Sudeten crisis
- says that Czechs can't be trusted/Czechs want war.

Maximum 1 mark for indicating content omission such as:

- British government put pressure on Czechoslovakia
- the result of this was the Munich Settlement.

Context 13: In the Shadow of the Bomb: The Cold War, 1945-1985

1. The candidate explains why the Cold War broke out after 1945 by referring to evidence such as:

from the source:
- Truman and Stalin did not trust each other
- USA had gained an advantage over the Soviet Union by developing the atomic bomb
- the Americans did not inform the Soviets of the development of the atomic bomb and did not consult over its use against Japan
- after the Second World War the Americans and Soviets were no longer united by a common enemy.

from recall:
- differences between American system of capitalism and Soviet communism always caused tension/mistrust
- the Soviet takeover of eastern Europe had angered the USA and its allies
- Churchill's 'Iron Curtain' speech had antagonised the Soviets
- the Marshall Plan contributed to divisions in Europe
- arguments between East and West over the fate of Germany/Berlin in the years following the Second World War
- Berlin Blockade, 1948-1949, deepened divisions between East and West.

2. The candidate describes the part played by the USSR in the Cuban Missile Crisis by referring to evidence such as:
- the Soviet Union had developed an alliance with Cuba following Castro's seizure of power and the failure of the Bay of Pigs
- with Castro's agreement, Soviet Union constructed missile launch sites on Cuba
- Soviet cargo ships with missiles on board headed for Cuba, despite American protests
- U2 spy plane shot down by Soviet missile over Cuba
- Khrushchev thought he could take advantage of youth and inexperience of American President, Kennedy
- Khrushchev eventually backed down in the face of American blockade/resolve
- Soviet missiles were removed from Cuba in exchange for the removal of American missiles from Turkey.

3. The candidate evaluates the usefulness of **Source B** as evidence of why the process of détente had come to a halt by the early 1980s by referring to evidence such as:
- primary source from 1983, a time when the process of détente had halted
- author was the American President who was directing/influencing foreign policy at the time/possible bias, from an American perspective

- written to explain why he wants to strengthen American military power/end period of détente
- says there is a need to end freeze on building nuclear weapons.

Maximum 1 mark for indicating content omission such as:
- Soviet invasion of Afghanistan had contributed to end of the process of détente/American boycott of Moscow Olympics had strained relations further.

HISTORY INTERMEDIATE 2 2011

PART 1 THE SHORT ESSAY

Scottish and British

Context 1: Murder in the Cathedral: Crown, Church and People, 1154-1173

1. The candidate explains why Henry II and Archbishop Becket quarrelled so violently by referring to evidence such as:
   - Becket resigned as Chancellor/Henry felt betrayed
   - Becket defended the Church against the King
   - Criminous Clerks – Henry believed that all clergymen who committed a crime should be tried in the King's Court, whereas Becket believed that they should be tried in a Church Court
   - The Constitution of Clarendon – Becket refused to sign the document outlining the powers of the Church and agreeing to obey the king
   - Northampton Trial – Becket refused to attend court/Henry charged him with contempt of court
   - Becket fled to France before he could be sentenced/lived in exile for six years
   - Becket sought the protection of the Pope and Henry's enemy Louis VII against the King during peace talks in France, Henry refused Becket the royal kiss/Becket refused to accept the King's authority "Saving our order"
   - Becket excommunicated the Archbishop of York when he crowned the King's son
   - Becket excommunicated the bishops involved in the coronation when he returned to England
   - the personalities of the two men were very different.

Context 2: Wallace, Bruce and the Wars of Independence, 1286–1328

2. The candidate explains why some Scots were reluctant to accept the Maid of Norway as their ruler by referring to evidence such as:
   - she was a child – others would have to rule on her behalf and there could be disputes
   - she was a child and could possibly die – an adult ruler would be better
   - she was a girl – some people did not believe that a female could rule/give noblemen orders
   - she was a girl – some people did not think that a girl could lead an army into battle
   - she was in Norway – would she understand Scotland and be able to rule it?
   - she needed a husband – a Scottish husband could cause jealousy
     – a foreign husband could lead to Scotland being taken over
   - other nobles – Balliol and Bruce – had ambitions to rule
   - potential for civil war to break out
   - concern that Edward I might exploit the situation.

Context 3: Mary, Queen of Scots and the Scottish Reformation, 1540s-1587

3. The candidate explains why Mary, Queen of Scots, was forced to abdicate in 1567 by referring to evidence such as:
   - people thought she had been involved in the murder of her husband, Darnley
   - she had married her husband's murderer, Bothwell
   - people thought she was involved with Bothwell before the murder
   - she allowed Bothwell to prevent a fair inquiry into Darnley's death

- some people did not agree with a female ruling
- some people did not want to have a Roman Catholic as ruler
- some Roman Catholics were disappointed by her lack of support for their religion
- some nobles had plans to take over the government for themselves.

Context 4: The Coming of the Civil War, 1603-1642

4. The candidate explains why the reign of Charles I was opposed in Scotland by referring to evidence such as:
    - Charles demanded that Ministers accept and use the Prayer Book
    - resentment at the Act of Revocation whereby church or royal property which had been alienated since 1540 was taken back by the crown
    - resentment of Charles' coronation in Edinburgh eg High Church ceremony, employed Anglican forms
    - reaction/opposition to the introduction of Laud's Prayer Book, 1637/St Giles riots
    - reaction by the Scottish clergy on the requirement to wear gowns and surplices (Laud's Canons)
    - abolition of the Presbyteries/threat of dissolution
    - General Assembly not allowed to meet
    - Bishops were to be introduced into the Scottish Church
    - rejection of Canons included in the national covenant of 1638.

Context 5: "Ane End of Ane Auld Sang": Scotland and the Treaty of Union, 1690s-1715

5. The candidate explains why some people thought that Scotland would benefit from a Union with England in 1707 by referring to evidence such as:
    - a Union would end arguments about the Succession between England and Scotland
    - a Union would ensure the Protestant Succession and keep the Stuarts out of Scotland
    - a Union would stop the English and Scottish governments falling out with each other
    - a Union would prevent future wars between England and Scotland
    - a Union would open up English markets to Scottish businessmen
    - a Union would open the English Empire to Scots
    - a Union would ensure Scotland no longer suffered disproportionately when England went to war against France or Spain
    - the Equivalent would inject some much needed cash into Scotland
    - a Union would guarantee the Protestant Church in Scotland.

Context 6: Immigrants and Exiles: Scotland, 1830s-1930s

6. The candidate explains why life was difficult for many Irish immigrants to Scotland between 1830 and 1930 by referring to evidence such as:
    - Irish immigrants had to do the lowest paid work
    - many could not speak English
    - they lived in the slums of the industrial cities – details of overcrowding, poor sanitation, disease
    - immigrants were accused of keeping down wages or of stealing jobs
    - immigrants were accused of violence/causing crime
    - victims of discrimination, violence, press hostility
    - there was suspicion of the Catholic religion in a predominantly Protestant country
    - Irish immigrants felt that the education system was anti-Catholic
    - some Scots felt that Irish were unpatriotic eg during Great War.

Context 7: From the Cradle to the Grave? Social Welfare in Britain, 1890s-1951

7. The candidate explains why the Liberal Government reforms of 1906-1914 were important in improving the lives of children and the elderly by referring to evidence such as:
    - Education (Provision of Meals) Act provided free meals to the poorest children
    - by providing meals for the children they were able to concentrate better at school
    - Education Act 1907 – Medical inspections – allowed for the identification of health problems in school children
    - clinics were introduced into schools in 1912 to provide treatment for children with health problems
    - 1908 Children's Act (Children's Charter) provided legal protection for children eg protection from abuse
    - Children's Charter gave the abolition of the death sentence for children, segregation of child and adult prisoners
    - Children's Charter gave protection from smoking and drinking
    - 1908 Old Age Pensions Act provided pensions for those over 70, relieving the fear of ending their lives in the poorhouse/workhouse
    - pensions were to be paid for through general taxation, meaning the old people did not have to make contributions to qualify – especially helpful to women
    - pensions were paid through the Post Office relieving the stigma of the hated Poor Law – many more people claimed pensions as a result
    - Acts for children and the elderly showed that the government was taking responsibility for the most vulnerable in society.

Context 8: Campaigning for Change: Social Change in Scotland, 1900s-1979

8. The candidate explains why Scottish education in the 1930s was in need of reform by referring to evidence such as:
    - the school leaving age was 14/children left very young without qualifications
    - children could be physically punished/belted by teachers
    - maximum class size was 50 in state schools
    - pupils sat a 'qualifying' exam at 11 to determine their academic ability/which school they would go to/working class children largely disadvantaged by this
    - 3 year junior secondaries concentrated on practical subjects/pupils were prepared for the workplace/pupils gained no qualifications
    - 5 year secondary schools taught academic subjects for university entrance/exams
    - girls and boys followed different curricula – girls did domestic science, boys did technical subjects
    - schools were often poorly equipped/buildings were often old and inadequate but there was no money to improve them
    - there were very few grants to enable poorer students to go to university so many did not go/Carnegie Trust helped to fund 40% of students/37% were working class
    - there was no proper organised scheme of adult education because of lack of central funding.

Context 9: A Time of Troubles: Ireland, 1900-1923

9. The candidate explains why the Unionists were against the Home Rule Bill by referring to evidence such as:
    - Unionists considered themselves British not Irish and had an emotional attachment to Britain
    - Unionists believed it would end their way of life and that they would be less prosperous under Home Rule eg lower wages, poorer health care etc
    - feared the shipbuilding and linen industry based in Belfast would be damaged

- feared Ulster would have to bear the financial burden of the rest of Ireland which was poorer and dependent on the farming industry
- feared Ulster would be cut off from trading markets in Britain and the Empire
- feared the government in Dublin would be influenced by Roman Catholic Church
- feared the Protestant religion would be forced into decline
- feared Home Rule would eventually lead to full independence.

European and World

Context 1: The Norman Conquest, 1060-1153

10. The candidate explains why there was so little opposition to William I after 1066 by referring to evidence such as:
    - victory of William's forces at Hastings
    - death of Harold at Hastings
    - most Anglo-Saxon nobles died at Hastings
    - Anglo-Saxons lacked a native king
    - Anglo-Saxon opposition was weak and scattered
    - William's easy capture of London
    - brutal crushing of any opposition in the north (Harrying of the North)
    - building of castles across the kingdom as secure bases for his forces
    - development of the feudal system.

Context 2: The Cross and the Crescent: The First Crusade, 1096-1125

11. The candidate explains why people joined the First Crusade by referring to evidence such as:
    - the Pope was extremely influential and encouraged people to go on Crusade
    - many believed that it was their duty to recapture Jerusalem and help their Christian brothers
    - the promise that all sins would be forgiven was an attractive idea
    - preachers such as Peter the Hermit encouraged peasants to go on Crusade
    - peasants also went on Crusade because they hoped that they would have a better life in the East. "Milk and honey"
    - some knights were extremely religious and wanted to serve God eg Raymond of Toulouse
    - some knights saw an opportunity to gain land for themselves in the East eg Bohemond/Baldwin
    - some knights went on a crusade because they wanted to use their military skills in the East eg Tancred
    - some knights went on a crusade because of peer pressure/to represent the French royal family eg Hugh of Vermandois.

Context 3: War, Death and Revolt in Medieval Europe, 1328-1436

12. The candidate explains why the Black Death had serious consequences for England by referring to evidence such as:
    - one third of the population died
    - high casualty rate caused a shortage of labourers
    - some villages became derelict
    - disastrous effects on agriculture eg animals died, crops rotted in the fields
    - trade was interrupted
    - affected the attitudes of survivors eg less deferential towards the church
    - led peasants to demand higher wages
    - likely factor in the unrest which led up to the peasants revolt.

Context 4: New Worlds: Europe in the Age of Expansion, 1480s-1530s

13. The candidate explains why Christopher Columbus was important in European exploration by referring to evidence such as:
    - he used his wide sailing experience to support existing arguments about route to Japan
    - persevered for many years to find backers to undertake first voyage (8 years in Portugal, 7 years in Spain)
    - first to take a new route, sailing west to reach the east
    - he had excellent navigational skills (dead reckoning) to set and follow his course
    - voyage found/proved there was land to the west
    - founded the first Spanish settlements in the New World, in Hispaniola
    - claimed new territories for Spain/Spanish crown
    - made Spain (and subsequently Portugal) rich
    - made four voyages to the New World, discovering Caribbean Islands, Venezuelan Coast, Honduras
    - kept detailed accounts of voyages to add to knowledge of places and peoples.

Context 5: "Tea and Freedom": The American Revolution, 1763-1783

14. The candidate explains why the colonists were able to achieve victory in their war against the British by 1783 by referring to evidence such as:
    - poor leadership of British forces eg Howe, Cornwallis
    - tactical errors made by Britain eg Yorktown, Saratoga
    - British army was small in number/had to rely on mercenary forces
    - British soldiers were not properly trained/equipped to cope with terrain and conditions
    - colonial army was effectively led by George Washington
    - colonists had greater forces/able to call on minutemen when required
    - colonists benefited from assistance from foreign powers
    - attacks by French and Spanish weakened/distracted British forces
    - assistance from French and Spanish navies gave colonists control of the seas.

Context 6: "This Accursed Trade": The British Slave Trade and its Abolition, 1770–1807

15. The candidate explains why the Middle Passage was such a dreadful experience for slaves by referring to evidence such as:
    - slaves were held on board using tight pack/loose pack system
    - disease was common on ships – dysentery due to poor sanitary conditions
    - lack of fresh air – slaves held for long periods below deck
    - crew were often cruel towards slaves
    - female slaves often suffered sexual abuse from the crew
    - food was limited and bland/unfamiliar to slaves – some had to be force fed
    - slaves taken above deck and whipped to make them exercise
    - slaves would witness deaths of fellow slaves/evidence from the case of the Zong.

Context 7: Citizens! The French Revolution, 1789-1794

16. The candidate explains why so many people were frightened of the Committee of Public Safety in 1793 by referring to evidence such as:
    - opponents of the Jacobins were labelled as 'traitors' to France
    - Committee of Public Safety could issue warrants of search and arrest
    - Committee set up Revolutionary Tribunals – only they could order the death sentence

- evidence often came only from secret informers
- trials and executions were quick and uncontested/accused were not entitled to lawyers or right of appeal
- accusation meant the assumption of guilt in vast majority of cases
- many thousands of people were executed by guillotine or other means
- Committee enforced order in the Provinces with great brutality.

Context 8: Cavour, Garibaldi and the Making of Italy, 1815-1870

17. The candidate explains why the 1848-49 revolutions failed to bring about Italian unification by referring to evidence such as:
- Charles Albert was initially reluctant to put himself forward as head of the nationalist movement
- Austrian army was superior – due to the failure of the Austrian revolutions the Austrian army was re-enforced
- Pope Pius XI abandoned the nationalist cause
- peasants could not be relied upon to support the nationalist cause/nationalists lacked mass support
- nationalists were divided and could not work together eg divisions between supporters of Mazzini, Charles Albert and the Pope
- there was not enough foreign support to help the nationalist cause
- Charles Albert was wrong to say that Italy could 'go it alone' (fara de se)
- French intervention crushed the Roman Republic
- Regionalism was strong
- more organisation, planning and military strength would be needed to advance the nationalist cause
- Italian nationalists now focused their attention on Piedmont as it held on to its constitution.

Context 9: Iron and Blood? Bismarck and The Creation of the German Empire, 1815-1871

18. The candidate explains why the 1848-49 revolutions failed to bring about German unification by referring to evidence such as:
- the Frankfurt Parliament could not agree on the size of Germany – Kleindeutschland or Grossdeutschland
- the Frankfurt Parliament lacked clear, agreed objectives and argued minority views at great lengths
- King Frederick William of Prussia refused to take the crown of Germany
- the Frankfurt Parliament was leaderless/lacked a strong leader
- Austrians withdrew their delegates from the parliament after Frederick William's refusal and other states soon followed
- the Parliament did not have an army to enforce its decisions
- the old rulers of Germany still had control of their armies and used them to restore power
- by 1849 Austria had recovered its political power and was willing to use its armies to destroy any further revolutions
- Kings and other Heads of State did not see unification as being in their interest
- by 1850 Austria had persuaded most of the old rulers to renew the German Confederation
- after Erfurt, Austria was again dominant in Germany with a policy to keep Germany divided.

Context 10: The Red Flag: Lenin and the Russian Revolution, 1894-1921

19. The candidate explains why the Provisional Government had lost popular support by October 1917 by referring to evidence such as:
- Provisional Government was not elected so lacked legitimacy/failed to hold elections
- Provisional Government failed to end the war/war going badly/failure of June offensive
- Provisional Government failed to give land to the peasants
- Provisional Government failed to help unemployed or raise wages
- Provisional Government failed to solve food shortages
- Provisional Government could not govern without co-operation of Petrograd Soviet
- Order Number One – soldiers should obey officers only if the orders did not contradict decrees of the Petrograd Soviet – weakened the Provisional Government's authority with the army
- Lenin returned and proclaimed the 'April Theses' (peace, bread, land) refusing support for the Provisional Government
- Provisional Government looked ineffective during Kornilov Revolt.

Context 11: Free at Last? Race Relations in the USA, 1918-1968

20. The candidate explains why the attitudes of Americans towards immigration changed after 1918 by referring to evidence such as:
- growing fear of social unrest in aftermath of Russian Revolution
- fear that Communism may spread to USA
- worry about increasing numbers of immigrants from southern and eastern Europe
- concern that immigrants would take jobs
- concern that immigrants would depress wages
- concern that immigrants would be used to break strikes
- concern that immigrants would create pressure on scarce housing
- feeling that new immigrants were inferior eg illiterate
- feeling that USA could no longer take unrestricted numbers of immigrants
- feeling that immigrants were involved in organised crime
- influence of WASPs.

Context 12: The Road to War, 1933-1939

21. The candidate explains why Britain did not want to go to war with Germany in the 1930s by referring to evidence such as:
- war was unpopular with the British people because of the losses of 1914-1918
- there was a strong pacifist movement in Britain eg White Poppy campaign
- there was fear that "the bomber will always get through" leading to huge losses
- Germany had rearmed with powerful army, navy and air force
- Britain had failed to modernise Armed Forces/was militarily weak
- Chiefs of Staff warned that British forces could not deal with Germany, Italy and Japan
- Britain had no reliable allies – USA neutral, France unstable and Russia communist
- countries of the Empire warned that they might not support Britain in another European war
- Fascism was seen as a barrier to the spread of Communism.

Context 13: In the Shadow of the Bomb: The Cold War, 1945-1985

22. The candidate explains why the USA and USSR had begun the process of détente by the 1970s by referring to evidence such as:
    - the experience of the Cuban crisis in the 1960s had shown how close the superpowers had come to nuclear war
    - the end of the Vietnam War had reduced tension between the USA and Soviet Union
    - there were concerns that the arms race could spiral out of control
    - America and the Soviet Union were experiencing economic difficulties
    - the superpowers were keen to focus on spending more money on domestic priorities
    - anti-nuclear protest movements were growing in many countries
    - there had been widespread criticism of the Soviet Union's action in Czechoslovakia
    - Brezhnev and Nixon had a desire to improve relations between the superpowers
    - the leaders of both countries wished to portray themselves as peacemakers.

PART 2 HISTORICAL STUDY

Scottish and British

Context 1: Murder in the Cathedral: Crown, Church and People, 1154-1173

1. The candidate describes the actions taken by Henry II to increase his power when he became king in 1154 by referring to evidence such as:
   - castles built without permission were seized or knocked down
   - barons who disobeyed the king were dealt with severely eg Earl of York had his title taken from him
   - mercenaries/private armies sent back to Flanders
   - Assize of Clarendon introduced to deal with serious crimes eg murder, theft/ensure the law was the same throughout the country
   - Assize of Northampton introduced to deal with arson, forgery
   - trial by ordeal introduced with sentencing/punishment
   - Novel Disseisin introduced to deal with land disputes
   - corrupt sheriffs sacked and replaced
   - barons no longer allowed to hold office of sheriff
   - key personnel introduced to enforce law and order eg Jury/Justices in Eyre.

2. The candidate evaluates the usefulness of the source by referring to evidence such as:
   - primary source written during the time the code of chivalry was followed
   - author was an eyewitness/poets wrote about knights and chivalry
   - to criticise the behaviour of knights
   - they steal from the church and rob pilgrims/show disrespect to children and the elderly.

   Maximum 1 mark for indicating content omission such as:
   - some knights upheld the Code of Chivalry eg fought for the Church on Crusade
   - some knights also enforced the law eg were members of a jury.

3. The candidate explains why priests were important to the twelfth century by referring to evidence such as:

   from the source:
   - offered support and hope that life after death would be better
   - taught people how to behave/fulfil their Christian duties
   - carried out key ceremonies eg baptism, marriage, funerals
   - taught local boys to read and write/prepared them for a career in the Church.

   from recall:
   - heard confessions/issued penance for sins committed
   - carried out ceremonies such as communion/confirmation/last rites
   - enforced Canon law at local level
   - kept part of their tithe (harvest) to give to the poor during times of need.

Context 2: Wallace, Bruce and the Wars of Independence, 1286-1328

1. The candidate evaluates the usefulness of the source by referring to evidence such as:
   - primary source written in 1298, at the time of the Battle of Falkirk
   - Walter of Guisborough is an English chronicler – possible bias
   - the chronicle is to describe what happened at Falkirk/celebrate English success and show Scots as cowards
   - it states that the Scots were in schiltrons/the Scots cavalry fled.

   Maximum 1 mark for indicating content omission such as:
   - Edward used his archers to break up the schiltrons
   - the Scots were defeated.

2. The candidate describes the events that led to the death of John Comyn at Dumfries in 1306 by referring to evidence such as:
   - Bruce arranged to meet with Comyn at Greyfriars in Dumfries
     or
     Bruce tricked Comyn to meet him at Greyfriars in Dumfries
   - Bruce accused Comyn of betraying him to King Edward
     or
     the two men began to argue about Comyn telling King Edward about Bruce
   - Bruce stabbed Comyn
     or
     Bruce hit Comyn with a sword
   - Bruce ran out of Greyfriars and told his companions what he had done
   - the monks carried Comyn to the altar
   - Comyn said that he would survive the wound
   - Bruce ordered his men to kill Comyn
     or
     some of Bruce's men killed Comyn
   - Comyn's blood spilled over the high altar.

3. The candidate explains why it took so long for Robert Bruce to be accepted as King of Scots by referring to evidence such as

   from the source:
   - he had to force many Scots to abandon King John Balliol
   - he had to force Scots to reject Edward II as overlord
   - Bruce was unable to force Edward II to change his mind
   - Bruce's efforts to spread the war to other parts of Britain were not successful.

   from recall:
   - it took a long time to drive the English out of their castles in Scotland
   - Bruce had been excommunicated so some people could not accept him as King

- the Comyns were long-standing rivals and the most powerful family in Scotland
- Bruce took several years to defeat the Comyns and their allies eg the MacDougalls
- Bruce's wars in Ireland had ended in failure at Dundalk
- Bruce's invasion of northern England had not forced Edward to accept him.

Context 3: Mary, Queen of Scots and the Scottish Reformation, 1540s-1587

1. The candidate evaluates the usefulness of the source by referring to evidence such as:
   - primary source written at the time the Treaty of Greenwich was broken
   - written by Knox, a Protestant leader/bias – says Arran "slipped away"/calls Cardinal Beaton "the Devil"
   - to describe how the Treaty of Greenwich was broken/to criticise Arran
   - tells that Arran changed his religion/broke the Treaty with England.

   Maximum 1 mark for indicating content omission such as:
   - some Scots were alarmed by the demands of Henry VIII and wanted to break the Treaty
   - Arran had been offered a duchy in France for changing sides – Chatelherault.

2. The candidate explains why the Scots rebelled against Mary of Guise in 1559 by referring to evidence such as:

   from the source:
   - she took stronger action against Protestants
   - she made more use of French officials
   - she had more French soldiers in key strongholds in Scotland
   - she wanted to introduce a new tax in Scotland.

   from recall:
   - Scottish Protestant Lords became more organised as "Lords of the Congregation" to challenge Mary
   - they wanted to challenge the Roman Catholic Church in Scotland eg Beggars' Summons
   - Knox returned and fuelled religious controversy – iconoclastic outrages in Perth
   - Scots feared that Frenchmen would be settled in Scotland and Scots sent to France
   - Scottish nobles resented Frenchmen taking Scottish jobs which they wanted.

3. The candidate describes the events that led to the execution of Mary, Queen of Scots in 1587 by referring to evidence such as:
   - 1580 the Pope's policy of encouraging plots against Elizabeth made English Protestants think Mary was a menace – especially since her son and heir was a Protestant
   - 1585 after several plots, the English government passed a law stating that Mary would be executed if she was actively involved in any plot against Elizabeth
   - 1585 Mary was moved to Chartley where English spies discovered how letters were smuggled
   - 1586 Babington contacted Mary to inform her of his plans to kill Elizabeth and help Mary to escape
   - Mary replied to Babington and agreed to Elizabeth's death
   - The incriminating letter was intercepted by Elizabeth's spies
   - Mary was arrested, put on trial and sentenced to death
   - Elizabeth hesitated to execute her cousin, the death warrant was concealed amongst a pile of letters and Elizabeth signed them all
   - 1587 February Mary was executed at Fotheringay.

Context 4: The Coming of the Civil War, 1603-1642

1. The candidate describes the changes in the way Scotland was governed after 1603 by referring to evidence such as:
   - Scotland was ruled by the Privy Council
   - Privy Council ensured that the King's will was followed in Scotland
   - Parliament was brought under strict Royal control
   - Parliament was run by a small committee called the Committee of Articles (Lords of the Articles)
   - Committee of Articles (Lords of the Articles) only could suggest new laws for Scotland
   - the King chose Lords and bishops to become part of the Committee of Articles (Lords of the Articles)
   - the King controlled the membership of the Committee of Articles (Lords of the Articles)
   - King was now based in London – 400 miles away and rarely visited.

2. The candidate explains why there was opposition to the methods used by Charles I to raise money by referring to evidence such as:

   from the source:
   - Charles raised money without reference to the Parliament
   - introduction of the forced loan 1626-27
   - imprisonment of knights without a fair trial for refusal to pay
   - ship money collected from counties without coastlines.

   from recall:
   - Hampden case. John Hampden was tried and found guilty for refusing to pay ship money
   - Charles sold monopolies and patents which meant the traders had to pay to take part in that trade or be forced out
   - forest fines charged people who lived on former royal forest land
   - collection of customs duties without Parliament's consent.

3. The candidate evaluates the usefulness of the source by referring to evidence such as:
   - primary source from 1642, the year the Civil War broke out
   - Thomas Wiseman was present in London at the time of the 'arrests'/possible bias as Wiseman appears to support the Houses of Parliament
   - to describe the events of the 'arrests', criticise the actions of the king
   - says Parliament has wrongly accused bishops of high treason/supports Parliament's right to be angered.

   Maximum 1 mark for indicating content omission such as:
   - Charles' abuse of Parliamentary privileges – not allowed into Parliament unless invited
   - reference to other reasons for outbreak of war eg Charles' grievances regarding the impeachment of Stafford and Laud, the Grand Remonstrance, Nineteen Propositions rejected by Charles in 1642.

Context 5: "Ane End of Ane Auld Sang": Scotland and the Treaty of Union, 1690s-1715

1. The candidate describes Scotland's economic problems in the years before the Union by referring to evidence such as:
   - farming in Scotland was very poor
   - the "Ill-years" had affected Scotland's harvests
   - people were unable to pay rents, landowners were short of money
   - Scotland did not produce many goods to trade with abroad
   - Scots were excluded from trading with England's colonies
   - the wars between England and France had reduced Scottish trade with France
   - Scotland never gained from peace treaties at the end of these wars

- Scotland had invested a lot of money in the Darien Scheme
- Scotland had lost all of this money when Darien failed.

2. The candidate explains why opponents of the Union were unable to stop it being passed in Scotland by referring to evidence such as:

   from the source:
   - they were not well organised (eg Squadrone Volante)
   - they placed trust in Hamilton who was unreliable
   - the government had sent secret agents to promote the Union
   - the government offered money to people to support the Union.

   from recall:
   - the government threatened Scottish trade if the Union was not passed
   - the government offered titles to people who supported the Union
   - the government offered jobs to people who supported the Union
   - the government made its officials support the Union or they would not be paid
   - the government had soldiers in northern England and Ulster ready to go to Scotland
   - the Equivalent made money available to Scotland.

3. The candidate evaluates the usefulness of the source by referring to evidence such as:
   - primary source written a few years after the Union
   - written by Daniel Defoe who had been an English spy and who was there at the time/possible bias
   - to highlight the bad effects of the Union
   - it describes how money and jobs are going to England/Scottish manufacturers are ruined.

   Maximum 1 mark for indicating content omission such as:
   - the Malt Tax and Customs and Excise were unpopular
   - Scots were beginning to trade freely with English colonies.

Context 6: Immigrants and Exiles: Scotland, 1830s–1930s

1. The candidate evaluates the usefulness of the source by referring to evidence such as:
   - primary source from the time of the potato famine/poverty/mass immigration
   - a British magazine but showing an accurate/sympathetic image of conditions
   - to show that there was poverty/starvation in Ireland
   - women and children dressed in rags/very thin/bare-foot.

   Maximum 1 mark for indicating content omission such as:
   - many died at this time
   - prospect of work in Scotland
   - other factors eg push and pull.

2. The candidate explains why so many Highland Scots emigrated by referring to evidence such as:

   from the source:
   - landowners encouraged tenants to emigrate to gain greater profit from sheep
   - farming was difficult due to poor soils and weather
   - the failure of the potato crop
   - Highlanders preferred foreign countries to Scottish cities.

   from recall:
   - the fishing industry was in decline
   - kelp making was no longer profitable
   - landowners cleared their tenants from the land
   - cities such as Glasgow and Edinburgh funded Highlanders to emigrate.

3. The candidate describes the ways emigrants created Scottish communities in their new homelands by referring to evidence such as:
   - Scots built communities in remote places
   - they built schools as they valued education
   - they built churches and stuck to their Presbyterian religion
   - many went into business and industry
   - they retained their culture eg Burns suppers, Highland games
   - they created cultural societies eg Caledonian Society
   - they gave Scottish place names such as Nova Scotia
   - some continued to speak the Gaelic language.

Context 7: From the Cradle to the Grave? Social Welfare in Britain, 1890s–1951

1. The candidate evaluates the usefulness of the source by referring to evidence such as:
   - primary source produced at a time of poverty
   - Aberdeen organisation representative of an industrial city which would experience more poverty/possible bias because of attitudes shown eg only targeting the 'deserving poor' – sober and industrious
   - to show their willingness to help the 'deserving poor'/sober and industrious who may become ill
   - says drinking and laziness are causes of poverty/only those willing to work and stay sober are to be helped.

   Maximum 1 mark for indicating content omission such as:
   - other causes of poverty as the fault of the individual such as gambling
   - some believed everybody should be helped/poverty was not always the fault of the individual (low wages/size of family/irregularity of work).

2. The candidate explains why the Second World War changed people's attitudes towards welfare reform by referring to evidence such as:

   from the source:
   - rationing helped encourage the idea of universal sharing of the nation's food supply
   - the government were assisting all those suffering bomb damage – rich and poor
   - classes were mixing in society who previously had little in common
   - war highlighted problems that could be overcome by government action.

   from recall:
   - the poor health of some city children evacuated to the country highlighted the problems of poverty
   - suffering of war caused a determination to create a better society once the war was over
   - other reforms had been made by the government during the war such as free health care for war wounded and bomb victims, Emergency Milk and Meals scheme etc
   - war raised awareness of continuing social problems (experience of evacuation), which many assumed had disappeared and that only the government could tackle
   - Beveridge report, published in 1942, set out principles for government intervention and was very well received.

3. The candidate describes the limitations of the Labour Government reforms of 1945-1951 by referring to evidence such as:
   - not everyone was covered by the National Insurance Act, only those with a certain level of contributions
   - Social Security payments were felt to be inadequate by 1949/more people applied for national assistance
   - the NHS became too expensive and prescription charges had to be introduced in 1951
   - not enough new hospitals to meet the demands of a modern health service

- insufficient new housing to replace damaged housing and for the demobilisation of the 5 million service men and women
- quality of housing not a priority eg 37% of homes still had no fixed bath
- limitations of school building programme eg concentration on primary schools rather than secondary (only 250 by 1950s)
- limits of education provision eg 11+ was seen as unfair, affecting future job opportunities for those who failed to get into grammar schools.

Context 8: Campaigning for Change: Social Change in Scotland, 1900s-1979

1. The candidate evaluates the usefulness of the source by referring to evidence such as:
   - primary source produced in 1914 when militant suffragette activity was at its height/public disapproval of suffragette tactics at its height
   - produced by the British Museum which would be a potential target/had been attacked by suffragettes, so unsympathetic
   - to control behaviour of women visitors
   - states that women must be accompanied by men who will guarantee their good behaviour/states that unaccompanied women must bring a letter from a responsible person who will guarantee their good behaviour.

   Maximum 1 mark for indicating content omission such as:
   - references to other militant activities eg arson, attacking pillar boxes
   - other paintings were attacked in Glasgow and Birmingham
   - most women were not militants/many men supported suffragettes
   - Cat and Mouse Act.

2. The candidate describes the effects of the economic slump in Scotland in the 1920s and 1930s by referring to evidence such as:
   - the unemployment rate rose nationally to almost 15%
   - traditional industries/shipbuilding, iron and steel, coal mining, textiles went into severe decline
   - unemployment was worst in areas dependant on traditional industries eg 50% in Motherwell, Dundee in early 1930s
   - over 400,000 Scots emigrated in the 1920s
   - new political affiliations developed eg Communism, Nationalism
   - availability of cheap unskilled labour discouraged investment in new technology
   - Trades Unions organised a series of strikes and demonstrations protesting at job and wage cuts
   - unemployed workers went on hunger marches to Westminster
   - the Means Test was introduced/families were split up
   - central Scotland was made a 'Special Area' for government assistance in 1934

3. The candidate explains why more Scots used the countryside for recreation between the wars by referring to evidence such as:

   from the source:
   - new organisations such as youth hostels, cycling clubs set up
   - cheap motor bikes enabled access
   - the unemployed joined climbing clubs
   - Scottish Rights of Way and Recreation Society supported walkers' rights.

   from recall:
   - cheap cycles (£5) became easily available
   - second hand cars became easier to buy
   - cheap day trips to the countryside by coach increased
   - National Trust for Scotland (1931) opened up gardens and castles/estates for visitors
   - publicity/public information about outdoor recreation.

Context 9: A Time of Troubles: Ireland, 1900-1923

1. The candidate evaluates the usefulness of the source by referring to evidence such as:
   - primary source written at the time of the Easter Rising executions
   - author in position of authority in Ireland would be aware of public opinion – possible bias
   - to condemn the executions/warn of potential unrest
   - executing leaders has increased support and sympathy for rebels/people are angry at British reaction.

   Maximum 1 mark for indicating content omission such as:
   - support grew for Sinn Fein as a result of the executions
   - Unionists supported action taken by the British government.

2. The candidate describes the terms of the Anglo-Irish Treaty of 1922 by referring to evidence such as:
   - Ireland given same legal status within the Commonwealth as other countries such as Australia, Canada and New Zealand.
   - Ireland to be known as the Irish Free State
   - the British King was to be represented in Ireland by a Governor-General
   - all members of the Dail were to swear an oath of allegiance to the British King
   - Britain would still use Irish ports for the Royal Navy/to help with the defence of Britain and Ireland
   - Britain to look after Ireland's coast for the next five years
   - a Boundary Commission was to be set up to decide the exact boundary between Northern Ireland and the Irish Free State
   - a Council of Ireland was to be set up if and when Northern Ireland decided to join the Irish Free State.

3. The candidate explains why the Free State Army won the Irish Civil War in 1923 by referring to evidence such as:

   from the source:
   - used artillery supplied by the British to attack Republicans
   - won back Four Courts/other important buildings
   - Republican leaders captured and executed
   - support of the Catholic Church/public.

   from recall:
   - amnesty announced by Irish government, some Republicans surrendered
   - Republicans outnumbered
   - Republican leader Liam Lynch killed
   - De Valera surrendered and accepted partition.

PART 3 HISTORICAL STUDY

European and World

Context 1: The Norman Conquest, 1060-1153

1. The candidate explains why William became a successful leader of Normandy by referring to evidence such as:

   from the source:
   - William was a capable soldier from an early age
   - he was prepared to use ruthless methods when necessary
   - he recognised his need for allies
   - he married the daughter of the powerful Count of Flanders.

   from recall:
   - William defeated an attempted French invasion in 1054
   - he was a skilled tactician eg out manoeuvred King Henry at Mortemer
   - he increased the size of Normandy by taking over Maine
   - he arranged for his sister to marry the Count of Ponthieu.

2. The candidate compares the sources by referring to evidence such as:

The sources fully agree

Source B	Source C
• David was responsible for founding many abbeys	• he encouraged the work of Cistercian monks at Melrose and Kinloss
• David established a series of royal burghs	• David established many of Scotland's most important towns
• he put down a revolt against him in Moray – Anglo-Norman knights helped strengthen his rule	• he put down rebellions against his rule

3. The candidate describes the features of Norman government which were introduced to Scotland after 1124 by referring to evidence such as:
   • knight service eg members of the jury in law courts
   • sheriffs appointed to deal with administration, finance, military affairs and hold courts
   • government by royal council
   • creation of burghs to encourage trade through markets and fairs
   • royal officials appointed eg chancellor to look after royal records and keep great seal
   • law officers appointed who also introduced the Jury of Inquest
   • constable appointed as the King's military officer
   • encouraged Normans to settle in Scotland.

Context 2: The Cross and the Crescent: The First Crusade, 1096–1125

1. The candidate compares the sources by referring to evidence such as:

The sources agree completely

Source A	Source B
• stole food and possessions from Jews	• homes robbed and valuables stolen
• forced Jews to change religion and become Christian	• Jews forced to give up faith and become Christian
• slaughtered Jews	• attacked and killed Jewish men, women and children

2. The candidate explains why Emperor Alexius and the Crusaders had a poor relationship by referring to evidence such as:

from the source:
• Emperor Alexius freed the Muslims inside Nicaea
• Emperor Alexius insulted the Crusaders/did not let them plunder the city and take a share of the treasure
• Crusaders no longer willing to keep oath of loyalty
• Crusaders agree to keep any land captured for themselves.

from recall:
• Crusaders blamed the Emperor for failure of the People's Crusade
• Crusaders unhappy at their treatment at Constantinople eg Crusaders only allowed into city in small groups/forced to take oaths/supplies withheld
• Baldwin kept Edessa and did not return it to Emperor Alexius
• Bohemond kept Antioch and did not return it to the Emperor
• Emperor Alexius did not help the Crusaders at Antioch.

3. The candidate describes the capture of Jerusalem in 1099 by referring to evidence such as:
   • Crusaders entered Jerusalem after nine days of fasting and praying
   • Crusaders used battering rams to weaken the city's defences
   • Crusaders used siege towers to climb the city's walls
   • Godfrey's men were the first inside the city
   • a Crusader called Letold killed the guards and let the other Crusaders in
   • the Crusaders killed everyone inside the city: men, women and children
   • the Jewish inhabitants of the city were burned in the synagogue
   • houses and temples were robbed
   • the bodies of the dead were searched for valuables and burned.

Context 3: War, Death and Revolt in Medieval Europe, 1328–1436

1. The candidate explains why the French were defeated at Crecy by referring to evidence such as:

from the source:
• the French army was forced to fight uphill
• French crossbows took time to reload
• French cavalry were forced back by a hail of arrows
• French foot-soldiers were trampled by their own men.

from recall:
• the English longbow was superior to the French crossbow
• speed and accuracy of longbow men
• effective leadership of Edward III
• bravery of the Black Prince during the battle

2. The candidate describes the Jacquerie risings in France 1358 by referring to evidence such as:
   • uprisings began near Beauvais in May 1358
   • uprisings spread through north eastern France (Valois, Amiens)
   • peasants sacked and burned castles
   • French nobles were killed
   • the rising was put down by Charles of Navarre
   • the peasant army was defeated near Meaux in June 1358
   • savage reprisals were taken against the peasants
   • caused nobles to accept the authority of the French King in order to support and maintain their position.

3. The candidate compares the sources by referring to evidence such as:

The sources mainly disagree

Source B	Source C
• chateaux and churches across north-west France were sacked	• recovery of French lands had not been destructive
• Charles VII worried about a new English attack	• Charles was worried at first but built strong defences and encouraged attacks in the channel
• English still controlled Calais	• English had to pour resources into defending Calais

Context 4: New Worlds: Europe in the Age of Expansion, 1480s–1530s

1. The candidate describes the improvements in technology which made the voyages of discovery possible by referring to evidence such as:
    *   development of new ship types eg nao, caravel
    *   new sail arrangements – lateen sails
    *   the new mast arrangements – mizzen
    *   improvements to compass
    *   development of navigation equipment – astrolabe, quadrant, cross staff, log line
    *   improved cartography
    *   portolano charts
    *   more detailed rutters.

2. The candidate explains why Vasco da Gama's voyage was important for European trade by referring to evidence such as:

    from the source:
    *   crossed the Indian Ocean to Calicut
    *   brought back a cargo of spices
    *   increased profits – 60 times cost of voyage
    *   enabled trade to many lands – Ethiopia, Arabia, Persia, India.

    from recall:
    *   broke Arab-Venetian monopoly of the spice trade
    *   costs were brought down – middlemen cut out
    *   discovered new coast, ports
    *   enabled Portuguese to set up a base in Goa for trade further east.

3. The candidate compares the sources by referring to evidence such as:
    The sources agree completely

Source B	Source C
• their culture their religion and their civilisations were destroyed by the Conquistadors	• their existing religions were harshly dealt with/discouraged
• Kings who had gold and wealth were held captive and their people forced to pay ransoms in gold	• Europeans took gold and riches from New World peoples by any means, fair or unfair
• Europeans brought them new diseases which wiped them out in hundreds of thousands	• smallpox and measles spread rapidly and whole populations had no resistance and died

Context 5: "Tea and Freedom": The American Revolution, 1763–1783

1. The candidate describes what happened during the Gaspée incident in 1772 by referring to evidence such as:
    *   the British had been patrolling the seas to prevent smuggling/impose customs
    *   the British vessel Gaspée ran aground off the coast of Rhode Island
    *   the vessel was attacked by a crowd of local men
    *   the commander of the Gaspée was wounded by a musket shot
    *   the British government launched an investigation into the incident
    *   the inhabitants of Rhode Island refused to cooperate with the British investigation.

2. The candidate explains why many colonists had turned against British rule by 1776 by referring to evidence such as:

    from the source:
    *   people were persuaded by Paine that the British government were abusing the rights of the American people
    *   Paine's ideas were very popular/150,000 pamphlets were sold
    *   the King had rejected the Olive Branch Petition
    *   the British were using mercenary soldiers to help them run the colonies.

    from recall:
    *   anger at unfair taxation – Sugar Tax, Stamp Act etc
    *   colonists felt that actions of the British government were damaging trade
    *   anger among the colonists about the growing number of British soldiers in the colonies
    *   acts of violence by the British eg Boston Massacre
    *   lack of representation in the British parliament.

3. The candidate compares the sources by referring to evidence such as:
    The sources agree to a considerable degree

Source B	Source C
• Cornwallis' position at Yorktown was deteriorating fast	• Yorktown ended up being in a poor position
• American forces prevented Cornwallis' forces from moving inland	• American troops moved in quickly to contain Cornwallis
• the French defeated the British fleet in Chesapeake Bay	• the French defeated the British fleet in a naval battle near Yorktown

Context 6: "This Accursed Trade": The British Slave Trade and its Abolition, 1770–1807

1. The candidate explains why resistance was difficult for slaves on the plantations by referring to evidence such as:

    from the source:
    *   slaves were controlled by strict laws or codes
    *   slaves who escaped were hunted down
    *   slave risings lacked effective leadership
    *   slave resistance was crushed by the better armed and organised whites.

    from recall:
    *   plantation owners often used black overseers to help them maintain authority
    *   punishments for escaping were very severe and acted as a deterrent
    *   slaves lived in fear of being sold off/separated from their families if they broke the rules
    *   slaves had little or no education and could be brainwashed into accepting plantation life
    *   many islands were small and it was difficult for slaves to evade capture.

2. The candidate compares the sources by referring to evidence such as:

There is agreement between the sources

Source B	Source C
• the slave trade had many powerful supporters	• plantation owners had the support of important groups who promoted slavery
• British ports relied on the trade	• dozens of British ports, and surrounding areas relied on the slave trade
• many people believed that the trade had helped to make Britain wealthy and prosperous	• slave trade seemed vital to the continuing prosperity of Britain and the Caribbean Islands

3. The candidate describes the ways the Abolitionists tried to win support for their cause by referring to evidence such as:
   • Abolitionists formed the Society for the Abolition of the Slave Trade in 1778
   • published pamphlets/posters in support of their cause
   • mounted press campaigns
   • Josiah Wedgewood designed a range of goods to promote the cause
   • published accounts of former slaves, such as Equiano
   • lobbied Parliament and persuaded MPs (led by Wilberforce) to support legislation to end the slave trade
   • encouraged people to sign petitions
   • held public meetings
   • Clarkson – collected evidence of the barbarities of the trade
   • tried to persuade Christians that the slave trade was against the teachings of the Bible.

Context 7: Citizens! The French Revolution, 1789–1794

1. The candidate describes the complaints of the French peasants in 1789 by referring to evidence such as:
   • lack of support to overcome bad harvests and food shortages in the 1790s/famine in 1789
   • prices of goods rose very rapidly
   • peasants had to pay taxes such as the taille, vingtieme, gabelle
   • the landowners/nobles did not pay taxes
   • peasants had to pay money to the Church
   • peasants were subject to feudal services eg the corvee forced them to work on road building/repairs without pay
   • peasants were forced into long periods of military service
   • no political power – peasants made up a large percentage of the population.

2. The candidate compares the sources by referring to evidence such as:

The sources disagree

Source A	Source B
• honest reward for work	• wanted to get as much as they could for as little effort as possible
• lived only for wife and children	• cared only about themselves
• quiet and humble/wished only to live in peace	• violent and arrogant

3. The candidate explains why many French people were unhappy with the treatment of the Catholic Church during the French Revolution by referring to evidence such as:

   from the source:
   • the Catholic Church was to be brought under state control
   • Church lands were sold but the government kept the money
   • priests became state servants rather than Church servants
   • Protestants would be allowed to vote for Catholic Bishops/Bishops to be elected

   from recall:
   • Catholic religion was no longer the official religion
   • the Pope's authority was being undermined
   • Catholic clergy were made to swear an oath of loyalty to the Assembly
   • Robespierre introduced a new official state religion.

Context 8: Cavour, Garibaldi and the Making of Italy, 1815–1870

1. The candidate describes why Napoleon Bonaparte had an important influence on Italian unification by referring to evidence such as:

   from the source:
   • he created a kingdom in Italy in the North
   • he abolished internal customs barriers
   • he built roads across the Alps which brought Italians together
   • he encouraged the Italian language and literature

   from recall:
   • he created a national army
   • he appointed people of talent rather than social standing to high office which changed the way Italy was governed
   • trade became quicker and easier between the regions under his system of single weights, measures and currency
   • some were united in their opposition to his demands for tax, recruits for war and robbery of art treasures.

2. The candidate describes the events between 1850 and 1871 which led to the unification of Italy by referring to evidence such as:
   • involvement of Piedmont in Crimea War on side of Britain and France won support
   • Pact of Plombieres
   • War of Italian Independence – April-July 1859 defeated Austria
   • Battles of Magenta and Solferino and conquest of Lombardy
   • Peace of Villafranca
   • annexation of central Italian states
   • Garibaldi and thousand – expedition to Kingdom of the Two Sicilies
   • Garibaldi's handing over of conquests to Victor Emmanuel
   • alliance with Prussia and gift of Venetia, 1866
   • Franco-Prussian War 1870-71 and entry into Rome
   • money was raised through subscriptions and donations to help Garibaldi's Sicilian expedition.

3. The candidate compares the sources by referring to evidence such as:

The sources disagree

Source B	Source C
• Cavour was not always a supporter of a united Italy	• Cavour's ambition was always to unite Italy
• Cavour took advantage of opportunities rather than plan them	• Cavour was a great diplomat and brilliant planner
• Cavour acted to stop Garibaldi	• Cavour allowed Garibaldi to win the South

Context 9: Iron and Blood? Bismarck and The Creation of the German Empire, 1815–1871

1. The candidate describes the ways German national feeling grew before 1848 by referring to evidence such as:
    *   the German Confederation encouraged the growth of national feeling
    *   students held meetings to promote the ideas of nationalism and unity eg Karl von Hase
    *   Carlsbad decrees united students to the cause of nationalism
    *   the popularity of German artists, musicians and writers helped create a common identity/cultural nationalism eg Grimm Brothers, Beethoven
    *   the Zollverein brought economic co-operation between the states
    *   the Zollverein allowed good roads and railways to be built linking the states together and allowing ideas of common identity to spread through travel between the states
    *   economic growth in Germany strengthened the political position of the German states
    *   Prussia's dominance over the Zollverein/Austria's exclusion from the Zollverein strengthened Prussia's influence over the German states.

2. The candidate describes why Austria had lost her leading position in Germany by 1860 by referring to evidence such as:

    from the source:
    *   Austria unable to replace skilful Metternich
    *   Austria lost an important ally in Russia
    *   defeat by France destroyed Austria's strong military reputation
    *   industrialisation in Prussia had increased her economic growth and strengthened her position

    from recall:
    *   Austria's attempt to replace the Zollverein failed
    *   Austria was behind Prussia in industrial output/Prussia produced more than any country except Britain
    *   the railway network improved Prussia's military efficiency
    *   Prussia's economic strength increased as head of the Zollverein (Custom's Union)

3. The candidate compares the sources by referring to evidence such as:
    The sources agree

Source B	Source C
• his first task was going to be the re-organisation of the army to strengthen Prussia's position in Germany	• it was Bismarck's decision to reform the army which made Prussia dominant in Germany
• Bismarck wanted to seize an excuse to create war against Austria	• Bismarck planned to force Austria to go to war with Prussia
• Bismarck wanted to control the smaller states and unite Germany under Prussian leadership	• Bismarck aimed to extend Prussian power over the other German states to unite them with Prussia at the head

Context 10: The Red Flag: Lenin and the Russian Revolution, 1894–1921

1. The candidate describes the hardships faced by industrial workers in Russia before 1914 by referring to evidence such as:
    *   wages were low and working conditions were poor
    *   working hours were very long/12 hour shifts
    *   high number of deaths from accidents and work related health problems/poor diet
    *   poor living conditions/shared rooms in tenement blocks/barrack style buildings next to factories
    *   no privacy or private space/shared beds occupied in shifts/curtains in place of walls
    *   under surveillance by Okhrana/police spies infiltrated the unions
    *   did not have full voting rights
    *   strikes/protests often put down by police or government troops eg Bloody Sunday, Lena Goldfields
    *   food shortages.

2. The candidate describes why the Russian Royal Family had become increasingly unpopular by 1917 by referring to evidence such as:

    from the source:
    *   Nicholas and Alexandra were unwilling to give up autocratic rule
    *   Tsar did not let Duma run the country/largely ignored it
    *   Tsar left Alexandra in charge of the government which was disastrous
    *   Alexandra was influenced by Rasputin to sack ministers.

    from recall:
    *   Tsar took personal charge at the Front so was personally blamed for the heavy losses/general impact of war
    *   Alexandra was German and was thought by some to be a spy
    *   Rasputin was thought to be Alexandra's lover and this brought Royal Family into disrepute
    *   Alexandra ignored the growing problems faced by the workers.

3. The candidate compares the sources by referring to evidence such as:
    The sources disagree

Source B	Source C
• he made rousing speeches and raised morale/ensured the Red Army was well fed and properly armed	• he ordered the execution of one in every ten men in the regiment, as a warning to the rest
• he was an inspirational leader and was dedicated to the cause	• he was a ruthless leader who used strict discipline
• over 5 million men joined the Red Army of their own free will	• he forced people to join the Red Army to raise the number of troops

Context 11: Free at Last? Race Relations in the USA, 1918–1968

1. The candidate describes the activities of the Ku Klux Klan in the 1920s and 1930s by referring to evidence such as:
    *   campaigned against immigration in the 1920s especially Jews and Roman Catholics
    *   acted anonymously eg wore robes and hoods/activities took place at night
    *   used violence against opponents eg whippings/beatings/tar and featherings
    *   used intimidation of black Americans eg fiery crosses/house burnings
    *   lynching of black Americans ie murder of black Americans accused of committing crimes
    *   infiltrated government eg 16 senators gained election in 1920s with KKK help
    *   infiltrated state officials and police – especially in the Deep South and Oklahoma, Indiana and Texas
    *   large peaceful demonstrations eg 1928 March down Pennsylvania Avenue, Washington DC

- KKK was less active after 1925 as membership fell following allegations of corruption amongst Klan leadership
- attempted to disrupt trade unions which admitted black members eg CIO.

2. The candidate compares the sources by referring to evidence such as:

   The sources agree

Source A	Source B
• King's first step towards becoming the leading figure in the civil rights movement	• King became a leader of the civil rights movement
• Courts decided that segregation on Montgomery's buses was illegal	• US Supreme Court announced Alabama's bus segregation laws were illegal
• Montgomery remained a segregated town – white only theatres, pool rooms, restaurants	• most other services in Montgomery remained segregated

3. The candidate describes why Malcolm X was opposed to non-violent protest by referring to evidence such as:

   from the source:
   - Malcolm's mistreatment in his youth gave him different attitudes towards Whites from Martin Luther King
   - he became influenced by the ideas of Elijah Mohammed who preached hatred of white people
   - he believed that support of non-violence was a sign that Black people were still living in mental slavery
   - he believed violent language and threats would frighten the authorities into action.

   from recall:
   - Malcolm X claimed that even Whites who appeared friendly were 'wolves in sheep's clothing'
   - he believed that non-violence deprived Black people of their right to self-defence
   - he claimed that peaceful protest gained little for most Black people
   - he didn't think non-violent campaigns tackled the problems for Blacks in northern cities.

Context 12: The Road to War, 1933-193

1. The candidate explains why Hitler wanted to rearm Germany in the 1930s by referring to evidence such as:

   from the source:
   - Germany was defenceless
   - surrounded by hostile countries
   - strong Germany would restore balance of power
   - to defend Europe from the threat from the east.

   from recall:
   - France had built the Maginot Line
   - Communism/Russia was a threat to Germany/Europe
   - an army would be to unite all Germans/create Greater Germany/gain Lebensraum
   - an army would be necessary to regain territory lost at Versailles
   - gain popularity and economic growth for Germany.

2. The candidate compares the sources by referring to evidence such as:

   The sources disagree

Source B	Source C
• Sudeten German should return to Germany	• Sudetenland had never been part of Germany
• Sudeten Germans resented being part of Czechoslovakia since 1919	• Sudeten German unrest originated in early 1930s
• persecuted as ethnic minority	• treated with respect

3. The candidate describes events in 1939 that led to the outbreak of war between Britain and Germany by referring to evidence such as:
   - Germany invaded Czechoslovakia in March 1939 breaking the Munich Agreement
   - Great Britain sped up her rearmaments programme/led to conscription
   - Hitler demanded the return of Danzig from Poland
   - Germany demanded permission to build a road and railway line through Poland
   - Britain promised to defend Poland if she were attacked
   - August 1939 Germany and Russia signed the Nazi-Soviet Non-Aggression Pact which left Hitler free to attack Poland
   - September Germany invaded Poland
   - Britain declared war on Germany.

Context 13: In the Shadow of the Bomb: The Cold War, 1945–1985

1. The candidate describes the events which led to the formation of the Warsaw Pact in 1955 by referring to evidence such as:
   - the Soviet take-over of Eastern European countries had increased tension between East and West
   - Soviet Union felt threatened by the West's actions – Churchill's Iron Curtain speech/offer of Marshall aid to all European countries
   - Berlin airlift had increased tension between East and West
   - Allies merged their zones to form West Germany, formalising the division of Germany, increasing tension
   - NATO was formed in 1949
   - NATO expanded in 1951 to include Greece and Turkey
   - USA forms SEATO in 1954
   - USA forms CENTO in 1955
   - West Germany joined NATO in 1955
   - Soviet Union felt increasingly surrounded
   - Soviet Union saw the Warsaw Pact as a means of exerting its control over Eastern Europe.

2. The candidate compares the sources by referring to evidence such as:

   The sources disagree

Source A	Source B
• the Soviet Union had the idea of installing a small number of nuclear missiles on Cuba	• Americans believed that the Soviets planned to place a large number of their missiles in Cuba
• Khrushchev did not want to start a war	• Americans regarded Soviet action as a warlike act
• purpose of missiles was just to defend Cuba from American attack	• missiles had an offensive purpose – pointed directly at major American cities

3. The candidate explains why American became involved in a full scale war in Vietnam by 1964 by referring to evidence such as:

from the source:

- France asked America for assistance in Vietnam
- America feared that Vietnam would become communist
- they believed that they could establish a friendly government in South Vietnam, under the leadership of President Diem
- America feared that a civil war was developing in South Vietnam.

from recall:

- America was increasingly concerned about the influence of China in south-east Asia
- there was a widespread belief in the Domino Theory
- there was a fear that other countries eg Thailand, Laos, Burma, Cambodia even New Zealand and Australia could fall to communism
- there was a general concern that America was falling behind in the Cold War at this time and needed to make a stand against communism
- 'advisors' had been in Vietnam to support the government of Diem since the early 1960s
- Gulf of Tonkin incident led America to become involved in a full scale war in Vietnam.

Hey! I've done it

© 2011 SQA/Bright Red Publishing Ltd, All Rights Reserved
Published by Bright Red Publishing Ltd, 6 Stafford Street, Edinburgh, EH3 7AU
Tel: 0131 220 5804, Fax: 0131 220 6710, enquiries: sales@brightredpublishing.co.uk,
www.brightredpublishing.co.uk

Official SQA answers to 978-1-84948-200-4
2007-2011